For my parents, Joan and Harry Hawkes

Contents

Acknowledgements

The author would like to thank her family, colleagues and students for their support and Jackie Jones of Harvester Wheatsheaf for her patience and interest in this project.

Introduction

In the nineteenth century the child became the focus of widespread attention in an unprecedented way, and, in England, the figure of the child and the theme of childhood became immensely popular literary topics. Indeed, it is generally agreed that it was only after the end of the eighteenth century that children became at all significant in literature.[1] Although a substantial amount of critical work has been done on children's literature, there seem nevertheless to have been relatively few attempts to examine the development and implications of the theme of childhood throughout the century in different literary genres. Those studies which explore the subject tend to limit themselves to a restricted selection of texts and authors, unanimously identifying the Romantic poets, Wordsworth, Coleridge and Blake, and, in the realm of the novel, Charles Dickens, as the initiators and best exponents of the myth of childhood which fast took root in the national consciousness and flowered throughout the century in imaginative fiction. The contribution and influence of these writers were undeniably extremely significant but the privileging of these names obscures a vast body of works published in the late eighteenth and early nineteenth centuries which centred on the child figure and had not only an immense contemporary readership but a far-reaching influence on later Victorian fiction writing. These were the moral and didactic tales and the widely disseminated religious tracts originating in the Evangelical movement, and the majority of them were written by women.

Although it was, and still is, frequently argued that women writers excelled in the depiction of domestic, family settings, they have been curiously neglected in studies of the portrayal of childhood. While any critical work is necessarily selective, it would seem that, on this subject, women writers are largely only included in the discussion in the context of children's literature, or compared unfavourably as in Peter Coveney's book *The Image of Childhood – The Individual and Society: A study of the theme in English literature*, first published in 1957 and one of the first surveys of the theme. Concerned largely with the development of the Romantic sensibility and its decline and distortion in the later nineteenth century, Coveney devotes the bulk of his discussion

1

and praise to male authors, with the exception of George Eliot. Given his
focus on the Romantic poets and their influence, this could be seen as
justifiable, but it is deeply disturbing that, in his consideration of the
development of the theme of the child in the novel, the other women writers
he discusses are always compared in pejorative terms. Although admitting the
significance of *Jane Eyre*, Coveney indicts the 'masochistic relish' and
'neurotic prose' with which Jane's physical and moral tortures are recounted.
Mrs Henry Wood and Marie Corelli are subjected to a sustained attack,
unusual in its vituperation. Even George Eliot does not fully escape this
alarmingly one-sided view, for what is seen to be a strength in Dickens and
Wordsworth, the subjective resonances in their portrayal of childhood which
become 'part of their wisdom', is adroitly deemed 'an unfortunate legacy',
debilitating and lacking a controlling intelligence in some of her work.[2] Robert
Pattison, in *The Child Figure in English Literature*, an attempt to establish a link
between the portrayal of the child and the concepts of the Fall of Man and
Original Sin, only gives detailed consideration to George Eliot, although other
women are mentioned in the context of children's fiction.[3] David Grylls' book
on the parent-and-child relationship, *Guardians and Angels*, assesses a range
of women writers of children's literature, but discusses only Jane Austen as
one of four major writers of novels for adults.[4] Women writers fare rather
better in Richard N. Coe's stimulating work *When the Grass was Taller*, which
ranges widely in time and place, but this is concerned only with the
autobiographical 'Childhood'.[5] R. Kuhn's very thought-provoking *Corruption
in Paradise: The child in Western literature* is also breathtakingly ambitious
in its range, but in concentrating on themes and motifs, he effectively
divorces the texts from their specific national, social and historical contexts
which, with reference to the nineteenth century, is, as I hope to demonstrate,
a barrier to fully understanding much of the import of the portrayal of the
child.[6]

Even with the changing climate of opinion over the last few decades about
the significance of hitherto underrated and marginalised women writers,
relatively little attention has been paid to their portrayal of the child and
childhood at different points in the century. Moreover, even feminist critics
have not explored to any great extent the significance of women writers of
books for children or for a dual readership of adult and child, perhaps because
it has not until recently been regarded as 'serious' literature, with the result,
since this was an area in which many women were able to find a voice in the
early nineteenth century, that they have become doubly disadvantaged. Yet
large numbers of women throughout the century wrote sensitively, poignantly,
amusingly, with pity, sympathy and rage, about the delights and miseries of
childhood and, like their male counterparts, used the figure of the child as a
vehicle for personal, social and spiritual polemic. This study seeks, therefore,
to redress the balance by attempting to identify the main approaches towards

this theme and to assess the contribution of a succession of women writers to the nineteenth-century mythology of childhood.

The literary texts which form the basis of this study were written against the background of an eventful and rapidly changing social and economic climate and an equally varied and challenging climate of ideas, which generated conflicting, controversial, passionately espoused and often highly subjective attitudes towards the nature of children, their education and upbringing and their role in society. It is not the object of this study to present a detailed analysis of the social, legal and historical implications of these attitudes, a task which has been provocatively carried out by a number of writers to date.[7] However, although the relationship between literature and life is at all times a problematic one, it is necessary to grasp the significance of certain factors which had considerable bearing on the literary portrayal of childhood in order to understand fully the purpose and nature of a given narrative and assess its effectiveness in a literary climate which favoured realism, especially as many of the texts considered here were written as a direct response to prevailing conditions and views which thus influenced, in often radically differing ways, both content and approach.

Demographically, children were a very important element in nineteenth-century society. Early censuses carried out in England and Wales reveal that throughout the period the proportion of the expanding population aged 14 and under was never less than one-third.[8] Not only did these growing numbers present enormous social problems but increased the ferment of debate about the nature, position and treatment of the child which had been gathering momentum over previous centuries. In his important and controversial book, *Centuries of Childhood*, Philippe Ariès argues that the 'discovery' of childhood as a separate phase of existence was bound up with the developing concept of the family as opposed to the community life of the Middle Ages, when children were commonly sent away from home to serve as apprentices at the age of 7.[9] The belief, based on economics, that children were a subsidiary element in the adult world had been bolstered by religious attitudes founded on St Paul's view that childish thoughts and behaviour were irrelevant and should be put away as soon as possible.[10] As the essential 'difference' of children began to be realised, so they increasingly came to be seen as a source of interest and amusement for adults and by the seventeenth century, emotional ties between parents and children in the domestic environment had been strengthened and a considerable degree of moral solicitude had been generated, with the child seen as an 'imperfect adult' who needed to be carefully guarded and educated to develop its reason.[11] Children were now given schooling rather than bound to apprenticeships, so that the actual period of childhood, associated with domesticity and freedom from adult responsibilities, was extended.

The eighteenth century is generally seen as an important period of change in the recognition of the child's 'special nature', with the proliferation of schools for the offspring of well-to-do families, greater concern for health and hygiene, increased provision of amusements, toys, entertainments and a new emerging literature to stimulate the child, and a decline in physical brutality (although the latter was revived in the nineteenth century).[12] The decline in the infant mortality rate in the late eighteenth century is sometimes adduced as a factor affecting attitudes in that more emotion could safely be invested in a child if it was likely to survive, but this conclusion has been called into question on the basis of evidence from earlier centuries and from the nineteenth, when the incidence of child deaths was still extremely high and in fact, as will be seen, became the source of much sentimentality.[13] At the same time, children were being abused and exploited as they had always been and indeed continued to be: among the working classes, they were still sold into prostitution or as chimney-sweeps, sent out to beg, were drugged, beaten and abandoned, and at other levels of society were ill-treated, isolated and exposed to cold and starvation in the name of their moral, spiritual or intellectual good.

The same period also brought to the fore the debate about the education of children which was to have a strong influence on social and literary attitudes at the beginning of the nineteenth century. Influenced by the tenets of rationalism, the concern with education in the eighteenth century lay with developing the child into a rational adult as efficiently as possible. In his influential 'Essay concerning Human Understanding' (1690) and 'Some Thoughts concerning Education' (1693), John Locke saw the child as a *tabula rasa* whose reason had to be cultivated by careful nurture and advocated an upbringing which developed a healthy body as well as a character that was rational, moral and just. Knowledge came most effectively from experience, so the child's senses should be actively employed rather than dulled with the cramming of facts and second-hand knowledge by rote learning. Significantly, he also argued that the desire to learn must be evoked and the acquisition of knowledge should be made a pleasurable activity rather than imposed by fear or force, and should be adapted as far as possible by the educator to the child's capabilities which should be studied carefully.[14] The revolution which came about in educational thinking in the mid-eighteenth century with the works of Jean-Jacques Rousseau, who drew on the ideas of Locke, had far-reaching consequences for the literary portrayal of the child in England as in France. In *Émile ou de l'éducation* (1762), which describes the upbringing of an individual boy by his tutor in rural seclusion, Rousseau argued that the child was important in itself rather than as just an embryonic adult, and that because closest to nature, had natural purity and sensibility and innate tendencies to virtue. The child's identity and nature, different in kind from that of adults, because children have their own way of thinking and seeing things, should therefore be carefully studied, in all their different stages, and the child's good qualities developed by experimental learning under careful adult supervision rather than being made to conform to adult, social standards.[15] Aggressively anti-book-learning, Rousseau also rejected conscious teaching of facts and urged that the child should be encouraged to learn by experience and by the contact of the senses with the world. His classic and often quoted example is that if a child breaks a window, it should be made to sleep in the draught, rather than being physically punished or subjected to abstract moral argument which a child cannot understand, and will thus acquire natural wisdom. A shocking aspect to many of his readers was his rejection of the Christian view of innate evil, deriving from the doctrine of Original Sin, explicit in his argument that children had an innate innocence and that deviation from virtue came from the influences of society.[16] In his *Confessions* (1782–89), Rousseau further explored his view of the continuity between the self of childhood and the adult, which allowed the latter to be explained and understood in terms of early experiences. These views not only inspired the Romantic cult of the child, but also a whole progressive school of thought on education which flourished in the second half of the century. Some 200 treatises on education were published in England before 1800.[17] But Rousseau's secular approach inevitably also outraged Christian views on the importance of obedience and of moral indoctrination from an early age and were denounced in England by Christian apologists as the subversive work of an infidel.[18]

Rousseau's influence in England quickly became modified and diluted. Richard Edgeworth, the influential educational theorist, for example, who in his initial enthusiasm brought his son up in the Rousseau manner with less than spectacular success, changed his allegiances to a much more controlled, rational programme of education.[19] In fact, the rational moralists of the late eighteenth century in England often brought together in their educational works the general views of both Locke and Rousseau, emphasising in particular their shared recommendations of the importance of the tutor (which may or may not be the parent) and that learning should be an active, constant and engaging pursuit. Rousseau's view of the innocent child was even more influential on those writers who developed the cult of Romantic sensibility and installed the child as the symbol of primal innocence in danger of corruption by the world.

As general concern about children broadened in the nineteenth century in literature and in life, two clearly discernible parallel responses became apparent in England which can be conveniently summed up as the concepts of 'Original Innocence' and 'Original Sin', the one deriving from the writings of Rousseau and the Romantic poets, and the other from the influence of the religious revival launched by John Wesley, the founder of the Methodist movement, which also affected the Church of England and became known as the Evangelical revival.[20] The former, also in effect having its roots in

Christian beliefs, notably Christ's reverence for the inspired innocence of little children, was given impetus by Wordsworth's depiction of childhood as the 'seed-time of the soul', a time of superior integrity, spontaneity and sensitivity:

> . . . our childhood sits,
> Our simple childhood, sits upon a throne
> That has more power than all the elements.[21]

Wordsworth's evocation of the Platonic myth of the child's immortal nature in his Ode on *Intimations of Immortality* (1802), the visionary character of childhood 'trailing clouds of glory' which has to give way when it comes into contact with the 'shades of the prison-house' of reality, became central to the nineteenth-century mythology of childhood. His survey of his own upbringing in the *Prelude* (written before 1805 but published posthumously in 1850), which was both an extremely personal work and an attempt to establish universal truths about childhood and the nature of human life, shared Rousseau's insistence on the significance for the adult of childhood experience and emphasis on the relationship between the child and nature as a fundamental prerequisite for moral growth. The regret that comes with age at the loss of the child's spontaneous joy in nature and intense imaginative powers implied that the child was, in fact, superior to the adult.[22] Such a view directly influenced the progressive idealisation of the image of the child in the nineteenth century and the web of subjectivity and sentimentality which came to adhere to it. This sentimentality is amply illustrated in much Victorian pictorial art, where children are frequently depicted in idealised rural settings, with animals or old folk, or as sad-eyed, ragged urchins against a foggy London background.[23] As a result of the social and political ferment of the end of the eighteenth century, the spiritual and intellectual conflicts and the atmosphere of national and personal doubt and questioning, the child became a potent literary symbol of the subjective exploration of the self, of the writer's sense of uncertainty and vulnerability, and of simplicity, innocence and feeling in the face of the increasingly dehumanising industrial age. William Blake in his *Songs of Innocence* (1789) and *Songs of Experience* (1794) celebrates the joy of childhood and denounces the forces which deny the expression and fulfilment of it, both a harsh, materialistic society and a cold, dehumanised Christianity.[24] The Romantic concept of the child was to be increasingly pressed into service as a vehicle for social protest as it became clear that there was a gross disparity between this image and the reality of nineteenth-century life.

The other prevailing view of the child, stemming from the Calvinist belief in innate depravity, which retained its power in England through the Evangelical revival, stressed the need for strict discipline, constant watchfulness for sin, the early breaking of the child's will and absolute obedience to parents.[25] Since the individual was polluted through having been conceived in sin and could be saved only by faith and the conviction of his or her own sin, constant self-examination and early conversion were highly desirable. The enduring popularity of Bunyan's *The Pilgrim's Progress* (1678, 1684) and James Janeway's *A Token for Children: Being an exact account of the conversion, holy and exemplary lives, and joyful deaths of several young children* (1671–72) testifies to the tenacity of such beliefs in the early nineteenth century. Indeed, Janeway's terrifying exhortations and examples of obsessively pious children had their counterpart in the admonitions and little prodigies of nineteenth-century Evangelical writing, as will be demonstrated in my second chapter.

These two trends converged to a certain extent as the Romantic view gained ground – the belief in the revitalising power of the childhood vision was transmuted in Evangelical literature, for example, into the redemptive power of the child who converts an adult with pious words and actions, and the child as symbol of fragile innocence was to play an important role as the helpless victim of a godless society. The complex implications of this dual approach and its ramifications for the portrayal of the child in literature are one of the central issues to be explored in this study.

There is a large amount of evidence which suggests what life was really like for children in the nineteenth century.[26] James Walvin, in his study *A Child's World: A social history of English childhood 1800–1914*, in particular offers a lively, readable and well-documented account of conditions which can only be very briefly summarised here. In the middle classes and above, almost obsessive attention was paid to children and, in life as in literature, the duality outlined above manifested itself in the otherwise apparently paradoxical attitude of extreme severity in discipline and punishment and an intense sentimental affection resulting in spoiling, petting, parading and shielding from the world. Obedience to parents was paramount (although the day-to-day care of children of wealthier families was generally left in the hands of servants): along with the eulogies of childhood joys, the dictum that children 'should be seen and not heard' originated here. Education took place either at home in the hands of tutors and governesses, especially in the case of girls, or at boarding schools and private academies. In both cases, the standards of education varied enormously, and in the schools so did the living conditions, often being spartan and humiliating.

The careful nurture and protection from the world were not, however, true for huge numbers of children. Among the working classes, indifference, ignorance and brutality were the consequences of poverty, hunger and overcrowding. As can be seen in much of the art of the period, the children of the poor frequently looked far older than their years.[27] Education, available only in the ragged schools, voluntary schools, Sunday schools and schools in factories or workhouses, was poor and sporadic, and in some areas non-existent. The Industrial Revolution intensified the cynical exploitation of child labour. The death toll was still huge: half of the children born in 1831 died within five years.[28] This was due to rampant disease, especially typhoid and tuberculosis, and common children's illnesses like measles, scarlet fever, whooping cough and, in the second half of the century, diphtheria, which afflicted all social classes but were fermented by neglect and living conditions in the crowded, polluted urban environments; and to hunger, overwork and the widespread use of opiates. The crimes against children perpetrated by parents, baby-farmers, teachers and employers gradually became serious concerns eventually warranting parliamentary interference. Acts regulating working conditions, the Education Act of 1870 which recognised that education should be provided by the state for all children, the setting up of rehabilitation schemes for children in trouble (who could still be hanged in the early years of the century for stealing a loaf and were routinely imprisoned or transported) and the provision of parish relief in the workhouses were among the efforts made throughout the century to improve conditions for children who up to this point had little legal status and few legal rights. Yet well-to-do parents could still, to all intents and purposes, treat their children how they liked, as many autobiographies and autobiographical novels testify, for oppression and cruelty could be mental and emotional as well as physical. The rapid advances in the latter part of the century – the Prevention of Cruelty Act (1889), the Poor Law Adoption Act (1889) and the Custody of Children Act (1891) – helped further to defend the interests of the child, although there was continued anxiety about the role, authority and rights of parents, and many problems persisted well into the twentieth century.[29]

How, then, did nineteenth-century writers set about representing the experiences of the child? A considerable number of the texts to be discussed in the following chapters testify to the fact that many women writers, like their male contemporaries, sought to interpret the child and convey childhood experience in the light of preconceived spiritual, philosophical or literary ideologies and models. In some cases, this can be seen to correspond to a need in the adult writer to believe in and endorse a certain mythology of childhood. The individual writer's own preoccupations and aims are therefore often of crucial significance. Frequently, the writer's own experience in childhood, or indeed as a parent, guardian or teacher, can be seen to inform their approach in a profoundly subjective manner. This, of course, may be true of writers of either sex (Charles Dickens' attempts to exorcise his shame and anger about his experiences in *David Copperfield* and *Great Expectations* are obvious examples), but it is particularly true of women, for whom literature became a valuable means of openly exploring their responses to the gendered identity and roles imposed on young females by society from a very early age. In texts where the child figure is used as a vehicle for a didactic message or as a symbol (of the victims of the cynical greed of the industrial age, for example), it is often the case that the picture presented may be little more than a stereotypical one, with little sense of the individual reality of the child's personality. Nevertheless, the best writers succeed in making such child characters transcend their stereotypy and emerge as credible human beings too. Furthermore, such stereotypes were frequently challenged, revised or rejected altogether, thus subverting the reader's expectations and creating both plausible characters and new ways of looking at childhood. The writer's response to the portrayal of childhood is also illuminated by the handling of the ways in which current mythologies of childhood inform the views and behaviour of the adult characters in their fiction.

The greatest problem facing a writer who seeks to depict the outlook of the child or the world of childhood is that of narrative focus. 'What do we know of that which lies in the minds of children? We know only what we put there,' wrote Anna Jameson in 1854.[30] A superficial survey of texts depicting children might suggest that the dominant narrative approach is that of the adult looking at the child lovingly or critically, with condescension or sympathy, commenting upon and interpreting the child's behaviour and thoughts from without, from an adult perspective. Given the difficulties of adequately representing the complexities of childhood experience, this is the most commonly chosen approach. There are, after all, considerable differences between recounting *what* children experience and actually evoking and reproducing the nature of that experience and the child's perception of it, which, as the Romantics saw, is different in quality and kind from that of adults, despite the fact that both reader and writer may have undergone, and retained clear memories of, something similar in their own childhood. In *The Mill on the Floss* (1860), George Eliot asks: 'Is there anyone who can recover the experience of his childhood, not merely with a memory of what he did and what happened to him . . . but with an intimate penetration, a revived consciousness of what he felt then – when it was so long from one Midsummer to another?'[31] The freshness and imaginativeness of childhood perception, the intensity with which the child may experience joy, frustration and sorrow, even in trivial matters, and their reactions of wonder, perplexity or indifference to new experiences like birth and death are unique and resistant to adult interpretation. Wordsworth was adamant that it was an impossible task for the adult to recapture 'the glory and freshness of a dream': 'the things which I have seen I now can/see no more'.[32] It is, moreover, difficult to convey adequately from the child's point of view, in adult language, an experience which the child may not be able to comprehend fully or articulate, given the child's more limited linguistic range, or which, in the case of a very young child, may be pre-verbal. Many of the earliest experiences a child encounters are, after all, sensory ones which words can rarely evoke to the same effect. Efforts to overcome these difficulties by employing the language of the child are rarely satisfactory, as will be seen, for they are often coloured by the author's subjective and idiosyncratic view of childhood and may be merely cute or embarrassing. Katherine Mansfield, for example, voiced a common reader reaction in her remark that 'the kind of sentimental writing about a virginia creeper and the small haigh [sic] voices of tainy [sic] children is more than I can stick . . . It's so much worse when the spelling is wrong.'[33] Yet some authors did make strenuous efforts to capture the quality of childhood experience and transmit it through their writing. The various narrative strategies used to accomplish this – whether consistent or sporadic, spontaneous or self-conscious, a complete immersion in the viewpoint of the child or a mixture of perspectives – are an important part of my concern here.

With such an immense topic, it has been necessary to establish clear parameters from the outset. First, the definition of childhood was a very fluid one in the nineteenth century, the concept of adolescence being a more modern phenomenon. Any such definition also has class implications. Thus, young people of 16 or 18 from well-to-do families may still have been living dependent lives in the home (a situation which, for females, may in effect have lasted a lifetime) or, in the case of young gentlemen, in full-time education, while among working-class children few childlike qualities were discernible in children of 8 or 9 who had perhaps already been working for a year or more to earn their own living and help support their family.[34] Physical and emotional maturity and even sexual awareness and experience also differed across classes and throughout the century. The definition of childhood in literature reflected this vagueness, and my own boundaries are correspond-ingly flexible. While avoiding those texts which are essentially concerned only with the adolescent, because this presupposes significant differences of content in terms of dilemmas, ambitions and relationships, and presentation, my upper limit has generally been the mid-teens. Thus, I have considered novels of self-development only where the childhood period of the protagonist's life forms a substantial and particularly revealing part of the whole text. Similarly, I have omitted many texts where the portrayal of the child or childhood does not play a central part: texts, for example, which explore problems of parenthood where the focus of interest is the adult protagonist or where the existence of the child only serves to illuminate adult relationships or dilemmas.

In the interests of control I have limited myself to prose writing, although poetry is occasionally used to corroborate or illuminate my findings. Although I have chosen to draw on works ostensibly written for a young readership as well as those written for adults, not only because women were pre-eminent here, but because they illustrate widely held assumptions about the nature of childhood and in their turn established popular narrative conventions, my criterion for selection has been that of dual readership, considering for the most part those texts which it can be demonstrated were widely read and enjoyed by adults too, especially the newly literate or parents reading to and with their children. In many such texts, it is clear that the author has an eye on the reactions of an adult as well as a child reader. I have also included some discussion of the autobiographical works of a small number of the writers whose fiction forms part of my argument, where the childhood of the writer can be said to play a significant role in their self-portrayal. Many autobiographies explore childhood years in order to throw light on the author's present self or as a means of eliciting a desired response from the reader to elements in the past or present, and the anxiety that many nineteenth-century women writers clearly felt about their public role and their reticence about so openly promoting their own achievements can be seen to spill over into their portrayal of their childhood selves. Roy Pascal in *Design and Truth in Autobiography* argues that the great nineteenth-century novels are 'unthinkable without the great autobiographies' and that writers' awareness of the implications of the uninterrupted development from childhood to adulthood generated the interest in the *Bildungsroman*, or novel of self-development, in an age characterised by the bourgeois preoccupation with the individual.[35] Any portrayal of childhood has reference, to some extent, to areas of experience which are universal as well as specific to the individual writer, and in the case of women writers, whose experiences would, in some respects, have echoed those of many of their readers, their retrospective self-analysis would have had particular appeal, evoking a self-awareness and insight into conventional attitudes not encouraged by traditional female roles. It is also clear, intriguingly, that autobiographical writing was influenced in return by literature, and I hope to show that literary constructs were manipulated in the act of self-portrayal, traditional images of childhood being enlisted or subverted to create a personal mythology to serve the author's purposes.

Many of the points raised above will be further explored in the following chapters which, with this social, historical and literary background in mind, examine the image of the child and childhood in the works of women writing at different stages throughout the century. The extent to which they helped to create stereotypes and subsequently accepted, rejected or modified them and created new ones, explored the implications of gender and were influenced by the rising feminist consciousness in the issues they wrote about, will hopefully throw more light on the importance of the child in nineteenth-century literature.

Chapter 1

Early lessons for life:
The child of reason

The Giddy Girl

Miss Helen was always too giddy to heed
What her mother had told her to shun;
For, frequently, over the street in full speed,
She would cross where the carriages run.

And out she would go to a very deep well
To look at the water below;
How naughty! to run to a dangerous well,
Where her mother forbade her to go!

One morning, intending to take but one peep,
Her foot slipp'd away from the ground;
Unhappy misfortune! the water was deep,
And giddy Miss Helen was drown'd.

Elizabeth Turner, *The Daisy, or, Cautionary Stories in Verse*
Adapted to the Ideas of Children from Four to Eight Years Old (1807)

In the late eighteenth and early nineteenth centuries, the figure of the child acquired new and far-reaching significance in the work of writers of rationalist and moral tales. This interest stemmed from the increasing concern with the nature of the child and the realisation of the importance of upbringing and education in formative years for the moulding of the adult human being, for moral and ethical training of the individual would lead eventually to the general improvement of society. Although such tales were intended for young readers, the authors seem to have written them with the dual audience of child and adult parent or tutor in mind, aware that it was adults who purchased the books and read them to and with their children. Indeed, many of the authors also wrote texts for adults in a similar vein.

The majority of authors of juvenile literature at this time were women, a number of whom, like Mary Wollstonecraft, Barbara Hofland, Sarah

Trimmer and Anna Laetitia Barbauld, also ran their own educational establishments. There are easily identifiable reasons for this. First, moral or didactic zeal was seen as an acceptable motivation for putting pen to paper and thus entering the public domain, an especially important factor for women who needed a respectable means of earning a living. The production of morally didactic literature was also still within the sphere of women's accepted domestic role as educator within the family circle. Writing for and about children was thus seen as appropriate for women and the depiction of domestic settings easily within the reach of most women's limited experience. Moreover, moral and didactic tales, like the tremendously popular religious tracts later, were relatively easy to produce for the inexperienced and aspiring writer, often being variations on a basic formula.[1]

In most such tales, influenced by the work of the French writers Madame de Genlis (*Théâtre à l'usage des jeunes personnes*, 1779, and *Les Veillées du Château*, 1784) and Arnaud Berquin (*L'Ami des enfants*, 1782–83), and by Sarah Fielding's *The Governess, or, Little Female Academy* (1749) in which education is seen to be a moral process based on experience rather than the indiscriminate cramming of facts, the focus of the text is a child who is seen as an imperfect creature needing to be trained and socialised, who receives moral, social and factual instruction and is exposed to experience under the watchful eye of an apparently omniscient adult mentor, usually a tutor or parent figure. In keeping with the urge to educate which dominated the age, the reader is in this way instructed together with the fictional child. The pen was thus seen as a powerful instrument for influencing the character of young readers (for good *or* ill, as critics of imaginative literature who fulminated against the insidious effect of fairy-tales vociferously pointed out). The portrayal of childhood, in thus serving a didactic purpose, is always clearly subservient to the writer's aims rather than being explored for its own sake. In many late eighteenth-century moral tales, like the works of Mrs Barbauld and Mrs Trimmer, the didactic aim is dominant, so that the plots are minimal and contrived, the dialogue stilted and the characters are mere cardboard figures.[2] The portrayal of the child's experience is restricted to the narrator's external, adult and frequently patronising viewpoint with little or no real attempt to enter the child's mind, such that the language and activities of the child and the arguments of the text are coloured by adult perceptions. The processes of reason and learning by experience are foregrounded and other aspects of the child's nature – imagination, fancies, fears and, above all, individualism – tend to be suppressed. The focus is on establishing the ideal child model and the reader is constantly aware of the author looking over his or her shoulder just as the formality and earnestness of the narrative voice shows itself to be aware of the dual audience of child and approving adult.

Didactic books for the young often took the form of dialogues, with the child's questions being answered by an adult, in which the direction of the child's inquisitiveness is artificially manipulated by the author to lead to the desired educational outcome, often beyond the limits of credibility. The 'conversation' in works such as Elizabeth Sandham's *Summer Rambles or Conversations, Instructive and Entertaining for the Use of Children* (1801), Jane Marcet's *Conversations on Chemistry* (1806) and *Mary's Grammar Interspersed with Stories and Intended for the Use of Children* (1835) or Lady Eleanor Fenn's *Rational Sports: In Dialogues passing among the children of a family Designed as a hint to mothers how they may inform the minds of their little people respecting the objects with which they are surrounded* (*c.* 1783), may simply expound facts or moral attitudes, or, in a slightly more complex plot construction, be designed to illustrate and correct the development of bad habits and point out the dangers in thoughtless behaviour. The children enter submissively into rational discussion with the adult, respond eagerly to facts and invariably accept the adult's point of view and advice. The most influential of this type of book was *Evenings at Home, or, The Juvenile Budget Opened* (published in six volumes between 1792 and 1796), by Mrs Barbauld and her brother John Aikin: a compilation of stories, dialogues, plays and poems full of useful instruction on matters of science, manufacturing and the achievements of famous men like Josiah Wedgwood and Richard Arkwright. As in similar texts, the children of the family are constantly instructed, such that even the making of a cup of tea becomes the stimulus for a disquisition on chemical processes. Despite the insistent note of rationalism and materialism, the children do speak and react in a more lively and natural manner, which, together with the range of subjects covered, must account for the continuing popularity of the work throughout the nineteenth century.

Another very popular format was the contrast between two children who are the personification of good or bad, sensible or foolish; an effective if psychologically implausible method of illustrating the results and rewards of different behaviour patterns. The prototype for this approach was Thomas Day's widely read *The History of Sandford and Merton* (1783), partially influenced by Rousseau's *Émile*, in which Harry Sandford, the sensible and industrious farmer's son, is constantly praised for his diligent response to his rational education (in which the child is encouraged to learn from experience of the consequences of his acts) unlike the rich, idle, illiterate and rebellious Tommy Merton who eventually reforms and follows Harry's example. For younger children, cautionary verses which could be easily assimilated and remembered, were composed by writers like Ann and Jane Taylor and Elizabeth Turner, from whose collection *The Daisy, or, Cautionary Stories in Verse Adapted to the Ideas of Children from Four to Eight Years Old* (1807), the poem cited at the head of this chapter is taken. The emphasis in such verses is usually on common sense and obedience, and the consequences of thoughtlessness or defiance are swift, dire and graphically expressed, playing on children's deepest fears. Thus giddy Miss Helen anticipates Maggie Tulliver as a young girl who goes against her mother's wishes and drowns; the boy who plays with the poker is badly burned; and little Jack who ran too far from home to play, is lost and must spend the rest of his life as a chimney-sweep.

Although the desired responses of the young readers are clearly signposted (the names of the characters often leaving no room for doubt as to the example to follow), it is interesting to speculate in passing about children's actual reaction to such small paragons as Little Steady in one of Lady Eleanor Fenn's dialogues from *Cobwebs to Catch Flies, or, Dialogues in Short Sentences, Adapted to Children from the Age of Three to Eight Years* (*c.* 1783), entitled 'The Stubborn Child', who proclaims that 'I am never happy when I have been naughty' and that 'I will not say Why, again, when I am told what to do: but I will always do as I am bid directly.' Little Steady is contrasted with Miss Wilful who questions and disregards Mr Steady's advice about a dog that bites, and, though predictably wounded, is reported to have asserted that 'she would get a pair of thick gloves, and then she would tease Pompey', an attitude consistent with her name but which strikes the modern reader as having a humorously subversive note.[3] As Rousseau pointed out in his discussion of Aesop's fables, children are often inclined to identify or sympathise with the wrong character, the naughty, wicked or defiant being more interesting because livelier and, perhaps, more true to life than the very good.[4] This was a problem which must have exercised many writers of juvenile literature, but which few at this period succeeded in solving satisfactorily. Despite the simplistic didacticism of such texts, however, they can be compared with books for children which are extremely popular in our own time. Mrs Trimmer's use of a family of robins as a paradigm for human behaviour in her *Fabulous Histories, Designed for the Instruction of Children, Respecting their Treatment of Animals* (1786), republished frequently in the nineteenth century as *The History of the Robins*, for example, uses the same basic device as late twentieth-century texts in which errors of judgement or character faults are illustrated by animals, tank-engines or imaginary creatures like the Wombles, the Magic Roundabout characters and those very close relations of Little Steady and Miss Wilful, Roger Hargreaves' Mr Men – Mr Forgetful, Mr Greedy, Mr Nosey, and so on.

In the Georgian period, then, the approach was largely a secular one, promoting the values of good sense, reason, diligence, family loyalty and duty, enterprise, honesty and obedience. William Pinnock's *Catechism of Morality* (*c.* 1827) expressed succinctly the principles of contemporary moral education, dividing human duties into the Personal ('to promote our own permanent security and happiness'), namely Cleanliness, Economy, Industry, Temperance, Contentment, Prudence, Self-Examination, Self-Improvement and Self-Government, and the Relative ('for the permanent security and happiness of society in general'): Obedience, Gratitude, Civility, Benevolence, Charity, Veracity, Honesty, Candour and Justice. These, in fact, were the values, underpinned to different extents by reason and religion, which continued to inform not only the education of the child, but the literary portrayal of childhood, throughout the rest of the nineteenth century.

It is illuminating to consider briefly a further example of a work for young readers based on rationalist principles from the pen of a writer better known for her revolutionary approach to the position of women in her society, Mary Wollstonecraft. In the preface to her *Original Stories from Real Life with Conversations Calculated to Regulate the Affections and Form the Mind to Truth and Goodness* (1788), Wollstonecraft states that 'these conversations and tales are accommodated to the present state of society; which obliges the author to attempt to cure those faults by reason, which ought never to have taken root in the infant mind' and, professing little faith in parents 'for the present generation have their own passions to combat with, and fastidious pleasures to pursue, neglecting those pointed out by nature', stresses her belief that example is more important than the cramming of facts, for 'example directly addresses the senses, the first inlets to the heart; and the improvement of those instruments of the understanding is the object education should have constantly in view, and over which we have most power'.[5]

The short episodes concern Mary (14) and Caroline (10), the daughters of wealthy and neglectful parents who, after the death of their mother, are placed under the tuition of the severely rational Mrs Mason, 'a woman of tenderness and discernment'. The girls are ignorant and have been allowed to acquire bad habits: Mary has 'a turn for ridicule' and Caroline is vain and affected. To correct these, Mrs Mason never allows the girls out of her sight, subjecting them to a strictly regulated regime of constant instruction and improvement. All their failings and acts of thoughtlessness are picked up, no matter how small. During their frequent walks (a device regularly used by didactic writers as a means of furnishing new and endlessly varied opportunities for comment), she lectures them on moral behaviour, kindness to animals and the follies of greed, vanity and improvidence. The character defects held up for critical scrutiny are not just those that would traditionally have been thought appropriate for the edification of girls (vanity, idleness, affectation) but the universal and not specifically gendered faults of anger, lying, destructiveness, brutality, ridiculing other people, improvidence, rudeness to servants, irresolution, prodigality and false pride. Part of her method consists of the telling of traditional stories of example involving characters with names like Jane Fretful, Lady Sly and Mrs Trueman. She teaches her charges charity by taking them to visit poor cottagers and discussing the causes and implications of poverty in scenes which provide realistic pictures of eighteenth-century life. The girls also learn by experience: in chapter 9, 'The Inconveniences of immoderate Indulgence', Caroline, having stuffed herself with fruit, is left to suffer the painful consequences alone, then taken the next day for a walk during which they 'happen' to come across the pigs being fed at their trough, an occasion for appropriate remarks from the indefatigable Mrs Mason and the complete humiliation of the hapless Caroline. To underline her lesson, Mrs Mason commends the behaviour of Mary, who collected some of the fruit for her guardian, thus proving herself a 'friend' and not just a greedy child, for 'reasonable affection had conquered an appetite; her understanding took the lead, and she had practised a virtue'.[6]

Indeed, throughout the different episodes, virtue is synonymous with reason and thus the most important attribute for the child to acquire:

> a child is inferior to a man; because reason is in its infancy, and it is reason which exalts the man above a brute, and the cultivation of it raises the wise man above the ignorant; for wisdom is only another name for virtue.[7]

The highest praise the girls receive from Mrs Mason is 'you have done good this morning, you have acted like rational creatures'.[8] Such is Mrs Mason's influence that the girls' self-esteem depends totally on her opinion: 'her quiet steady displeasure made them feel so little in their own eyes, they wished her to smile that they might be something; for all their consequence seemed to arise from her approbation'.[9] Although Mary and Caroline are generally relatively silent in the text (it is Mrs Mason who does most of the talking), chapter 6 contains an interesting and comparatively rare instance in works of this kind, of the girls talking together alone about their relationship with their tutor-guardian. After being sent to bed for displaying their characteristic faults in company, they discuss the situation, acknowledging the unswerving justice of Mrs Mason's treatment of wrongdoing and displaying a curiously ambivalent mixture of fear and admiration: 'I declare I cannot go to sleep, said Mary, I am afraid of Mrs Mason's eyes . . . I wish I were as wise and good as she is.' Though apprehensive of what might happen the next morning, they declare that they are happier than they ever were at home. The all-powerful yet just adult mentor figure is seen, despite the awe she inspires, as a thoroughly desirable role model: 'I wish to be a woman, said Mary, and to be like Mrs Mason.'[10]

Like many of her contemporaries, Wollstonecraft is firmly critical of the fantastic in children's literature, which is seen as a deviation from reason and the truth, in a way which seems to reveal a disregard for the imaginative needs of the child. Her recommendation of Sarah Trimmer's *Fabulous Histories* comes with a caveat: Mrs Mason allows Caroline to lend the book to a friend only if she can make her first understand that 'birds never talk'. The almost paranoid fear of the insidious effects of imbibing the improbable and untrue is found even in the works of writers who employed the fantastic in their works, as Mary Jane Kilner demonstrates in her disclaimer in *The Memoirs of a Peg-top* (c. 1805), to the effect that 'when a story is written or told where things inanimate are represented as talking or acting it must be known to be only supposition; as in reality wood cannot feel, nor iron think'.[11] The urge to warn against the dangers inherent in excesses of the imagination had particular significance in the case of women writers who, in their aspiration to be recognised as making an important contribution to their society, needed to emphasise their seriousness and rationality and thus to distance themselves and, through their writing, future generations of young girls, from the traits all too commonly associated with their sex: the emotional, the irrational and a tendency to indulge in sensations.[12]

The best writer of moral tales is undeniably Maria Edgeworth (1768–1849), whose entire literary output of juvenile fiction, moral tales for adolescents, tales of fashionable life and adult novels (including her best-known work, *Castle Rackrent* (1800), which portrays the consequences of errors in estate management) were illustrative of the educational views she shared with her father Richard Edgeworth, in collaboration with whom she produced the widely influential *Practical Education* (1798). The theories promulgated in this work were based on the conviction that the education of children was the duty and divine mission of parents and that it was most effective when it involved the hearts of children, stimulating their imagination and desire to learn by the activities of daily life. Influenced by the works of Rousseau and Madame de Genlis, *Practical Education* was regarded as radical in a number of ways: its fundamental premise of child-centred learning recommends lessons in the natural sciences and in practical crafts, urges higher education for girls and states that children should not be forced to learn what they cannot readily understand, criticising mere cramming with facts by rote learning. The most significant criticism levelled at the book during the nineteenth century, however, was of its almost entirely secular approach. It is still an extremely interesting work for students of the period, for it contains detailed observations and anecdotes of children's responses to the process of learning, which Maria Edgeworth was well qualified to portray, as one of a family of twenty-two children (her father married four times) who participated in the education of her siblings and was in the habit of reading her stories to them and taking careful note of their reactions. The Edgeworth children spent most of their time with the adults and had free access to instructive books, maps and educational toys.[13]

That Maria Edgeworth clearly understood and had sympathy with the nature of children is apparent in her preface to her first collection of tales, *The Parent's Assistant* (1796), where she writes that 'only such situations are described as children can easily imagine, and which may consequently interest their feelings. Such examples of virtue are painted, as are not above their conceptions of excellence, and their powers of sympathy and emulation.'[14] Like Wollstonecraft, she rejected the use of fantastic elements such as fairies and giants, but was fully aware of the need to make her stories dramatically interesting to capture the child reader's interest at the same time as instructing them: 'The history of realities, written in an entertaining manner, appears not only better suited to the purposes of education, but also more agreeable to young people than improbable fictions.'[15] Her attempt to portray childhood experience within a didactic framework in a way with which children could identify in fact makes the best of her work far superior to that of her contemporaries in terms of freshness, directness, humour (an element conspicuously lacking in other educational texts) and a recognition of the pleasures and sorrows of the child's world. Unlike the little automata of much didactic fiction, her child characters, though for the most part seen from the outside by the observing adult narrator, more nearly approximate to real living creatures.

For Edgeworth too, a favourite format is the conflict of contrasts; the good, sensible and diligent child struggling against a worthless or malicious opponent. Although it could be argued that with such a polarisation the characters inevitably cannot have any real psychological complexity or development, the situations she features are dramatised very realistically, her 'good' children are made attractive and not nauseating prigs, and her 'bad' characters are credible in their contexts.[16] One of her most enjoyable tales, *Simple Susan*, which appeared in the 1800 augmented edition of *The Parent's Assistant*, contains many of the ingredients which made the stories popular with both children and adults, and influential on the work of later writers.

Set in a village in the border country between Shrewsbury and Oswestry, Shropshire, it is constructed on the pattern (which was to become increasingly popular) of the virtuous poor child who by good sense and industry achieves success and happiness. As in many such tales, the device of an ailing, incapacitated parent, in this case Susan's mother, thrusts the child's efforts into the foreground. The family's situation is made worse by the threat of Mr Price, an honest farmer, being drafted into the militia. The responsibilities of womanhood, the work of caring for home and younger siblings, thus fall early upon Susan who, described as 'modest, sprightly and industrious', is admired by the whole village for her gentleness, unselfishness and sweet temper. Although she performs her many tasks with exemplary energy, neatness (a highly prized quality in the Edgeworth world) and grace, the emphasis on her simplicity, her down-to-earth, decent, humane virtues unsullied by self-consciousness, arrogance or worldly ambition, and her childish delight in play, music, nature and animals make her an attractive and positive character rather than a sickly sweet mouthpiece of platitudinous sentiment. Her qualities are portrayed in a practical context, her prudence, dexterity and initiative displayed in her earning enough money by baking and selling her own bread to help buy a substitute for her father for the militia. She is seen to be ever ready to help others in a quiet, unassuming manner and her friends, the other village children, help her in return. An interesting aspect is the endorsement of her energy and enterprising nature, characteristics especially approved by Edgeworth in girls as well as boys. Although Susan's activities are based on traditional female chores, cooking, sewing, childcare and nursing the sick, she also shows a modest business capacity and is seen to be capable of standing up for herself.

Susan is contrasted with Barbara Case, the spoilt, hypocritical and self-seeking daughter of a grasping, litigious attorney, who in turn is the enemy of Mr Price. This double contrast demonstrates the significance of upbringing for both Susan and Barbara are clearly the products of their family background. Susan has been well brought up despite poverty and Barbara's bad manners are explained, if not excused (and she is not allowed to redeem herself within the confines of the text), by her father's neglect. In Edgeworth's indictment of the grasping cynicism of the middle classes, a theme common in literature of this period and mediated here through the actions of the child characters, false gentility and aspiration to status are doubly opposed to the true nobility of the farming community and that of the aristocracy. Barbara, who once played with the local children, has now become artificially 'refined' and reaps no happiness from her malice towards Susan, in which she is seen merely to follow her father's example. As in other of her tales, far from seeing parents as infallible, Edgeworth shows how the child's tendency to imitate adults can result in their being seriously led astray in moral terms.

The Price family fortunes are aided by the intervention of the local squire and his sisters who, taking a fancy to Susan because of her reputation and modesty, buy her a gown, provide a job for Mr Price and are instrumental in returning Susan's pet lamb and guinea-hen, procured by devious and callous means by Mr Case and his daughter. The question of the nature of charity was to become a burning issue in the nineteenth century and, as will be seen, duty towards the poor was a principle stressed by rational moralists and Evangelicals alike. Thus the upper-class representatives here are seen as benevolent, just and generous to the truly deserving poor: 'those who wish well to their neighbours surely deserve to have well-wishers themselves'.[17] A characteristic part of the moral here, as in other tales of the Georgian period, is that the virtuous receive material rewards for themselves and their family as well as universal respect and approval.

Susan's 'simplicity' is thus not a pejorative term but a commendation of her unsophisticated virtues, allied with common sense and a generous spirit, which ultimately overcomes the self-interested wit and cunning of her adversary.

> Those who never attempt to appear what they are not – those who do not in their manners pretend to anything unsuited to their habits and situation in life, never are in danger of being laughed at by sensible, well-bred people of any rank, but affectation is the constant and just object of ridicule.[18]

Although her age is nowhere mentioned (one imagines her to be about 12), it is the refreshing spontaneity of Susan's childlike nature and her eager participation in the activities of the village children that help to evoke such a delightful picture of a rural childhood. The main action takes place around May Day, at which Susan is to be the May Queen, a treat she is forced to forgo through nursing her mother, and much is made in the narrative of the simple delights of gathering flowers and dancing and singing to the tunes of pipe and harp. The cheerful and affectionate relationship between Susan and her little brothers and the other children is unsentimentally realistic and their language, behaviour and interests credible and engaging. The story demonstrates Edgeworth's awareness that, as she states in *Practical Education*, 'the happiness of childhood peculiarly depends upon their enjoyment of little pleasures'.[19] The role of animals in the life of a child and the importance of looking after their welfare is not just presented as an abstract moral principle, but becomes a vital element in the plot. Susan's love for her pet lamb and her silent, dignified grief at the prospect of its slaughter are touchingly portrayed in a scene all the more effective for its brevity and lack of heavy sentimentality, and the huge significance of such an injustice in a child's world has the capacity to move young, and not-so-young, readers alike.[20]

Lazy Lawrence, one of the original tales in the 1796 edition of *The Parent's Assistant*, presents a similar narrative pattern featuring a boy protagonist. The industry, imagination and initiative of young Jem, spurred on by the love of his horse, Lightfoot, whom he fears may have to be sold, help to support both himself and his widowed mother. Once again, the moral cause and effect are clearly established: good deeds lead to opportunities for work, and diligence and self-reliance are rewarded. Like Susan, Jem earns the patronage of a benefactress who becomes interested in and encourages his honest efforts, so that the eventual material rewards for his family are not seen as charity, which might be deemed to foster idle sponging. Jem's opportunities for work are, as a boy, more wide-ranging than Susan's; he sells fossils which he has collected himself, runs errands, digs gardens and develops a flourishing trade in home-made heath mats, all of which are consonant with healthy boyish activities. Thus, self-help leads to the greater personal satisfaction of self-made success, supported, as before, by respectful assistance from an aristocratic patron.

Energetic endeavour is, moreover, its own reward, for Jem is always merry and never bored, idle and tempted to dishonesty like the contrasting figure in this tale, the eponymous Lawrence, whose self-indulgence and laziness (faults firmly laid at the door of his neglectful, drunken, alehouse-keeper father) result in disgruntled listlessness and, eventually, bad company and mischief. Having conspired to steal Jem's hard-earned silver coins, Lawrence is caught and sent to prison where he too learns to become hard-working and motivated. A factor, worthy of note, which betrays a typically Georgian class-consciousness is the one-dimensional portrayal of the stableboy who leads Lawrence into trouble, a 'low-life' character seen as a hardened wretch who in the end is transported to Botany Bay, whereas Lawrence gets only a month in Bridewell for the same misdeed.

As with Susan, Jem's artlessness and delight in activity, play as well as work, and his strong attachment to an animal, make him an attractive vehicle for Edgeworth's moral. His speech is portrayed simply but without condescension or artificiality and the reader is often given access to his thought processes. When his mistress promises that she will undertake to dispose of as many mats as he can make, his unsophisticated reaction is nicely captured: '"Thank'e, ma'am"', said Jem, making his best bow, for he thought by the lady's looks that she meant to do him a favour, though he repeated to himself, "Dispose of them, what does that mean?"'[21] Edgeworth also uses Jem's internal musings as a means of demonstrating his character and forwarding the plot: '"Perhaps I could make a mat",' he ponders, after hearing of his mistress's need for one. The portrayal of Lawrence is also interesting, and more complex than that of Barbara, for all his wickedness is seen to stem directly from having nothing worthwhile to occupy his time, and he suffers the torments of a guilty conscience the night after helping to steal Jem's money. Moreover, he is allowed to transcend the effects of his upbringing, recognise his errors and profit by Jem's example. In both *Simple Susan* and *Lazy Lawrence*, the youth of the protagonist is crucial to the moral for it is seen as important that good habits should be learned and developed early in life.

The Orphans, from the 1800 edition of *The Parent's Assistant*, takes this general narrative pattern to its extreme. The parent figure is removed altogether by death, and the oldest female child, Mary, aged 12, becomes a little mother to her siblings. This favourite theme, especially, it would seem, of women writers of the time, is developed here in an interesting manner characteristic of Edgeworth's work, for Mary not only assumes all the domestic tasks and preserves the unity of the family against considerable odds but, together with her little brothers and sisters, discovers and develops a thriving cottage industry in the manufacture of soft indoor shoes. This achievement is more notable because of the dire circumstances of the little group of orphans, which are even more grim than in other tales, for they are reduced to living, a touch improbably, in a makeshift home in the ruins of an old castle and even the girls of 6 and 7 have to go to work at a paper mill to earn a few pence. The origins of the shoe manufacturing reveals an amusing touch of characterisation, for it is because of her brother Edmond's discomfiture in the stockings and heavy shoes he is obliged to wear in his new job as a serving-boy that Mary first makes a pair for him with soles of plaited hemp. Such is their popularity that the children of the village are soon happily employed in helping Mary produce more. Once again, impetus to success is given by a benefactress who sees Mary's potential and provides her with flax to spin, hence the means of earning a living and becoming self-reliant while retaining dignity and self-respect. The merry industry of the children is contrasted with the idle, trust-to-luck attitude of an old woman beggar who spends her time looking for buried treasure. In a plot contrivance which is admittedly difficult to swallow, it is Mary who finds a real pot of gold in the shape of a hoard of Roman coins and whose honesty in handing them over earns her and her family a new home as a reward. Despite this problematic twist in the plot, one of the most attractive features of this tale is the portrayal of the self-sufficiency and family affection of the community of children who, though engaged in the task of survival, still retain the spontaneity of childhood in their reactions.

Although childhood is seen to be hard for Edgeworth's protagonists and living conditions generally meagre, poverty also confers the blessings of family closeness and happiness denied to the middle-class foils. Material comforts and entertainments are few but her child characters find their own pleasures in music, play and nature. Moreover, the economy of her narrative serves to minimise the grim implications of their situations, like the actual effects of hunger and cold and long hours at work for the little ones in *The Orphans*, for example. In all these stories what the child learns, through experience and the exercise of reason, is a pattern for life. Unlike other writers, Edgeworth makes her child protagonists fairly dynamic and not just the passive recipients of instruction. She was certainly breaking new ground in making her young female characters robust and active, independent and self-supporting. In other tales in *The Parent's Assistant*, the children save their families, trap burglars, perform feats of courage (see, particularly, *The White Pigeon* and *The False Key*) and even, anticipating a popular theme of later Victorian fiction, teach adults a moral lesson, as in *Forgive and Forget* and, implicitly, *Simple Susan*. While it can be argued that her characters are all cast in a similar mould and, in their behaviour, often seem like small adults (in their clear-headedness, single-minded determination, powers of concentration and lack of hesitation or vacillation for example), they are in many respects more like real children than is the case in most contemporary fiction, and are far more acceptable and engaging than many later Victorian child prodigies of virtue. Edgeworth proved herself adept at identifying and reproducing the joys, anxieties and fears of childhood. Although there is little attempt, as yet, despite the focus on the child's experience, to see the world consistently through the child's eyes, Edgeworth does provide a glimpse of her protagonists' reactions to their situations and of the development of their characters through their thought processes, which must have proved a far more effective method of conveying the message to the young reader than had been hitherto employed. Her narrative voice, moreover, is direct and natural and does not display the stiff, overtly teacherly tone characteristic of other early moral tales, yet does not condescend to younger readers in terms of the range of vocabulary.

Another of Edgeworth's popular approaches, more in line with the type of narrative her contemporaries were producing, was to illustrate a child learning a lesson about a personal character defect such as selfishness or lack of thought. The emphasis is on learning by experience and reasoning, bolstered by reproof and explanation, a process firmly placed in the security of a supportive, middle-class family context. The tales in *Early Lessons* (1801) are based on such character-forming instruction, tracing the progression from ignorance to knowledge and self-awareness as four children, Harry, Lucy, Rosamond and Frank, are forced to endure the consequences of their own actions and choices. Frank, as a boy, is exposed to more practical lessons: he is given his own little hut, taken to see candles made and beer brewed, learns to be brave and efficient and is energetic, eager and engaging. Rosamond, although her lessons are more concerned with inner values, is a very believable creation. A lively, impetuous but well-meaning child, she suffers in one of Edgeworth's best-known stories, *The Purple Jar*, for her obstinate desire to possess a beautiful jar she has seen in a chemist's shop instead of the new pair of shoes she badly needs and which her mother wants to buy. The mental tussle she undergoes between her recognition of the need for shoes and the desire for the jar is well portrayed, resolving itself in favour of the ornament although she is aware that this means she cannot have new shoes for another month:

> 'that's a very long time indeed! You can't think how these hurt me; I believe I'd better have the new shoes. Yet, that purple flower-pot. Oh, indeed, mamma, these shoes are not so very, very bad! I think I might wear them a little longer, and the month will soon be over. I can make them last till the end of the month, can't I? Don't you think so, mamma?'[22]

Her speech and reactions are realistically impetuous and egotistical. When her mother says that she will buy only the shoes or the jar, Rosamond responds instantly: '"Dear Mamma, thank you – but if you could buy both?"' She soon learns her mistake as her feet suffer appallingly and she has to forgo outings as her parents refuse to take her anywhere in her broken, shabby shoes, but her mother, in unnerving and unflinching rationalist manner, will not relent until Rosamond is able to acknowledge and understand her error. The emptiness of Rosamond's fancy is underlined when the jar turns out to be plain glass filled with purple liquid, a fact her mother knew all along. Thus, Rosamond learns painfully to examine her priorities more carefully and to admit she was wrong, although she remains convincingly childlike: '"however I am sure – no, not quite sure, but I hope I shall be wiser another time"'.[23] The modern reader finds it difficult to warm to Rosamond's cool and imperturbable mother who could perhaps have made her point without allowing her child's physical distress to go so far. However, like Mary Wollstonecraft in her portrayal of Mrs Mason, with her emphasis on rationality at the expense of affection and emotionality in the child-and-parent (or governess) relationship, Edgeworth seems to be revealing a desire to play down what were regarded as the traditional feminine aspects of nurturing in favour of more traditionally masculine attitudes to education, in order to demonstrate the seriousness of her approach.[24]

Similarly, in *The Birthday Present* (*The Parent's Assistant*), Rosamond makes an elaborate filigree paper basket for her spoilt cousin Bell while her sister Laura chooses to give her pocket money to a poor lacemaker whose work has been ruined by the actions of a callous footman in the street. In a subsequent discussion with her father about the basket, Rosamond is forced to realise that making a useless object for someone she dislikes simply because they expect a gift on their birthday was a poor use of her time, energy and resources and that benevolence to the poor is a more admirable form of generosity. *The Birthday Present* is an interesting tale because more of the child's viewpoint is portrayed and the reader is made to identify with Rosamond as her present, lovingly made, is first scorned, then carelessly destroyed. In contrast to the implacable rationalism of her parents who believe, among other things not likely to endear them to the child reader, in not distinguishing birthdays from other days, Rosamond's reactions appear more believably human and childlike. Her eagerness and absorption during the making of the gift and her anxiety lest it should be damaged before she can bestow it earn our sympathy in the face of her father's fastidious distaste at the flimsy result of her efforts. (He even goads her by suggesting that it is less useful than the purple jar!) Similarly, we cannot fail to identify with her anguish as his clever manipulation of her spirited attempts to justify her actions by his superior wit and ability to argue reduce her to the conclusion that she has been a fool. Events, however, inevitably prove him correct, for Bell has learnt the habits of 'tyranny, meanness and falsehood' from her maidservant and quickly succeeds in breaking the basket, thus demonstrating, on more than one level, its uselessness. Moreover, Rosamond's desire to please is seen as, to a certain extent, self-reflective, for she wanted her godmother to witness and praise her generosity. Nevertheless, she comes, convincingly, to recognise her error and finds greater satisfaction in praising the true, unselfish generosity of her sister.

This type of tale is more overtly didactic than those of *The Parent's Assistant* but here, too, Edgeworth displays her ability to capture the child's responses, and the dialogue is arguably even more natural and spontaneous. Frank, too, speaks in a register with which the child reader could identify, although he is also given a more adult language in some of his more intensely moral enunciations.[25] In her *Moral Tales* (1801), written for adolescents, we find some equally attractive portraits of children in a similar comfortable middle-class setting. The comical Charles in *The Good Aunt*, for example, is led by an injudicious visitor to affirm roundly that he prefers a bear and a learned pig (characters from his storybooks) to his tutor. The criticism is, of course, of the adult's stupidity in contrast to the child who, quickly realising the situation he has been placed in, asks his aunt '"Am I a fool?"' *The Good French Governess*, a tale which contrasts a bad and a good system of education, contains an interesting insight into a child's choice of plaything which, though very much in line with Georgian rationalist thinking, would strike a chord with modern progressive parents too. The 8-year-old Herbert is everyone's despair, 'a little surly rebel, who took pleasure in doing exactly the contrary to everything that he was desired to do, and who took pride in opposing his powers of endurance to the force of punishment'.[26] His parents' habit of introducing him to visitors as 'Rough-head' understandably makes him bashful and 'averse to polite society', and prone to seeking out the company of servants instead. When the new French governess, a woman of decidedly progressive educational ideas (which Edgeworth perhaps associated with her nationality), takes Herbert and his little sister Favoretta, a pretty, spoilt child who is lively and happy in company but idle, spiritless and pettish when alone, to a 'rational toyshop', an emporium stuffed with wonders, Herbert pounces upon a wooden cart which he likes precisely because it stimulates his imagination and provides an outlet for his energies, unlike the more elaborate toys, limited in their entertaining power, preferred by Favoretta. He also gets enormous pleasure from planting radish seeds and observing, and eventually eating, the results. Thus he learns patience and how to occupy himself fruitfully while having fun, through the now familiar method of rational teaching and material reward.

Although her adult novels are more concerned with adult situations and problems, it is in *Harrington* (1817) that we find what is perhaps Edgeworth's most successful attempt at entering a child's mind and portraying the long-lasting effects of childhood experience on an impressionable personality. In this novel, written in response to criticism of her earlier stereotypically unfavourable portrayal of Jews, the protagonist, Harrington, embarking on an exploration of his past, traces his fear and hatred of Jews to a specific experience in his childhood. This is indeed one of the earliest examples of a protagonist attempting to reconstruct the past to explain his or her present self, thus affording more direct access to a child's experience, a narrative strategy used to excellent effect in works like *Great Expectations* and *Jane Eyre*.[27] He begins with the memory of an event when, aged 6 years old, on his first evening in London, sleepy and with his senses overexcited, he is struck by the sight from his window of the light of the lamplighter's torch flaring on 'the face and figure of an old man with a long white beard and a dark visage', carrying a large bundle and repeating 'old clothes' in a low, abrupt, mysterious tone.[28] Although the good-natured Jew smiles up at the child, he is terrified by his nursemaid's threat that 'old Simon' will come up and carry him away in his bag. The pernicious influence of uneducated servants on children is a recurring theme in the work of both Edgeworth and Wollstonecraft, and was a characteristic preoccupation of the age.[29] The gullible child is quite naturally deeply dismayed, 'the old man's face had changed in an instant', and Fowler, the vicious nursemaid, seeing the effectiveness of her threat, continues to play on the child's fears such that the very mention of old Simon reduces him instantly to passive obedience. Her threat is endorsed by further stories of murders and abductions of children allegedly perpetrated by Jews (Edgeworth is quick to assert that such tales would not be believed 'these days') and, sworn to secrecy by her fear of his mother's reprimand, the young Harrington soon becomes her slave. The portrayal of his sleepless nights spent in 'indescribable agony of terror', in which he sees 'faces around me grinning, glaring, receding, advancing, all turning at last into the same face of the Jew with the long beard and terrible eyes' and imagines the sack full of the mangled limbs of children ('it opened to receive me, or fell upon my bed, or lay heavy on my breast, so that I could neither stir nor scream') most effectively conveys the child's experience of impotent anguish and the way in which the seed of an idea planted in a child's mind can acquire horrendously momentous importance and potentially damage the tender psyche.[30]

Although there is some poetic justice in the fact that Fowler now has to sit with her small charge till he falls asleep, her attempts to remedy the harm she has done are fruitless, for, as Edgeworth explains, the 'power of association' prolongs Harrington's terror despite her remonstrations for 'my imagination was by this time proof against ocular demonstration', reducing him to a state of hysteria in old Simon's presence.[31] The situation becomes more hopeless when the Jew is paid to stay away from the house, for this, when the word gets around, sparks off the regular appearance of many fake Jews such that Harrington is made to feel a sort of magical persecution. Although this apparently reflects the traditional literary representation of Jews as rogues, it is in fact the crime of Fowler, the prejudice of his father and the emerging character of Harrington himself, now noticeably warped by his upbringing, which are held up to criticism here. In time, the child's 'sensibility' is seen by others as a sign of genius and 'as often happens with those who begin by being dupes, I was in immanent danger of becoming a knave' for he becomes increasingly guilty of exaggeration and affectation.[32]

The rest of the novel depicts Harrington's development as he unlearns his prejudice through a series of varied and often not very convincing encounters with Jews. The first episode in which, now a schoolboy, he is moved to defend a persecuted Jewish pedlar boy on the grounds of common humanity, sets the pattern when it transpires that the boy is the son of old Simon but conceals the fact because of Harrington's well-known aversion. The novel has been criticised for its contrivances and improbabilities and the overstrained nature of the author's attempt to right a social injustice, but its power and value lie in the utterly convincing insight into a child's view of experience and the assertion of the fundamental role played by the memory of such formative moments in the moulding of personality. The role of memory is in fact twofold, for as Edgeworth affirms: 'we must condescend to be even as little children, if we would discover or recollect those small causes which early influence the imagination and afterwards become strong habits, prejudices and passions'.[33] Memories can be thus, as Harrington finds, both the cause of evil and the means of undoing it. This novel demonstrates most convincingly Edgeworth's conviction of the importance of the sound education of both heart and mind, a view which exerted considerable influence on more complex psychological portrayals in later nineteenth-century literature. As Vineta Colby remarks:

> All the little Jane Eyres and David Copperfields and Maggie Tullivers and Richard Feverels were pupils in the schoolroom of the 'education of the heart' for which Maria Edgeworth and her sister-novelists like Susan Ferrier or Jane Austen were supplying curricula and texts.[34]

Among these literary sisters, Jane Austen (1775–1817) is normally seen as pre-eminent, but where the portrayal of childhood is concerned she is not, in fact, the most significant. Of course, her main concerns are other, notably the fortunes and misfortunes of young women as they come to greater self-knowledge and understanding of others on the only path to personal fulfilment open to them, the memorably described 'pleasantest preservative from want', marriage.[35] In fact, she wrote to her niece, Anna, in 1814 that 'till the heroine grows up, the fun must be imperfect . . . One does not care for girls till they are grown up.'[36] Yet Austen certainly shared her contemporaries' interest in the effects of education and upbringing and the socialisation of children. When they appear in her novels, however, children are of relatively minor importance, and her depiction of spoilt or unruly children is a means of directing criticism at the irresponsibility or lack of common sense or good breeding of the parents. Often she uses children to represent the financial and moral responsibilities of a family as a social unit, or merely as a device for throwing light on the character or behaviour of an adult figure or for furthering the plot, like little Charles in *Persuasion*.

Where Jane Austen does engage more fully with the nature of childhood itself, it is as a brief, though invariably insightful, explication of the origins of a protagonist's character and a prelude to her more central concern, the consequences of upbringing in adulthood. The gently ironic description in *Northanger Abbey* (published 1818) of Catherine Morland's failure to match up to the late eighteenth-century ideal of childish femininity evokes a delightful image of a strong-willed, active and imaginative individual:

> She had a thin, awkward figure, a sallow skin without colour, dark lank hair, and strong features; so much for her person, and not less unpropitious for heroinism seemed her mind. She was fond of all boys' plays, and greatly preferred cricket, not merely to dolls, but to the more heroic enjoyments of

infancy, nursing a dormouse, feeding a canarybird, or watering a rosebush. Indeed she had no taste for a garden, and if she gathered flowers at all, it was chiefly for the pleasure of mischief, at least so it was conjectured from her always preferring those which she was forbidden to take.[37]

At 10, Catherine is seen to shirk her lessons, show little talent for music or drawing, and in many respects continues to subvert the stereotypical ideal of more rigid literary models:

> What a strange unaccountable character, for with all these symptoms of profligacy at ten years old, she had neither a bad heart nor a bad temper, was seldom stubborn, scarcely ever quarrelsome, and very kind to the little ones, with few interruptions of tyranny. She was, moreover, noisy and wild, hated confinement and cleanliness, and loved nothing so well in the world as rolling down the grassy slope at the back of the house.[38]

Though improving in looks and manners at 15, Catherine still prefers cricket, riding and running about to sitting sedately at her work or books, except for storybooks. The behaviour which made her childhood happy is not, however, when unmodified by reason, decorum and good sense as she gets older, good training for the future. Her impetuosity and unconventionality and her exposure to imaginative literature at an impressionable age while 'in training for a heroine' thus combine to form the perfect psychological climate for the events which follow, as Catherine becomes more and more embroiled in what she believes to be a situation straight out of a Gothic romance. She is now open to criticism as self-indulgent, craving emotional excitement and lacking sense and prudence; her childhood energy has become unrestrained and misdirected and when channelled entirely through her imagination leads her into errors of judgement in reading the real world. Under the influence of a loving and rational male, Henry Tilney, Catherine eventually learns to control her feelings and see and deal with things clearly and with greater maturity.

The description of Fanny Price's childhood in *Mansfield Park* (1814) is similarly presented to illustrate the formative power of early experience and, though brief, is a perceptive and moving portrait of a lonely, sad child, insecure and lacking in a sense of self-worth. Brought to live with relatives, Fanny is 'afraid of every body, ashamed of herself, and longing for the home she had left, she knew not how to look up, and could scarcely speak to be heard, or without crying'.[39] Forlorn and fearful, she is mortified and condescended to by her cousins and has a lowly opinion of her own claims. Missing her siblings and neglected and unvisited by her own family (except once by her brother William on whom she dotes), Fanny learns to hide her tears beneath a passive manner, till the friendship of her cousin Edmund Bartram helps to reconcile her to her situation and she becomes less afraid and, in the family's eyes, more 'acceptable'. Fanny's early sensitivity, tentativeness and craving for affection prefigure, however, her adult character which is exemplary in its modesty, thoughtfulness, capacity for endurance and selfless goodness, as does the contrast with her cousins who have plenty of learning and are full of facts but lack the ignorant Fanny's 'common acquirements of self-knowledge and humility'.[40]

Fanny's plight in some ways foreshadows that of later unhappy, deprived literary children like Jane Eyre and Maggie Tulliver, as the theme of the effects on the child of uncaring or misunderstanding parents or relations became an increasing concern in the nineteenth-century novel. Although Angus Wilson has seen *Mansfield Park* as the first novelistic description of the neglect of a lonely child, this is not the case.[41] As early as 1788 Mary Wollstonecraft had given a touching portrait of just such a lonely child in her novel *Mary: A fiction*, which contains many autobiographical elements. Left to her own devices and neglected by a sickly, vain mother who fears competition from her daughter, Mary becomes, like so many literary females after her, a great reader and observer of nature, watching the clouds and gazing at the moon (a recurring motif in nineteenth-century literature symbolising the female's frustrated longing for self-development) and dwells largely in her imagination, identifying more with the supernatural than the human: 'The wandering spirits, which she imagined inhabited every part of nature, were her constant friends and confidants.'[42] Just as Wollstonecraft seems to have become a prey to unhealthy introspection in her sense of herself as unloved and unappreciated, the desperate need for a focus for Mary's loving instincts results in the danger of her becoming a 'creature of impulse, and the slave of compassion'.[43] The development of her sensibility is directly laid at the door of her parents' neglect: 'Could she have loved her father or mother, had they returned her affection, she would not so soon, perhaps, have sought out a new world.'[44] Although she learns to do good to others, it is not without passing through much tribulation, a reflection, to some extent, of the author's own unsettled life.[45]

A similar picture of a child who finds relief for her grief at feeling unloved in running wild in the fields and park of her home is painted by Wollstonecraft's daughter, Mary Shelley, in her remarkable novel *Matilda*, written in 1819. In a first-person narrative, Matilda describes the lack of real contact between herself and her cold aunt in this evocative image: 'to a timid child she was as a plant under a thick covering of ice; I should cut my hands in endeavouring to get at it'.[46] Instead she spends hours alone with nature, dreaming, her emotions become focused on inanimate objects and books replace human intercourse. Her grief and longing generate fancies which often revolve around her desire to be reunited with her absent father. One such fantasy, which both looks back to eighteenth-century sentimental novels of adventure and forward to much later feminist fiction, is of setting off to seek her father throughout the world disguised as a boy, although, as she wryly comments, she never found the courage to depart. When her father, whose love for his daughter appears to be of an almost incestuous nature, drowns himself, Matilda lives a withdrawn existence, despite the presence in her life of a young poet, a situation which suggests complex personal preoccupations on Mary Shelley's part.[47] Indeed, the provocative nature of the novel may account for the fact that it was never published in her lifetime.

The technique of manipulating contrasting characters to illustrate the consequences of an exemplary or unsatisfactory upbringing employed so widely in books for children was also taken over in the early nineteenth century by writers who were directing their work at the adult market. Susan Ferrier (1782–1854), for example, in her much underrated novel *Marriage* (1818), depicts the raising of twin girls, the daughters of the self-willed, capricious Lady Juliana who marries against her father's wishes and finds herself immured in a remote Scottish castle. One of the twins, Mary, rejected by her mother, is sent to be fostered at the home of Mrs Douglas, Lady Juliana's sister-in-law and an unaffected, rational woman, where she thrives 'blest in the warm affection and mild authority of her more than mother', while her sister, Adelaide, is brought up to be as vain, wilful and self-indulgent as her mother.[48] Their different paths and fortunes in life, often humorously depicted despite the clear didactic aim, demonstrate Ferrier's praise of the virtues of a prudent, thrifty, active upbringing as opposed to the unsatisfying emptiness of a luxury-loving, socialite existence. As in other contemporary educational fiction, the self-indulgent and ambitious are punished and the wisely brought-up, modest and unself-regarding child is well rewarded with a happy and fulfilling life. The emphasis, as in Austen's novels, however, is once again on the results, and although the elements and relative merits of both types of upbringing are commented upon by other characters at length, the actual portrayal of the children's experience is minimal, the main action of the second half of the novel being concerned with their subsequent fortunes as young women.

Such a straightforward contrast is used as late as 1876 by Mrs Linnaeus Banks (Isabella Varley, 1821–87) in *The Manchester Man*, where it is united with the theme of factory work in the form of conflict between an honest, industrious apprentice, Jabez Clegg, and the spoilt, idle manufacturer's son, Lawrence (perhaps influenced by Maria Edgeworth's character). Despite his inauspicious start in life (he is picked out of the flood waters of the River Irk by a poor but kindly and hard-working Manchester tanner), Jabez becomes a model apprentice and eventually wins the love of his master's daughter, while his antagonist, Lawrence, is suitably punished for his cruel and patronising superiority by, among other things, a ducking in a horsepond.[49] A fascinating novel for its description of early nineteenth-century Manchester, and for its inclusion of historical events, notably the Peterloo Massacre of 1816, one of the darker moments of Manchester history, its fundamental

moral and technique are essentially the same as in Edgeworth's stories seventy
years earlier. Indeed, the recognition by writers of the effectiveness of such
a technique is evidenced by its continued use, often with much greater
degrees of sophistication, throughout the century, as the Jane Eyre/Blanche
Ingrams, Mary Garth/Rosamond Vincey, Maggie Tulliver/Lucy Deane pairs
illustrate.[50]

The early nineteenth-century concerns apparent in the portrayal of
childhood and the role of children in literature were significantly developed
by Harriet Martineau (1802–76), an extraordinarily prolific writer, lionised
in London literary society and in the United States and best known for her
nine volumes of *Illustrations of Political Economy* (1832–34). Her most
important fictional work was written in the 1830s and 1840s and in a number
of ways she can be seen as a bridge figure between the Georgian and Victorian
ages.[51] Her preoccupation with the nature and importance of education,
similar in kind to that of Maria Edgeworth, is evidenced in her letters and in
Household Education (1849), a kind of manual designed for what she called the
'Secularist order of parents', in which she emphasises the role of everyone in
the home in training the young child's character and moulding its future
behaviour. By means of an extremely perceptive analysis of a child's hopes
and fears, often drawing on her own experience as her autobiography (to be
considered later) reveals, she gives sensible advice on how to inculcate
qualities like patience, truthfulness, conscientiousness and affection, recommending fresh air, cleanliness, exercise, discipline and manual and domestic
work for boys and girls alike. Her affinity with Maria Edgeworth is apparent
in her early moral tales for young people which exemplify the results of
influences in childhood and advocate personal effort. In *Principle and Practice,
or, The Orphan Family* (1827), 'a plain unaffected narrative of the exertions
made by a family of young persons, to render themselves and each other happy
and useful in the world', aims echoing the recommendations in Pinnock's
Catechism, the protagonists learn to survive by looking to their own industry
and moral will, and in *Five Years of Youth, or, Sense and Sentiment* (1831), she
contrasts the differing effects of an unconventional upbringing by their
widowed father on two young girls.[52]

Building on the success of Edgeworth's little heroes who fight injustice and
overcome obstacles, Martineau went on to depict in her work for older
children *The Playfellow* (four volumes containing *The Settlers at Home, The
Peasant and the Prince, Feats on the Fjord* and *The Crofton Boys,* 1841) truly
heroic deeds by children who undergo quite severe trials when they are
suddenly exposed to dangerous situations in strange and hostile environments.[53] In the first volume, *The Settlers at Home,* in which the windmill of a
family of Dutch immigrants is swept away by floods, the Linacre children,
mistakenly believing themselves to be orphaned, learn to trust in Providence
and fend for themselves in the ruins of their home with bravery, patience and

fortitude. The day-to-day efforts of Oliver (11) and Mildred (9) to cope with the crumbling building, the construction of a raft, the difficulties of finding food and the conflict with another boy, the family's enemy Roger Redfern who initially tries to survive alone on a nearby hilltop but finds solitude unpalatable and joins the others in their struggles, are vividly portrayed in what is still a super adventure story. The reader shares the boys' enthusiasm as they devise ways of transporting objects they find via a basket on a rope and their anxieties as the flood waters invade their small living space. There is no maudlin sentimentality in the mutual affection, concern and support of the family; even the death of their baby brother is handled with a sensitive realism. They experience demoralisation, grief and fear but little self-pity and certainly not the passive, pious resignation dear to many Victorian writers. Roger, though mischievous, destructive and lazy (he wishes that hares ran around ready-roasted) is not seen as irredeemably bad and is transformed when motivated in a positive, practical way. Mildred plays the little-mother role, but with energy and endurance despite her exhaustion, while Oliver, the oldest, takes charge and achieves considerable self-development in the process:

> Oliver seemed to have grown many years older since the flood came. He was no taller, and no stronger; indeed he seemed today to be growing weaker with fatigue, but he was not the timid boy he had always appeared before he spoke like a man; and there was the spirit of a man in his eyes. It was not a singular instance. There have been other cases in which a timid boy has been made a man of, on a sudden, by having to protect, from danger or in sorrow, some weaker than himself.[54]

The novel is all the more appealing because of the focus on the details of the children's lives isolated from the adult world. Their drastic situation in fact empowers the children, for they have to learn to make decisions and act positively, independent of adult help, to ensure their survival. There is one adult who shares their trials, the servant Ailwin, but she is a superstitious, ignorant and fearful woman who, apart from her physical strength, is more helpless than the children, and a source of much of the humour in the text.

In *Feats on the Fjord*, a young herd-boy helps to rescue his fellow servant Erica's lover from an island on which he has become trapped and eventually, because of his bravery and ingenuity, is allowed to lead a party of twelve men in an attack on a pirate schooner which is threatening the community on the fjord. The early chapters depict an amusing episode during the betrothal feast of Erica and Rolf which captures delightfully, by invoking the boy's viewpoint, the inquisitive, half-bold, half-fearful nature of Oddo. Sent to carry a large portion of cake and a mug of ale out into the snow as an offering to the local spirit, Nippen, Oddo is tempted to taste, and eventually consume, the cake himself. His curiosity further urges him to hide in the hopes of seeing the spirit approach while he speculates hopefully that Nippen will make allowances for the absence of the cake. He is successively alarmed by the echo of his own voice, fooled into believing that a fox which comes to sniff at the ale is the spirit in disguise, and eventually so frightened by the shriek of a large owl that he turns to flee. His merriment at the belief of his grandfather, master and guests that he has been carried off by the spirit, 'chained astride the wind', soon changes, however, to guilt and apprehension when the event is seen as a bad omen. His brave deeds thereafter are motivated to a large extent by his feelings of responsibility and desire to atone, and with the safe return of Rolf and the defeat of the pirates, the community learns a lesson about the evils of superstition and Oddo, like Oliver, graduates to manhood.

The dramatic settings and active heroism of these tales, exploring the children's responses to situations in which they have to rely on their own resourcefulness and courage, unguided and unprotected by a parent or benevolent adult (and in which passive obedience and book-learning play no part) can be seen as the beginnings of an important change of direction in terms of style and subject matter in juvenile literature. Martineau does not in any way talk down to young readers, although she speaks to them easily and directly, avoiding the ponderously instructive tone used by her contemporary Frederick Marryat in his sea adventure story for children, *Masterman Ready* (1841–42) and the chauvinism of R. M. Ballantyne's *The Coral Island* (1858).[55] Although she occasionally points a moral in her own voice, as in the passage quoted above, she generally allows the values she wishes to endorse to emerge from the events of the story themselves.

The inclusion in her tales of a number of sick or maimed children is another aspect which links Harriet Martineau firmly to the Victorian age but their role in her narratives and her approach to the question of infirmity are noticeably different. Her own frequent and extended periods of illness and the deafness from which she suffered from childhood naturally interested her in a theme which was generally neglected and, later, frequently romanticised in literature. Even more repugnant to her was that infirmity, loss of a faculty or limb, or deformity was all too often associated with some kind of moral deficiency.[56] In her tales, blind, deaf and crippled children learn courage, patience and acceptance of the Divine will, but she is also concerned with the practical problems and the children's own perception of their plight, their fears and efforts to cope with their situation. This is, of course, a natural concomitant of her belief in the heroism of the weak and as such can, moreover, be seen to reflect another of her concerns, the predicament of females in her society, just as illness came to be a useful metaphor for women's powerlessness in later fiction. In *Cousin Marshall*, one of her *Illustrations of Political Economy*, Sally, an orphan, is progressively losing her sight and is prepared by her adoptive mother for eventual entry into an asylum for the blind. Sally's distress is seen to be based largely on her own earlier curiosity about the uniformed figures of the asylum children whom she had often followed in the streets to see how they managed to find their way about, trying to peep under their bonnets to glimpse their faces. This very believable anxiety about her own future situation is an interesting contrast to the sentimental-ised, ethereal sick children of the Little Nell school of fiction. When Sally reappears after a short while at the asylum, she has adapted well and seems cheerful and relatively independent.

By far the most interesting of Martineau's works in this respect is *The Crofton Boys*, volume 4 of *The Playfellow*, a coming-of-age story which deserves to be far better known. It is one of the earliest realistic pictures of school life, with characters and situations with which young readers could readily identify. The opening scenes of life in the Proctor family are natural and attractive and the relationship of Hugh, aged 8, with his older brother and sisters and his younger brother is portrayed in a refreshing and vivid manner. Hugh is light years away from the priggish little boys of the early moral tales: his energetic excitement as he rolls and stands on his head on the roof leads and his aching longing to go to school like his brother Phil and become a Crofton boy are still enormously appealing to the modern reader. His impetuous enthusiasm for life makes him unable to concentrate for long, however, and he is constantly in trouble for inattentiveness to his lessons. The agony he experiences over his inability to remember the correct answer to four times seven (he is involuntarily fixated on fifty-six), and his terror that the visiting headmaster of Crofton School will ask him the dreaded sum, demonstrate considerable insight on Martineau's part into the way that comparatively trivial matters can become an obsession in a child's mind.

The psychology of the portrayal of Hugh's responses when he eventually gets to school is equally impressive. After all his delighted anticipation, he finds that it is not as wonderful as he thought and life is fraught with problems. He feels embarrassed about washing and combing his hair, let alone praying, in front of the other boys in his dormitory (he is indignant about being called a Betty because he continues to part his hair neatly) and anxious about remembering not to kiss Phil as he would at home. He begins to long not to be noticed (for as the youngest new boy he is an object of interest), becomes more and more uncertain of himself and distressed because Phil ignores him, and sobs himself to sleep at night. Such is Martineau's skill at rendering these experiences in straightforward, believably childlike terms, that the reader shares each little agony with Hugh. Some relief and comfort materialise when he is befriended by an older boy, Dan Firth, who explains the conventions of school life to him, and that new boys are seen as girls 'till they show that they are little men'.[57] Thus begins a series of lessons by which Hugh becomes socialised in the school context.

Although he is able to earn some respect for his courage and spirit by rescuing another boy from a group of tormenters, it becomes clear to him that he has a lot to learn about schoolboy lore which forbids tale-telling, enlisting a master's help in difficulties with classmates or boasting about academic prowess. His inexperience and innocence lead him into many scrapes and errors: he gets chased by cows, mocked for talking about his sisters, cheated out of his pocket-money and caned for going out of bounds. He is gullible and easily led but gradually realises that he must learn discretion and to listen to his own reason and conscience. He remains haunted by his old problem of lack of concentration and Martineau evokes an exceptionally perceptive picture of the signs of disturbance caused by his anxiety: he suffers from feverish headaches, tiredness and frequently jumps up in the night. In all this he is sustained mainly by the memory of his mother and her advice to him, that if he trusts in God, he will not fail and will do his duty and bear his troubles like a man. As in other novels of the early Victorian era, parental authority is never questioned here and is synonymous with love and respect. The adoration of the kind, beautiful mother is also very characteristic of the times, although this novel is unusual in that Martineau gives more prominence to the mother's moral authority than is usually the case in male-authored school novels, where the masculine atmosphere of the institution is seen as the most formative influence on character.

Hugh is gradually able to cope and progress, learning how to play with other boys and to enjoy the acquisition of knowledge without flaunting it. As Dan tells him, a boy must be 'full of action – if he tops the rest at play – holds his tongue, or helps others generously – or shows a manly spirit without being proud of it', the whole school will be his friend.[58] Tragedy strikes, however, when Hugh is pulled off an icy wall and has to have his foot amputated. This shock event is handled frankly yet sensitively by Martineau for, although not ignoring Hugh's fears and moments of despair as he sees his dreams of becoming a soldier or a sailor devastated, her attitude is brisk and sensible as Hugh is made to confront the practical problems of coping with everyday life. She even tackles and explains his first shock of apparently experiencing feeling in his missing foot. Her message is that it is important not to create false hopes by denying the situation but to get on with life, the more unpleasant aspects soon thus becoming habit. There is no sentimentality about his injury, nor is he presented as a model of wisdom and spirituality for adults like Dickens' Tiny Tim in *A Christmas Carol* (1843). His mother's support is rational and calm as she talks to him of the need to please God by accepting and bearing his affliction. The novel is also noteworthy for the different slant Martineau puts on the subject of the attendant problems of invalidism. His mother fears that Hugh may get vain and selfish because of the regard he has earned from the other boys for refusing to reveal who pulled him from the wall, and through being petted for his bravery, and the implications of his accident for the other children are also addressed. There is a touching scene between Hugh and Phil in which the latter is faced with the question of his future attitude towards his brother at school and to consider his own values and loyalties. The psychology of Tooke, the headmaster's son, who caused the accident, is revealed in quite a complex network of reactions: he inwardly rejoices at Hugh's continuing misery over his lessons because this obscurely relieves him of his feelings of guilt over the real injury, while constantly fearing discovery.

Hugh has further to go along the path of self-development, however, for his disability is not seen as any kind of excuse. He is forced to confront his high-handed treatment of his sister, his selfishness over the company of his friends, his love of money and the temptation at times of discouragement or anger to reveal his secret about his assailant or use his injury as a means of getting indulgence. Once reintegrated into school life, he soon becomes more grieved by his failure in his lessons than by his foot, and the dialogues between Hugh and Phil, who agrees to help him not only out of kindness but because of the gratification of his own vanity, are among the most natural and lifelike in the book. Similarly, the depiction of his friendship with Holt is appealing as their mutual understanding and sympathy are developed. The two boys improve significantly through their interaction, the timid Holt gaining in spirit himself as he helps Hugh to maintain his courage. Eventually Hugh is offered the opportunity to go to India with Holt to work when he leaves school, a prospect which comes so close to his original desire to travel that he is able to feel almost glad that he lost his foot and discovered the new horizon of companionship and the chance for 'honourable duty'.

The school life depicted in this novel is clearly a microcosm of adult life and what Hugh learns is a sound pattern of moral behaviour for the future. It is also extremely realistic, as comparison with the far more famous but less readable *Tom Brown's Schooldays* (1857) by Thomas Hughes or Dean Farrar's *Eric, or Little by Little* (1858) will amply demonstrate. Not only are the narrative and dialogue straightforward and natural, but most of Hugh's experiences are the most common and universal dilemmas of school life (bullying, jealous rivalry, anxieties over work not done, tale-telling, breaking rules) still familiar to readers of twentieth-century school stories and, indeed, to fans of television's 'Grange Hill'.

Like many elements in her work, the preoccupation with the psychological implications of infirmity for all concerned relates to her own experience as a child. In her autobiography, completed in 1855 but withheld from publication till 1877, Martineau writes of her 'first great wholesome discipline' at the age of 8 in her friendship with a crippled child called Emily Cooper.[59] She relates that she herself suffered a great deal after her friend lost her leg, becoming nervous and morbid, and claims that her own deafness may have been partly caused by the stress and the 'exciting and vainglorious dreams of martyrdom' which troubled her nights. Although the experience led to the positive lesson of patience under pain and privation, she sees this as 'poor recompense' for the enormous suffering of the imagination. She expresses anger, too, at the attitude of Emily's parents who sought to deny the situation which led to constant self-sacrifice on Harriet's part because she felt obliged to keep her friend company all the time instead of playing with the other children. Her subsequent sense of guilt at her lurking fear of growing crooked herself through supporting Emily as they walked and at leaving her for a short time to join in a game, quickly became a kind of self-detestation. Nevertheless, she sees Emily's disability as one of the 'most favourable influences I had the benefit of after taking myself in hand for self-government'.[60] Of her own deafness which was first identified at the age of 12 and was very noticeable at 16, she writes in a characteristically matter-of-fact way, commenting on the bad management of deaf children and of the dangers she experienced of becoming either a bore or ridiculous. Apart from constant fatigue and irritability, her family's reluctance to face the truth led to more suffering. Nevertheless, she learned self-help and independence: 'Instead of drifting helplessly as hitherto, I gathered myself up for a gallant breasting of my destiny; and in time I reached the rocks where I could take a firm stand.'[61] By seeing her situation as an 'enterprise' and overcoming her impatience and fear of being dreaded by relatives and acquaintances as a 'nuisance', she was able eventually to contemplate her infirmity as the 'grandest impulse to self-mastery' and an opportunity for helping others.[62] Whether it is this sentiment felt at the time which informed her work or whether her later philosophy colours her view of her past self is, of course, uncertain but her concern for similarly disadvantaged people and the way they are treated is a deep and heartfelt concern throughout her work.

In conclusion, the literary child at the beginning of the nineteenth century was cast in a very definite ideal mould: sensible, serious, obedient, thoughtful, eager to learn, with a highly developed sense of filial piety and unselfish duty to others. The narrative viewpoint in early texts remains largely that of the adult, *in loco parentis*, as it were, in that the child's responses are conditioned by the needs of the moral or didactic aim and carefully controlled to the extent that even passages of dialogue smack of the adult's idea of what children ought to enjoy talking about. The first writers of moral tales for the young came under fire for their strait-jacket approach to learning and for their rejection of the imaginative elements of fairy-tales and fables. In 1802 Charles Lamb wrote to Samuel Taylor Coleridge in no uncertain terms of what he calls the vapid and insignificant contents of books by Anna Barbauld and Sarah Trimmer: 'Science has succeeded to Poetry no less in the little walks of children than with men. Is there no possibility of averting this sore evil?' He concludes: 'Damn them! – I mean the cursed Barbauld Crew, those Blights and Blasts of all that is Human in man and child.'[63] In Book 5 of *The Prelude* (published posthumously in 1850), William Wordsworth addressed to Coleridge (a popular recipient, it seems, of such complaints) a similar lamentation at 'a pest/That might have dried me up, body and soul', asking where they, as poets, would have been now if, instead of being allowed to wander freely over the 'open ground/of Fancy', they had been

> Attended, follow'd, watch'd, and noos'd,
> Each in his several melancholy walk
> String'd like a poor man's Heifer, at its feed
> Led through the lanes in forlorn servitude . . .

He goes on to contrast the 'monster', the 'dwarf Man', trapped in the 'pinfold of his own conceit' which such literature depicted and indeed produced, with his own ideal child:

> not too wise,
> Too learned, or too good; but wanton, fresh
> And bandied up and down by love and hate,
> Fierce, moody, patient, venturous, modest, shy[64]

It is tempting to speculate whether the vehemence of such criticism may have been fuelled by the fact that the majority of the writers concerned were female and immensely popular, although serious dissatisfaction with the moralists' approach also came later from women. Elizabeth Rigby in *The Quarterly Review* in June 1844, for example, castigates the authors of juvenile moral tales for their intrusiveness: 'From the moment you open the book the moral treads so close upon your heels as to be absolutely in the way.'[65] Thus, in attempting to capitalise on the accepted role for women as educators of the young and stressing the scientific, rational and severely moral in order to escape from traditional associations of the female with sentiment and frivolity, they in fact provoked criticism and ridicule, especially from the male literary establishment, aimed at precisely those aspects which were intended to render their work most acceptable as a serious contribution to educational debate.[66]

In the late Georgian and early Victorian periods, interest began to focus more sharply upon the actual personality of the child, with greater analysis of character foregrounded as a vehicle for depicting moral, and, as discussed in the next chapter, religious development. It was increasingly realised that for moral stories to be effective, imagination had to be reinstated and wedded to realism in the construction of interesting and convincing plots, and the portrayal of children had to become much more lifelike, exploring aspects of childish development hitherto ignored or suppressed by the moralists.

Chapter 2

Sinners and saviours:
The child of faith

> And when you're good and do not cry,
> Nor into angry passions fly
> You can't think how Papa and I
>   Love Baby
>
> And when you see me pale and thin
> By grieving for my baby's sin
> I think you'd wish that you had been
>   A better Baby.
>
>   Jane and Ann Taylor

Running parallel to the moral didactic tradition in the early nineteenth century and, eventually, far surpassing it in popularity, was the tradition of Evangelical writing. After 1800, new social tensions resulting from the Napoleonic wars, economic depression and general anxieties about the future led to a reassessment of the Enlightenment moralists' conception of the rational life and human happiness and to considerable concern about the role of religion in education in relation to the poor as well as the rich. With the fall from favour of French theories of education which had inspired the gradual secularisation of didactic works, it was felt by an increasing number of writers and educationalists that education should become subservient to religion and directed chiefly towards spiritual rather than temporal happiness, encouraging a careful and prolonged preparation for the afterlife. In 1802, Sarah Trimmer, one of the more orthodox of the turn-of-the-century didactic authors of children's books, wrote in her journal *The Guardian of Education* that 'one of the worst passions that can inflict the mind is *the pride of Human Reason*. Religion alone can rule them ALL and bring the Reason itself into subjection to the revealed will of God.'[1]

In this climate the Evangelical movement, a surviving strain of Puritanism, which already had fifty years of mounting influence behind it associated with the Methodist revival, began to come into its own.[2] Between 1810 and 1830 religious teaching in literature came to displace the older form of moral tale, although the trend had already begun at the end of the previous century in works for the young and the newly literate of not only Sarah Trimmer, but also Anna Barbauld and Hannah More. An important influence was the rise of the Sunday school movement, founded by Robert Raikes in 1785, for which Sarah Trimmer had been the first successful theorist and publicist.[3] Her exemplary tales and, more particularly, the Cheap Repository Tracts, organised by Hannah More who herself wrote fifty of them, published between 1795 and 1798, had an enormous impact on the rapidly increasing reading public, especially among the poor, and, as all commentators on the period agree, a fundamental influence on the form and content of the Victorian novel.[4] Tract fiction, much of it given as Sunday school prizes, in fact formed a large proportion of printed matter in the nineteenth century (as a visit to any secondhand bookshop, particularly in smaller towns, will reveal) and were read by all classes and by adults and juveniles alike.[5]

The essential doctrines of Evangelicalism were a belief in the burden of Original Sin, individual conversion and justification by faith, and the exercise of private judgement guided by the Bible.[6] Evangelicals were fervent believers who encouraged self-discipline, self-improvement, active evangelising and good works especially among the poor. Popular with all levels of society, the movement produced some of the most zealous philanthropic pioneers (like William Wilberforce) of the day. Though vivid and emotionally satisfying for their readers, the approach in tracts like Hannah More's *The Carpenter, or, The Dangers of Evil Company*, or Mrs Cameron's *The History of Margaret Whyte*, written for village Sunday schools, was essentially a very conservative one, preaching obedience, fortitude, patience and acceptance of the 'rightness' of a lowly position in society.[7] Much concerned with sin and the temptations of worldly ambition as the Evangelicals were, an extremely high standard of Christian behaviour was demanded of the poor among the readers (an attitude deriving much impetus, of course, from the fear of working-class dissatisfaction evoked by the French Revolution and the middle-class interest in preserving social order).

Once again, women writers were at the forefront of the Evangelical literary movement. As with the impulses lying behind the writing of moral and educational tales, women were able to justify their literary activities by making them serve the religious cause and thus gain reassurance about their public role as creators of imaginative literature at a time when there was a great deal of Evangelical distrust of fiction.[8] Indeed, to a large extent, the novel began to gain respectability through its association with the Sunday school movement. Many such writers were extremely prolific, like Hannah More who, it has been picturesquely claimed, began a deluge of 'literary shepherds' ready to feed the 'hungry sheep' of England, which would, particularly after the arrival on the scene of Mrs Sherwood's works, 'have fed the whole of Europe'.[9] Thus, the voicing of a spiritual authority akin to that which they were ideally encouraged to exert in the domestic sphere, was for women, in literature as in life, a source of power denied to them in other respects. Nevertheless, while they gained in popularity, the writers of tract fiction were also the focus not only for criticisms of their sometimes questionable literary ability, but also of accusations of patronising self-righteousness and intellectual and spiritual presumption. The vicious tone of the following comment from Thackeray indicates that his views on the content of Evangelical works were exacerbated by the gender of the authors:

> to our shame be it said, we Protestants have set the example of this kind of proselytism – those detestable mixtures of truth, lies, false sentiment, false reasoning, bad grammar, correct and genuine philanthropy and piety – I mean our religious tracts, which any woman or man, be he ever so silly, can take upon himself to write and sell for a penny, as if religious instruction were the easiest thing in the world . . . Oh awful name of God! Light unbearable! Mystery unfathomable! Vastness immeasurable! – Who are these who come forward to explain the mystery, and gaze unblinking into the depths of the light, and measure the immeasurable vastness to a hair? O name, that God's people of old did fear to utter! O light, that God's prophet would have perished had he seen! Who are these who are now so familiar with it? – Women, truly, for the most part weak women – weak in intellect, weak maybe in spelling and grammar, but marvellously strong in faith: – women, who step down to the people with stately step and voice of authority, and deliver their twopenny tablets, as if they were some Divine authority for the wretched nonsense recorded there![10]

The early tales of Hannah More and her contemporaries, many of whom were actively involved in establishing Sunday schools and were fervent supporters of charitable and missionary work at home and abroad, did indeed have relatively simple plots, designed to hammer home the message in no uncertain fashion, and, as in many of the educational tales, one-dimensional characters which were unsophisticated devices for teaching the morality of virtue rewarded and vice punished. Among these characters, however, the child was of central importance, underlining the notion that the readers were all God's children and illustrating the biblical view that 'except ye be converted and become as little children, ye shall not enter the Kingdom of Heaven'.[11] Moreover, it was strongly felt that it was important to inculcate religious habits of thought at as early an age as possible in order to make Christianity the focus of an active life, a view which not only influenced the shape of much children's literature, but led to the prominent theme of the child as an example to adults. As Sarah Trimmer argued in *The Good Schoolmistress*:

> For all persons of ranks and degrees, RELIGION is the principal concern, and . . . it is of the utmost importance to sow the seeds of piety in the minds of

children, and give them as early as possible, strong impressions respecting the being of GOD, the immortality of the soul, the certainty of a future state.[12]

The early tracts soon developed into longer tract tales for the young and newly literate and full-length Evangelical novels in which the writers attempted to incorporate their message in a more interesting and realistic picture of children's lives. Moreover, emotion, which had been frowned on by the rationalists, came back into fiction via the approval of religious sentiment, and was soon skilfully manipulated by authors, particularly in the form of pathos. In this respect, the Evangelicals had much in common with Romanticism.

In practice, the portrayal of the child in Evangelical writing revealed the duality which corresponded to the legacy of, on the one hand, the Puritan and Wesleyan traditions, and on the other, the Rousseau-istic and Romantic.[13] The child was thus either seen as the product of Original Sin and hence burdened by the innate depravity of mankind which had to be recognised, battled with and overcome through individual conversion before salvation could be achieved, or, particularly later in the century, as a version of the 'innocent' child, a symbol of purity and grace. The former was, like the child in the moral tales, the recipient of instruction from an adult, while the latter was often an instrument of religious instruction, and a guide and example who could help to save the souls of erring adults. The latter view became, in fact, a firm favourite with many Victorian writers, gaining ascendancy over the 'Original Sin' approach as the century advanced. Thus, Evangelical writing directly influenced the development of the nineteenth-century novel by widely determining readers' expectations with the construction of types and narrative devices which later writers found it expedient and effective to manipulate. For example, it can be argued that the novels of Charles Dickens, with their characters often representing clear-cut embodiments of vice and virtue, his sentimentalising of the child and his penchant for death-bed scenes, owe not a little to the conventions established by the religious tracts, despite his rejection of the view of the child as reprobate. A further and significant way in which the Evangelical works can be seen as influential is in the important reorientation of interest from behaviour to conscience and emotions, from the external to the inner child. The greater emphasis on the individual, on the habits of self-examination and the development of a finely honed sense of guilt, responsibility and duty can be seen to anticipate the 'confessional' and psychological novel. Moreover, the tradition of authorial intrusion to comment on desires and motivations remained a characteristic part of much subsequent fiction.

Careful consideration of some contrasting Evangelical works for the young and their parents which were among the most successful of their day will provide ample illustration of this connection. The impulse behind the promulgation of the 'Original Sin' view of the child, with its insistence on innate depravity and its constant and often gruesome reminders of the awful punishment awaiting those who fail to combat their faults in this life and assure their salvation in the next, was voiced by Hannah More thus:

> Is it not a fundamental error to consider children as innocent beings, whose little weaknesses may, perhaps, want some correction, rather than as beings who bring into the world a corrupt nature and evil dispositions, which it should be the great end of education to rectify?[14]

Hannah More was mildness itself in her recommendations, however, in comparison with some of her contemporaries. Perhaps the most famous exponent of this view was Mrs Mary Martha Sherwood (1775–1851), whose *The History of the Fairchild Family* of 1818 reached an enormously wide audience and was the object of both much praise and vitriolic criticism.[15]

Mrs Sherwood (née Butt), who ran a boarding school for young ladies in the 1820s after returning from India where she spent her early married life, was also the author of *The Infant's Progress* (*c.* 1814), a grim little text based on Bunyan's work, and demonstrated in all her fiction an extreme proselytising fervour and an unnerving dual fascination with piety and the macabre.[16] Her depiction of childhood in *The History of the Fairchild Family* is dominated by ever-present reminders of death and the fear of eternal damnation. Indeed, childhood is seen as a dangerous time when the seeds of damnation can very easily be irrevocably sown. Written for middle-class readers rather than the Sunday or charity school audiences, the novel features the prosperous and genteel family setting of a house in a lovely garden which suggests a kind of Edenic context for the lives of the Fairchild children: Lucy, aged about 9, Emily, about 8, and Harry, between 6 and 7. The primary concern of the narrative is the constantly imperilled souls of the children, and no event or occasion, however trivial, passes without being made the subject of a lecture on the importance of self-examination and obedience to the parental and Divine will. Like the moralists, Mrs Sherwood is conscious of speaking to both her child readers and their parents, and her narrative voice reflects an authoritative parent/child relationship. The family context clearly mirrors the notion of the family in Christ, with the parents as surrogates for God in their role of ever-present, benevolent severity.[17] Mr Fairchild makes the encouraging announcement to Henry that: "'I stand in place of God to you, whilst you are a child'" and "'I do not punish you, my child, because I do not love you, but because I wish to save your soul from hell'".[18] The Fairchild parents take exclusive charge of their children's education and the days are carefully regimented. Yet despite the rigidity of the didactic framework (the subtitle is *The Child's Manual, being a collection of stories calculated to show the importance and effects of a religious education*), the unattractive coolness of the parents whose endearments generally precede a warning or punishment and the unnatural nature of the children's readiness to quote biblical texts, keep diaries of their 'wicked' thoughts and discuss points of dogma and the spiritual condition of other people, there is considerable humour and interest, and much of the children's behaviour is credible and lively, combining their piety with a degree of robust naughtiness not generally admitted in the religious tract. (This is especially true of portraits of poor children, where very little in the way of childlike spontaneity is portrayed, which reflected and, implicitly, endorsed the fact that the young members of poor families frequently had to shoulder adult responsibilities of work and childcare and, consequently, had little time or opportunity for play.)

The details of the Fairchilds' daily lives provide us with a very vivid picture of the activities and amusements of children in the early nineteenth century. The introduction to the 1902 edition, which removed all the prayers, religious lectures and horrific elements, in fact underlines the universality of their experience:

> Lucy, Emily and Henry led what we should call nowadays very dull lives, but they were by no means dull little people for all that. We shall find them very living and real when we make acquaintance with them. They tore their clothes, and lost their pets, and wanted the best things, and slapped each other when they disagreed. They had their good times and their bad times, their fun and frolic and their scrapes and naughtiness just as children had long before they were born and are having now, long, long after they are dead![19]

The children are frequently seen talking together and, though affectionate, they also quarrel, as when Henry is not allowed to carry a doll because he once played at hanging it from a tree as a thief! Occasionally, the dialogue is presented in play form, which creates a dynamic immediacy. Their roles are, for the most part, traditionally gendered (Henry helps in the garden while the girls help in the house), and so, to a certain extent, are their faults: the main fault of Lucy and Emily is envy, of a new doll or of the fine clothes of a neighbour's child, while Henry is prone to overexcitement and boisterousness. They are all most at risk from the cardinal sin of disobedience, however, and the girls are by no means passive, sedentary creatures, but share equally in the naughtiness. There are some very funny scenes, as when Henry and Emily try to catch a tame magpie and end up breaking bounds by climbing onto the thatch roof of a barn, or when Henry falls in a tub of pigwash and infects everything he touches with an appalling stench. There are also some very dramatic moments: when their parents are away for the day, the children's routine quickly disintegrates and they become slack and careless. They wreck their tidy beds, overeat, argue, get dirty chasing a pig in the lane, go into a forbidden farmhouse and get slightly tipsy on the cider they are given, and tear their clothes playing on a swing in the barn which Mr Fairchild has forbidden them to use. When Emily falls from the swing and is seriously hurt, they are brought face to face with the realisation that their disobedience could have led to her death. Emily almost comes to grief again when she steals some damsons and, having spilled juice on her dress, washes it herself because she fears discovery and promptly catches a serious fever from which she nearly dies. Her dilemma as she repeatedly confronts and succumbs to temptation to take the damsons, despite the fact that she knows that God is watching her, is evocatively portrayed, as is the family's anxiety about her. Once again, naughtiness based on greed and deceit is seen to bring unhappiness on the whole family, and the children learn valuable lessons through their own experience. Henry is shut in an attic without food for succumbing to his 'sinful desire' for apples which causes him to be branded a thief and a liar, and soon learns that having your own way does not always make you happy when, envying the freedom of an unruly family he visits, he is chased by a bull and, though saved by the dogs, falls and bloodies his nose. Henry, also, has to confront his obstinacy at leisure when he refuses to learn his Latin because he fears he will not be able to cope with the harder lessons ahead, and is ignored by the family on his father's orders. On this occasion, Henry is helped by Charles Trueman, a thoroughly godly child who is resigned to, and indeed, welcomes, his impending death, and who helps Henry to understand the nature of his sin in disobeying his father's wishes.

The difference between these situations and analogous ones in the moral tales is that here the children's faults and passions are seen as potentially sinful and, if allowed to develop into adulthood, likely to damn their immortal souls. A clear line is discernible between naughtiness as a result of high spirits or thoughtlessness, however, and what might be construed as sin. In the story of Miss Crosbie and the green silk bonnets, for example, the children delight in making fun of the elaborate overdressing of an ugly, elderly visitor, but are subsequently shamed and moved to tears by her gifts to them of truly pretty silk bonnets. Disobedience, however, as has been seen, may lead to a terrible end, as in the case of the young spoilt daughter of a neighbour, Augusta Noble, who, because she has been brought up 'without the fear of God' and hence no notion of filial obedience, sets fire to herself by playing with candles and dies a ghastly death. They also learn through stories and through the example of adults. Mrs Fairchild, for example, talks of her own naughtiness in childhood and of how she was 'cured' by a visiting clergyman cousin. It is interesting to note, in passing, that it is usually the women characters who tell or read the improving stories; Mr Fairchild is wont to retire under a tree to read his book at such moments.

Despite the animated nature of many of these scenes, the modern reader is inevitably taken aback by the juxtaposed insistent haranguing both of character and reader, for prayers and sermons on guilt, contrition and punishment are scattered throughout the text, and by the extreme nature of the often terrifying theological disquisitions and exhortations. Of Augusta's death we learn that she may have been looking at herself in a mirror with her purloined candle (thus being guilty of vanity as well as disobedience) and that she was found all in a blaze from head to foot! The maid burnt herself very much in putting out the fire, and poor Miss Augusta was so dreadfully burnt, that she never spoke afterwards, but died in agonies last night – a warning to all children how they presume to disobey their parents! 'The eye that mocketh at his father, and refuses to obey his mother, the ravens of the valley shall pick it out, and the young eagles shall eat it' (Proverbs xxx, 17).

The 'worst part of the whole business' is seen to be the fact that Augusta remained unconscious and hence 'had not one moment for thought or repentance'. Her parents' dereliction of their religious duty is sternly underlined with the following animating text: '"Withhold not correction from the child; for if thou beatest him with the rod, he shall not die; thou shalt beat him with the rod, and shalt deliver his soul from hell" (Proverbs xxiii, 13–14)'.[20]

Moreover, the treatment to which the children are subjected, by way of correction, seems to amount, on some occasions, to a disturbingly sadistic mental cruelty on the part of the parents. Not only are they required to listen carefully to all the gruesome details of Augusta's death and attend her funeral (an event described in full with frequently interspersed texts on the transitoriness of life), but are taken by Mr Fairchild, proving himself to be a man of action, to witness the corpse of a murderer hanging on a gibbet because they have been caught fighting over a toy, and to see the dead body of the gardener in his cottage. Where their immortal souls are concerned, the punishment is identical for male and female children alike. In the former episode, the children are made to sit, terrified, close by the partly decomposed corpse swaying on the gibbet in the wind, its chains rattling, while Mr Fairchild tells them the history of the quarrel between two brothers which led to the murder of one, the hanging of the other, the insanity of the old mother and the dereliction of their house and grounds. When they visit the gardener's widow, the children's initial enthusiasm for seeing the corpse wanes as they approach the cottage and even more so when they catch the disagreeable smell, but they stand dutifully in front of the sight which is more ghastly than they had imagined. The severity of Sherwood's outlook strikes an unintentionally comic note here, however, as Mr Fairchild's grim homily on the decomposition of the body as a fitting punishment for Original Sin prompts the sorrowing widow's reply that 'it comforts me to hear you talk'! Sherwood's preoccupation with hell and damnation is abundantly clear at moments like these and some of the more horrific scenes of the first version of the novel were, in fact, later expunged and parts 2 and 3 were considerably less macabre in tone. It could, of course, be argued that modern readers find such scenes far more gratuitously horrible than Sherwood's contemporaries would have done, since they were then a commonly encountered part of life and that, in any case, they are no worse than the scenes to which children today are routinely exposed in their own homes by television news and films, let alone horror videos.[21]

Mrs Sherwood used a different narrative pattern to underline the same central points in her other extremely popular work *The History of Henry Milner: A little boy, who was not brought up according to the fashions of this world* (four parts, 1823–37). Here her child protagonist is an only child and an orphan who is brought up and educated from the age of 4 by an elderly clergyman tutor, Mr Dalben, in a house in a garden near the Malvern Hills, a safe and secure setting echoing that of the Fairchilds and, in Rousseau-istic fashion, actualising the separation from worldly society which is fundamental to the story. Our first glimpse of Henry, dressed in a white frock with his ringlets of fair hair peeping out from under a muslin cap and falling upon his neck, as he puts up his 'blooming mouth' to kiss the pale lips of his dying father, is unmistakably sentimental and an image of childhood which was to pervade much later nineteenth-century fiction. Evangelical doctrine is explicitly stated at the beginning as Mr Milner thanks the tutor for having taught *him* as a child 'what sort of little boys are those who will be admitted into the kingdom of Christ on earth, and who will be allowed to play upon the hills of the Millenium', not children with 'sinful, proud and ambitious hearts' such as 'we see now', but 'holy children who have received new hearts, and been made white in the blood of the Lamb, have been justified, sanctified and are at length admitted into glory'.[22] The rest of this very lengthy novel is concerned with the process by which Henry reaches this state of grace.

Although his life is more solitary and claustrophobic than that of the Fairchilds, Henry, too, is given attractive, boylike attributes: he loves an old bag in which he keeps his treasures – bits of string, old nails, penny pictures, etc. – likes playing with pieces of wood, is easily distracted from his lessons and gets into scrapes. When praised on a visit to the housekeeper's sister for his knowledge, he starts to show off, gets overexcited, chases the ducks, throws sods of grass at an owl and causes considerable alarm by climbing up a ladder onto the roof and pretending to ride an elephant. In a very funny scene, he discovers that his precious bag, which he had left lying around, has been thrown in the ash-hole because it contains snails, and he is pursued by the servant as he rescues it and, angry and dirty, drags it through the house. On this occasion, he is humbled after Mr Dalben convinces him that he has been guilty of carelessness ('next in degree, with respect to criminality, to intentional disobedience') and disrespect to his elders. It is stressed, however, that Henry knows 'no naughty words' or tricks, but that 'like all little children, who have not yet received new hearts, he was full of evil inclinations which he showed in many ways' for 'every child born of the family of Adam is utterly corrupt from his birth, and not able in himself to think one single good thought'.[23] Thus the notion that children have their own power of reasoning which should be encouraged and developed is rejected as conflicting with Scriptural revelation. It is Mr Dalben who plays the role of absolute parental authority in this text, and Sherwood makes her views on physical punishment perfectly clear. When Henry, who 'like other children, stood in need both of spiritual and bodily chastisement', shows his temper at the cat or refuses to say a particular letter when reading, he is beaten by his tutor who consoles him with the assurance that '"I love you too well to omit any means appointed by God for your soul's good."'[24] Although at 5 he is deemed too young to understand fully the 'danger and guilt of sin' (although Mr Dalben is at pains to try to explain it to him!), he understands a beating so that his tutor only has to call for the broom to subdue him. As in all Evangelical texts of this period, adult authority is seen as God-given and punishment, even quite severe physical punishment for the very young, as not only consonant with the utmost paternal tenderness, but a positive religious duty, for God

> thus arranging matters for little children, and directing in his holy book, that the chastisements of various kinds should be used if needful, clearly pointed out, that he did not expect persons at a very early age to be regulated by argument or reason, but by parental authority; and therefore, those parents who neglect the use of the power thus placed in their hands, are as guilty of despising the ordinances of God, as he who refuses to enter a place of worship, or denies the authority of the divine precepts concerning the sacraments.[25]

Salvation is thus seen to depend more on the habit of obedience than on self-examination, a tendency avoided in this novel.

At 6 Henry is more docile and humble with good manners, although he still has faults, particularly the failure to grasp the dangers of reliance on his own childish judgement instead of on that of his surrogate father (he falls from a bridge into a brook), lack of moderation in his activities (he is criticised, aged 7, for his preoccupation with a new kite '"lest this fancy thing does not bring you to sin, by throwing you off your guard, and leading you from your God"') and idleness over his lessons, the 'strong symptom of an unchanged heart'.[26] At this stage, the pattern of the narrative converges with that of many earlier didactic tales as Henry is taken for nature walks by Mr Dalben and lectured on the different categories of animals, insects, birds, reptiles, flowers and vegetables. Though full of scientific detail, these talks are inevitably given a religious turn, not just to illustrate the immanence of God in nature, but on a metaphorical level too, constantly reading the landscape for divine truths; thus, the process of grafting a tree is seen as comparable to the process of being born again by acquiring a new heart. At the end of part 1, Henry is seen to walk through a wood and out into the moonlight, a symbolic representation of his gradual emergence from spiritual darkness as he grows up and progresses through school and Oxford towards his goal of Holy Orders.[27]

Another of Mrs Sherwood's obsessions was with the 'threat' of Roman Catholicism, a fear she shared with many of her contemporaries, notably Charlotte Elizabeth Tonna, whose novel *Falsehood and Truth* (1841) explicitly states at the outset that its aim is to counteract popery. Sherwood's *Victoria*

(1833) depicts the theme of infant piety in a strongly anti-Catholic setting, as the child of the title is almost ensnared by the 'insidious teaching' of her Catholic governess but is saved in time by her brother, a Methodist minister, and is able to confront and shame her worldly parents. The first part of *The History of the Fairchild Family* boasts a similar tale of 'a Little Boy who, through God's Grace, turned his Parents to Righteousness', thus demonstrating that not even Sherwood always depicted parents as infallible, particularly if they were 'unsaved' themselves. In this respect, too, Sherwood was a precursor. In her earliest popular work, *The Story of Little Henry and his Bearer Boosy* (1814), drawing on her experiences in India, Sherwood had already manifested her interest in the notion of the missionary child and opened up new literary territory in fully exploiting sentimentality and pathos in a religious text. In her depiction of the orphan who has been brought up by loving Muslim servants and who, after being rescued from spiritual ignorance by an English girl who teaches him to seek salvation through reading the Bible, converts his bearer in turn, dying shortly afterwards, Sherwood took the children's tract a step forward by its colourful detail of an unfamiliar and fascinating setting and by establishing the figure of the pretty, neglected and spiritually endangered child who triumphs and brings comfort and an awareness of God's mercy to a benighted adult, a figure which was to become a powerful literary weapon in not only the Evangelical campaign but in the wider context of much subsequent fiction.

The theme of the role of children in Christian life was nowhere more intensively deployed than in Maria Charlesworth's novel for Sunday reading, *Ministering Children: A tale dedicated to childhood* of 1854. Although this text was written later in the century, Charlesworth (1819–80), the daughter of an Evangelical minister who based her whole life on active Christian principles, was much closer to the early Evangelicals in her style and subject matter. *Ministering Children*, which was immensely successful for many years and widely reprinted in England, the United States and continental Europe, conveys, in a series of interconnected episodes occupying some 420 pages, a picture of Christian life in action through the deeds of a number of young children, thus illustrating the novel's title-page motto: 'Out of the mouths of babes and sucklings Thou hast perfected praise (Matthew xxi, 16)'. The novel is interesting in that it foregrounds children not as the recipients of adult wisdom and biblical discourse but as the central, active exponents of the religious message. The narrative sets up a chain of good deeds, linking children of different ages and social standing in both a country town and a vaguely idealised rural environment, a pattern which affirms the notion of the community in Christ. Thus Herbert Clifford, the young son of the local squire, learns through a series of misjudgements and mistakes to be a 'ministering child' to villagers, while Rose, a farmer's daughter, learns true charity and inspires her father and sharp-tongued mother to value the Bible, and little Ruth, though deprived and hungry in her poor home, is by nature a ministering child, carefully memorising the words of the Scriptures and comforting with her pious stories and morsels of her own scanty food the last days of a dying child even less fortunate than herself. The message shines through clearly that good deeds, no matter how small or humble, as long as they are motivated by love, not only help others but ennoble the benefactor too, bringing giver and receiver close together in God's blessing. All the deeds and gifts portrayed illustrate the notion of 'love in action': this is seen as true charity in the sense of caring and sharing, not the cold charity of a thoughtlessly bestowed superfluous coin. Herbert Clifford comes to understand his personal poverty despite his family's considerable wealth and that it is the personal effort involved which renders a charitable act worthwhile. This, of course, was the old-style theory of individual philanthropy (visiting the poor and sick, reading to the illiterate and distributing food and clothing) which had, for centuries, been carried out in rural areas but which, by the time Charlesworth was writing, had already engendered considerable debate and disillusionment about its effectiveness in the face of escalating hardship and the unprecedented destitution in urban areas.[28]

In her preface, Charlesworth outlines the notion that informs the whole of her text:

> It must be allowed by all, that the present is a day of increased exertion in behalf of those who are in need; but much care is necessary that the temporal aid extended may prove, not a moral injury, but a moral benefit, to both the receiver and the communicator of that aid. May it not be worthy of consideration, whether the most generally effective way to ensure this moral benefit on both sides, would not be the early calling forth and training the sympathies of children by personal intercourse with want and sorrow, while as yet those sympathies flow spontaneously?[29]

The learning of the true nature of charity and the blessing of its exercise are seen as the most important and enriching event in the childhood of her various characters and they are never too young to start. The grocer's daughter, Jane, is inspired at a public meeting to which she is taken by her mother, to save her pennies and darn her old stockings for the little orphan, Mercy. The comparative hardship involved (she finds darning difficult and time-consuming and no longer has money to spend on herself) is not ignored by the author, but is manifestly outweighed by the delight and satisfaction she feels, sensations which will continue, we are assured, to bear fruit in the future: 'a child's large feeling on so small occasion may win a smile, but the occasion had touched the deep chord of human sympathy within her heart, and the vibration was long and full'.[30] Herbert finds enjoyable physical activity and purpose in helping to chop wood and plant flowers for the cottager, old Willy (his adopted object of charity), and is led to examine his view of himself and the responsibility of his position in society. Rose's charity to Mercy's family brings her own family together in their involvement. The deeds the children perform are consonant with conventional gender roles: the girls labour to fill personal and domestic wants, while the boys' contributions involve more masculine skills.

The misfortunes and social ills depicted are, significantly, such as children, with a little help from adults, might realistically be able to remedy – a cottager child has chilblained feet, a poor widow no fire or a broken door, an old man a leaky roof – and herein lie both the strength and the weakness of the book. Although this would have appealed to the child reader, such a focus on details makes the attitude towards the actual overall situation of the poor seem trivialised and often unbearably condescending to the modern reader. The real implications of hunger and hardship are obscured by sentiment and a facile assumption and magnification of the long-term value of such 'good works'. Thus a pair of laboriously knitted stockings, a handful of strawberries laid by a child's hand on the coverlet of a dying woman's bed or a barrow of logs are seen to transform, apparently, the lives of the needy as they bless the ministering children and cheerfully accept their lot. The lessons of patience, hope and trust in God, taught by the privileged as they spend a few hours talking about heaven to the poor, strike us as patronising and arrogant. Moreover, the charitable acts themselves occasionally seem to be unpleasantly self-regarding. For example, when Jane hears from her mother that God teaches the fortunate to know the needs of the poor, she feels 'lost in the thrilling awe of one who felt herself to have been chosen and taught of God, to supply the wants she had not known', which seems almost to imply that God has created the poor to give the rich a warm thrill of self-righteousness.[31]

The mixture of Romantic sensibility and a strong Evangelical tone is nowhere demonstrated more forcefully than in the characters of old Willy and Mary Clifford, who are typical foils to the child characters. The former was by now a familiar literary stereotype: the poor, helpless and kind old man whose earthly needs are the vehicle for Herbert's education in faith and charity. It should be noted, however, that Herbert has to rely on the physical strength, precious time and goodwill of the labourer Jem to carry out his projects, although he gets his allowance doubled by his admiring father for his achievements. Old Willy is permanently patient, trusting and resigned, despite numerous causes for distress, and, moreover, knows his place, an important attribute in the Evangelical scheme of things. His spiritual needs are catered for by Herbert's saintly sister, Mary, whose ministrations among the villagers are renowned such that when she dies, in a scene which would not have disgraced Dickens, the whole community is consumed by grief.[32] Indeed, with a pathos typical of the period, as old Willy and little Mercy meet in the evening by Mary's grave, the dead 'angel' becomes herself a kind of object of veneration and adoration to the child and the childlike old man, a bright star twinkling in the heavens. The figure of Mary is grossly idealised, but the image of the beautiful young person synonymous in death as in life with an angel, which owed so much to the early unsophisticated obituary tracts, was already well rooted in Victorian fiction. At the other end of the social spectrum, the death of Ruth, though summarily dealt with in comparison, carries equal pathos and meaning to those who witness it ('no-one knows the blessed sights that God's departing children see').[33] The legacy of this ministering child is the redemption of her coarse father who is moved to recognise, somewhat belatedly, his responsibilities towards his family.

Charlesworth's children are clearly viewed from an adult perspective only, and her narrative betrays a constant awareness of and desire for the approval of the adult reader. The children's attributes are desirable ones by adult standards: they are obedient, quiet, kind and thoughtful, and with one or two exceptions, contented in their poverty. The miserable are seen as being so largely because they have not yet found Jesus, a far greater poverty, in Evangelical eyes, than bodily starvation or pain. Yet for all its faults, the novel does contain much interesting detail about the daily lives of the children at different levels of society. There are nicely observed pictures of Rose helping with the baking, peeling apples, filling tartlets with jam and washing over the tops of the loaves with a feather dipped in beer, of the children putting on their white aprons to hurry to school, of teatime on washing-day in the family of ten children where Patience goes to work, and of Jane plodding through an endless three-quarters of an hour with her knitting-needles held in a tight and awkward grasp. The lively and eager impetuosity of Herbert is also attractive as he is repeatedly moved to make promises to old Willy which he cannot keep. We view him more sympathetically than Charlesworth perhaps intended when his plan to spend his next month's allowance on coal for the old man after he has thoughtlessly pushed his log into a ditch is dampened by his father's rational objections to such dependence on his purse rather than his ingenuity, and his allowance is confiscated into the bargain. His refusal to believe that his sister is dying and his avoidance of people who might confirm it are touchingly realistic.

With the character of Patience, introduced in the first chapter as a sad, apathetic child who sits silent and withdrawn in the schoolroom, Charlesworth displays a comparatively perceptive understanding of the psychological reality of deprivation. Because she is so downcast and shows no interest, she is unattractive to the school visitor who, not realising that her listlessness and failure to learn her lessons stem from hunger and despair, chides her for not loving God's holy word. Though neglected by all (including the author, it might appear, for she disappears from sight for large chunks of the novel and is excluded from the descriptions of the Christmases spent by the other characters because 'no time brought her gladness as yet'), the aptly named Patience's frozen heart is eventually brought back to life by the kind words of another rich young 'angel' figure, thus demonstrating that 'poor Patience had wanted more love than others not less'.[34] Although she goes temporarily to the workhouse which here as elsewhere in literature of the time, is seen by the poor as next in disgrace to the prison, Patience is in fact taken good care of and blossoms, becoming a ministering child by reading the Bible to other inmates.[35] Thus the notion of ministering is seen by Charlesworth as a matter of will and the spirit, and a way of life independent of social standing and material capabilities.

Despite the cosy sentimentality adhering to every page, the portrayal of childhood in *Ministering Children* must have been, to a great extent, an attractive one for juvenile and adult readers alike. The situations and settings are detailed, there is a lot of dialogue and a wide range of characters who keep reappearing, thus keeping the interest stimulated. There is also a wealth of descriptions of village life (although it is perhaps unrealistically placid and undramatic), nature, animals and the changing seasons, although here too, the details serve a moral purpose, pointing to the difference, for example, between the glowing cheeks of Rose as she walks happily through the snowy lanes with her basket of offerings and the pinched, cold face of the recipient, the 'little chilblained prisoner', wrapped in an old cloak in a rough cottage. While adults would have responded to the by now familiar and emotionally charged picture of the innocent godly child, child readers would have felt encouraged that they were seen as important and that their limited capabilities and efforts could be effective in the dynamic Victorian world. The text closes with the assertion that 'the youngest child of God who is able to understand anything, can learn to be a ministering child' and, indeed, many of the adult characters are moved and instructed by the children.[36] Their spontaneous impulses and reactions are frequently seen as superior to those of the less instinctive and more rational adults, and the 'personal influence everywhere' proclaimed in the preface is the result of the loving kindness which is quintessentially the province of the childlike spirit.

Despite the outmoded nature of its view, the immense success and far-reaching influence of *Ministering Children*, in both real and literary terms, are indisputable.[37] Furthermore, it demonstrates how the Evangelical view of childhood had changed in the thirty-six years since *The History of the Fairchild Family* first appeared, with a shift of focus from sternness and the fear of not achieving salvation to a much gentler emphasis on the child's capacity for piety and good works, a shift which corresponded to a gradual and widespread literary idealisation of the child. This trend was apparent in both children's and adult literature. In 1821, Mrs Sherwood's sister, Lucy Lyttelton Cameron, had depicted religious precocity with a strong sentimental flavour in her tract for young readers *Memoirs of Emma and her Nurse*, in which we read that it was 'pretty' (a word much favoured by religious writers to denote childish piety) to see the 4-year-old Emma going off quietly to pray whenever she feels tempted to be disobedient, and sitting on her father's lap, pointing towards heaven as she tells him what Jesus has prepared there for a 'little sinful baby' like her. The consciousness of, and longing for, death by an innocent child fast became a popular theme in later years.

The Children of Cloverley, an early work by Hesba Stretton (the pseudonym of Sarah Smith, 1832–1911), published in 1865, offers splendid evidence of how far the idealisation of the child had advanced. The story of two American children who are sent, when their mother dies and their father has to go to fight in the Civil War, to live with their cousins in a mining village in Shropshire, the novel contrasts the angelic and thoroughly unconvincing Annie with her more robust brother Ben and her worldly, wealthy cousins. From the first chapter, Annie talks of angels and heaven 'as if it were a home' (a favourite early warning signal that she will not survive beyond childhood), and urges all with whom she comes into contact to try to become like the brother or sister of the Lord by always doing God's will. Her influence on the adults in the novel is extreme and improbable. She eases the despair of the miners as they face destitution after the failure of the mine by starting a little school to teach them to read and so softens them that they turn aside from their drink when she speaks to them at the alehouse of God's mercy and the analogy between their plight and her own as a virtual orphan far from home. She so affects a reclusive spinster neighbour, who has lived a life of selfish indolence, with her wisdom, that she begins to pity the miners and eventually helps them to develop a new mine with her savings. '"Child', Miss Reynolds says to Annie, '"tell me if is too late for me to begin the work I have so long neglected. Am I too old to try to be the sister of the Lord Jesus?"'[38] Similarly, her self-absorbed cousins learn patience and the will to work after the disastrous financial repercussions of the mining troubles.

After a night of exposure on the hillside through being lost in a snowstorm, Annie gradually fades away, dying on Easter Sunday, as the sun rises and the last snow has gone, with her family and friends around her. She gives little personal bequests and advice to all as she dies and her last words repeat the words about Jesus which have run like a refrain throughout the text. Just before her death, her two wishes are granted: coal is found in the mine and her father returns safe from the war. The otherworldly nature and role of Annie are underlined at the end as one of the miners says that God 'sent this little child to be a pattern to us' and her cousin Dora paints a picture of angel children, one of whom has Annie's face.[39] Death, as in *Ministering Children*, is no longer seen as a punishment for wrongdoing, but as positive and desirable as a means of converting others, and the presentation is thick with pathos as both the dying child and the grieving adults are comforted with the promise of heaven and everlasting life.

In contrast, Annie's brother Ben is a more far realistic portrait. Seen as a 'truant child' because his faith is less steady, Ben's misery when deprived of the active labour he has been used to on his parents' farm in America and his angry resentment at being laughed at for his blunders at school are perceptively depicted in his stubborn insistence on removing his shoes and stockings and tramping home alone through the dust. When he has been caught by Miss Reynolds after letting her pig loose among her cabbages and is shut up in her attic for the night, he prays fervently to overcome his wilfulness, but only after his bravado as 'a citizen of the United States of America' has given way to hunger, tiredness and anxiety about the suffering Annie must be undergoing because of his disappearance. Even in such scenes where a child's reactions seem natural and spontaneous, the narrative voice is ever conscious of its instructive role, emphasising 'the folly and wilfulness' of his conduct, his 'foolish resentment' and 'very contemptible' desire to vex his cousin.

It was, inevitably, the relative lack of relation to actual lived experience, together with the well-nigh impossibly high standard of consistent, all-consuming piety which they set before the reader in language which, for the most part, was far from naturalistic in its precociousness and sugary sweetness, that caused such works to be severely criticised, despite their popularity and the often well-portrayed, even exciting settings. One reviewer, herself a writer of pious domestic novels, Charlotte Yonge, complained that such texts encouraged children to 'play' at religion, mouthing pious platitudes while wallowing in a false and potentially dangerous self-righteousness.[40] Indeed, emulation of such rigidly structured behaviour was seen to run the paradoxical risk of leading to irreverence, as Elizabeth Rigby had already warned in *The Quarterly Review* in 1844: 'it is too horrid to make religion a matter of *show-off*, which I really think these stories could teach children to be guilty of'.[41]

That the sentimentalised child was a favourite in more secular children's literature too is evidenced by the phenomenal success of Frances Hodgson Burnett's classic *Little Lord Fauntleroy* (1886) which has remained in print and has been turned into both films and television series. Using the fairy-tale rags-to-riches formula, Burnett (1849–1924) clearly draws on the Romantic image of the pretty, idealised child in her tale of the young American boy, Cedric, who becomes the heir to an English earldom, and with his frank, honest, disarming ways and romantic beauty enchants the people he meets and 'converts' his crusty old grandfather, the present earl, such that the ill-tempered, hard-hearted recluse becomes a caring and respected landlord who does many kindnesses to his tenants, suggested to him by his thoughtful and democratic nephew. Little Lord Fauntleroy was modelled on one of Burnett's own sons (which apparently caused him considerable embarrassment in later life) and with his velvet suits, lace collars and long golden ringlets, as he appeared in the illustrations to the text, became a fashionable model for many contemporary real-life children. Although the character of Cedric never changes, for his innate nobility remains the same despite his drastically altered circumstances, even when it looks momentarily that he is to be ousted from his inheritance by a rival claimant, he is by no means a prig and his conversation is plausibly childlike. He is not given to high-flown rhetoric, nor pious pronouncements, but speaks openly and candidly of what he feels. His simple, trusting character and sympathy for those less fortunate than himself are attributed to his upbringing by his mother whom he calls 'Dearest', and who fulfils the kind of idealised mother role Burnett presumably cherished herself. The old earl's eventual acceptance of his son's wife, whom he has disdained and tried to separate from Cedric, is brought about by the boy's obvious grief and his revelation, through his own behaviour, of his mother's superior caring and forgiving nature. The novel ends with Cedric's eighth birthday party where all his friends, high- and low-born alike, gather to express their love and respect for the little boy who has transformed so many of their lives.

Although Cedric is seen from the outside, he is not uncomfortably patronised by the narrator, nor held up for the amusement of adult readers in a demeaning way. Nevertheless, some of the humour deriving from situations in which adults are discomfited or put in their place by his ingenuous remarks and questions would probably only be fully discerned by an adult. In fact, although appealing to young readers with its straightforward language and depiction of a child's success, the novel also found an immense audience among adults. The motif of the child exerting a moral power for good has, of course, lasted into our own time in juvenile literature, and the 'righting of wrongs' theme in novels where children tackle social injustices or solve crimes are but worldly and thoroughly secularised versions of the same idea.

The theme of the innocent child as spiritual guide also appealed to novelists writing for adults whose reputations now far exceed those of most of the writers discussed in this chapter. Among the works of women writers, perhaps the most noteworthy example is George Eliot's pastoral moral tale, *Silas Marner: The weaver of Raveloe* (1861). Eliot (1819–80) had fervently espoused Evangelical doctrines in the 1830s in her adolescence, under the influence of a schoolmistress, Maria Lewis, and although she later repudiated many aspects of the faith, she retained the characteristically Evangelical preoccupation with duty and responsibility and the moral development of the individual, as well as an awareness of the effectiveness of some of their literary techniques. *Silas Marner*, though shorn of the overt religious trappings of the tract novels, draws on the same stylistic stereotypes and moral assumptions in the portrayal of the child Eppie and her relationship with the old man Marner. Her theme harks back overtly to Wordsworth, exemplifying the quotation from 'Michael' (1800) which prefaces the text:

A child, more than all other gifts
That earth can offer to declining man,
Brings hope with it and forward-looking thoughts[42]

Marner, who, after being betrayed by his fiancée and his best friend in his home town has become a miser and a recluse in the village of Raveloe, has his hoarded gold stolen by the ne'er-do-well son of the local squire. When the abandoned, opium-addicted wife of the squire's other son dies with her child in her arms near the weaver's cottage, the child wanders in and is found by Marner sleeping on his hearth. At first, the short-sighted weaver mistakes her golden hair for his own gold restored to him, then thinks she is a vision of his long-dead little sister, endowing from the start her strange and sudden appearance with quasi-supernatural significance:

> he had a clumsy feeling that this child was somehow a message come to him from that far-off life: it stirred fibres that had never been moved in Raveloe – old quiverings of tenderness – old impressions of awe at the presentiment of some Power presiding over his life.[43]

The bond between the child and Marner is instantaneous, based on the similarity of their predicaments as two lone and rejected beings. Marner chooses to keep the child as his own, despite his total lack of experience and knowledge of children. Such a relationship was, as will become clear in the course of this study, a favourite theme in Evangelical and secular fiction, the very helplessness and clumsy attempts of an old man to cope with the day-to-day needs of a child employed as a source of poignant humour and pathos which perhaps could not be so readily derived from a comparable situation involving an elderly woman. The beneficent influence of a child upon the adult psyche is explicitly stated thus:

> She was perfectly quiet now, but not asleep – only soothed by sweet porridge and warmth into that wide-gazing calm which makes us older human beings, with our inward turmoil, feel a certain awe in the presence of a little child, such as we feel before some quiet majesty or beauty in the earth or sky . . .[44]

Eppie's vulnerability and childish needs 'reawaken his senses', give meaning to his hitherto arid life and provide something outside himself and his love of gold to look forward to in the years ahead. The emphasis throughout is not on the character and spiritual education of the child, who is seen entirely from the outside, but on the redemption of Marner through his self-effacing affection and concern for Eppie:

> In old days there were angels who came and took men by the hand and led them away from the city of destruction. We see no white-winged angels now. But yet men are led away from threatening destruction – a hand is put into theirs, which leads them forth gently towards a calm and bright land, so that they look no more backward; and the hand may be a little child's.[45]

Although the language here evokes the Evangelical concept of the redemptive and purifying force of the innocence of childhood, Marner's redemption is, in fact, of a largely secular nature: Eppie is the blessing that saves him from his loneliness and reconciles and integrates him with his village neighbours. In a letter to her publisher, Blackwood, George Eliot stated that her intention was to set 'in a strong light the remedial influences of pure, natural human relations'.[46] Marner discovers that having a child is an immediate bond between people who may otherwise have nothing in common, for he is now always greeted with smiles and friendly questions and advice. The lesson mediated through Eliot's child figure is not that of Divine love, focused on the life hereafter, but one of universal love and harmony in this world: 'There was love between him and the child that blent them into one, and there was love between the child and the world – from men and women with parental looks and tones, to the red ladybirds and the round pebbles.'[47]

When Marner learns to see the natural world afresh through the child's eyes, as they discover the wild flowers, herbs and birds together, he simultaneously begins to recapture a lost link with his past self, his knowledge of the medicinal properties of herbs, thus creating a unity between past and present: 'As the child's mind was growing into knowledge, his mind was growing into memory: as her life unfolded, his soul, long stupefied in a cold, narrow prison, was unfolding too, and trembling gradually into full consciousness.'[48]

Despite the opportunity to live with her real father, now reformed and remorseful, Eppie, as a beautiful young woman (her refinement carefully attributed to her tender nurture rather than to her upper-class paternal background) chooses to stay with Marner, rejecting riches for love and familiar rustic ways. Eliot's novel ends, significantly, not with the death of the redemptive child, but with a wedding, as Eppie marries the neighbour's son and they come to live, happily ever after we are to assume, with Marner. The weaver himself, having returned to see his old home town and found his former home demolished, and with it his unhappy past, can now look to the future with contentment.

Eppie as a child is certainly portrayed in a stereotypically idealised way: she is characteristically golden-haired and pretty, with 'cute', amusing ways. This is less uncomfortable within the confines of an overtly moral tale, however, and the sentimentality is modified by the humour and anxieties generated by the situation as Marner, a self-sufficient old bachelor, struggles to come to terms with the realities of a small child about the place. Thus, when he has attempted to keep Eppie from straying while he is working by attaching her with a long strip of linen to his loom, she discovers the usefulness of a pair of scissors and toddles away. The reader follows the anxious Marner step by step as he combs the neighbourhood, fearing the worst, and shares his relief when she is found. His efforts to punish her gently by locking her briefly in the coal-hole backfire delightfully when Eppie, regarding it as great fun, promptly climbs back in herself after he has washed and changed her. In the same way, the romanticism inherent in the portrayal of his neighbour's little boy Aaron, 'an apple-cheeked youngster of seven', is demystified to some extent by the remark that 'Marner, on the other side of the hearth, saw the neat-featured rosy face as a mere dim round, with two dark spots in it'.[49] Eliot uses the same kind of technique in *The Sad Fortunes of the Reverend Amos Barton*, one of the stories in *Scenes of Clerical Life* (1858), in which she sympathetically depicts members of the Evangelical faith. One of Amos Barton's children, Dickey, another little boy with stereotypical ruddy cheeks and big blue eyes, is nevertheless portrayed with affectionate humour. Compare, for example, his reaction at his mother's funeral to a comparable scene in a tract tale or in *The History of the Fairchild Family*:

> Dickey had rebelled against his black clothes, until he was told it would be naughty to mamma not to put them on, when he at once submitted; and now, though he had heard Nanny say that mamma was in heaven, he had a vague notion that she would come home again tomorrow, and say he had been a good boy, and let him empty her work-box. He stood close to his father, with great rosy cheeks, and wide open blue eyes, looking first up at Mr Cleves and then down at the coffin, and thinking he and Chubby would play at that, when they got home.[50]

The small child's incomprehension of the true meaning and consequences of death are far more believably captured here than in many Evangelical tales where a child comforts grieving adults with pious words. Dickey's resilience and irrepressible childish high spirits are evident some months later when he is invited to stay by two of his father's parishioners, to ease Mr Barton's financial and emotional burdens:

> Every morning he was allowed – being well wrapped up as to his chest, by Mrs Hackit's own hands, but very bare and red as to his legs – to run loose in the cow and poultry yard, to persecute the turkey-cock by satirical imitations of his gobble-gobble, and to put difficult questions to the groom as to the reasons why horses had four legs, and other transcendental matters. Then Mr Hackit would take Dickey up on horseback when he rode round his farm, and Mrs Hackit had a large plumcake in cut, ready to meet incidental attacks of hunger. So that Dickey had considerably modified his views as to the desirability of Mrs Hackit's kisses.[51]

Eliot's tales thus suggest that the influence of Evangelical writing imbibed in youth affected even writers who appeared to have rejected the religious content of the tract tales.[52]

The sentimentality in both characterisation and language surrounding the portrayal of the child in writers for the young was, then, very much a reflection of a general contemporary taste and was in full flower in other purely secular sub-genres written for an adult audience, notably the romances and domestic 'thrillers', many of which were written by and for women and achieved great popularity in the second half of the century. A glance at the morally very conservative novels of Mrs Henry Wood (1818–87), like *East Lynne* (1861) and *The Shadow of Ashlydyat* (1863) confirms her penchant for the angelic, and preferably dying, child. In *East Lynne*, the drawn-out death of little William is seen as part of the retributive pattern which afflicts the transgressing wife and mother.[53] There is, indeed, an unpleasant sense of wallowing in the pathos as the author declares: 'Merciful, indeed, is God to dying children! It is astonishing how very readily, where the right means are taken, they might be brought to look with pleasure, rather than fear, upon their unknown journey.'[54] The last words of William as he contemplates heaven ('"I wonder how it will be? . . . There will be the beautiful city, with its gates of pearl, and its shining precious stones, and its streets of gold . . . It will be so pleasant to be there; never to be tired or ill again . . ."') may appear to echo the Evangelical tracts despite its suspicious emphasis on the colourful and luxurious, but in fact has more of sentimental titillation than of spiritual uplift as its aim.[55]

It seems plausible that the Victorians' love of angelic and innocent children was a lingering romantic nostalgia for their own lost childhood in the face of the increasing materialism of the industrial age, and the obsession with dying children in male- and female-authored texts a manifestation of the sense that such innocence and purity could not be preserved in life. The attribution, most commonly associated with Dickens, of intuitive wisdom and spiritual strength to children, especially the sick or dying, also found favour with women writers. Indeed, many must have welcomed the popular appeal of a subject which exploited the emotional and domestic, and was thus well within the bounds of what it was deemed suitable for a woman to write about, and elevated these concepts to a new level of importance. The next chapter will consider how the growing concern with the social problems of the period affected this theme and the portrayal of the child acquired a new dimension.

Chapter 3

Apprentices to misery:
The exploited child

Do ye hear the children weeping, O my brothers,
    Ere the sorrow comes with years?
They are leaning their young heads against their mothers,
    And that cannot stop their tears.
The young lambs are bleating in the meadows,
    The young birds are chirping in the nest,
The young fawns are playing with the shadows,
    The young flowers are blowing towards the west –
But the young, young children, O my brothers
    They are weeping bitterly!
They are weeping in the playtime of the others,
    In the country of the free.

'For oh,' say the children, 'we are weary,
    And we cannot run or leap;
If we cared for any meadows, it were merely
    To drop down in them and sleep.
Our knees tremble sorely in the stooping,
    We fall upon our faces, trying to go;
And, underneath our heavy eyelids drooping,
    The reddest flower would look as pale as snow;
For, all day, we drag our burden tiring
    Through the coal-dark, underground –
Or, all day, we drive the wheels of iron
    In the factories, round and round.
        . . .

Now tell the poor young children, O my brothers
    To look up to Him and pray;
So the blessèd One who blesseth all the others
    Will bless them another day.
They answer, 'Who is God that He should hear us,
    While the rushing of the iron wheels is stirred?
When we sob aloud, the human creatures near us
    Pass by, hearing not, or answer not a word.

And *we* hear not (for the wheels in their resounding)
    Strangers speaking at the door:
Is it likely God, with angels singing round Him,
    Hears our weeping any more?'
            . . .

They look up, with their pale and sunken faces,
    And their look is dread to see,
For they mind you of their angels in high places
    With eyes turned on Deity! –
'How long!' they say, 'how long, O cruel nation,
    Will you stand, to move the world, on a child's heart, –
Stifle down with a mailed heel its palpitation,
    And tread onward to your throne amid the mart?
Our blood splashes upward, O gold-heaper,
    And your purple shows your path!
But the child's sob in the silence curses deeper,
    Than the strong man in his wrath.'

Elizabeth Barrett Browning, *The Cry of the Children* (1844)

As seen in the last chapter, Evangelical writers were much concerned, in the early nineteenth century, with the moral and spiritual condition of the poor and inundated them with tracts designed to illustrate the divinely sanctioned nature of their lowly position, recommending humility and emphasising the principles of hard work and self-help. Hannah More's *The Shepherd of Salisbury Plain* (1795), for example, portrays the stereotypical situation of the 'rescue' by a philanthropist of a worthy rural worker and his family who have demonstrated that they are self-reliant and religious. These tales became increasingly less relevant, however, to the actual experience of the working classes in the fast-developing industrial and urban areas.

Hannah More also produced one of the earliest tales of what was to become a central concern in the nineteenth century, a grim picture of hardship in an industrial setting. *The Lancashire Collier Girl: A true story* (1795), allegedly borrowed from an anonymous contribution to *The Gentlemen's Magazine*, tells the story of two children, aged 7 and 9, who work with their father in a mine as 'drawers', pulling baskets of coal through the passages.[1] When he is killed in an accident and their mother becomes 'deranged', the destitute family are taken into the workhouse except for the eldest child, Mary, who prefers to continue earning her own living in the mine. Eventually her health is severely affected by working double shifts in order to earn enough to care for and subsequently bury her mother and two of her small brothers, such that she suffers 'strange and unpleasant imaginings', the consequence of 'bad food, and great bodily fatigue, joined with excessive grief'.[2] Although she is at first refused the less onerous post of underservant in a neighbouring household, the owner is persuaded to give her a chance by the pitmaster's praise of her good character and hard-working disposition, and she recovers her health and lives a contented life in her new environment.

The tale illustrates the need for the rich to overcome their often unfounded prejudice against people working in conditions likely to foster immoral behaviour, but also insists strongly on the virtues of self-reliance and propriety ('I think it may teach the poor that they can seldom be in any condition of life so low as to prevent their rising to some degree of independence, if they chuse [sic] to exert themselves, and that there can be no situation whatsoever so mean, as to forbid the practice of many noble virtues') and the fundamental importance of religion ('This story may also encourage the afflicted to serve and trust God in every extremity').[3] For the reader who is aware of the real horrors of child labour in the nineteenth century, it is difficult at times to realise that the tale is not meant to be read ironically. More's insistence on the willing subordination and contentment of mine workers like Mary seems to strike a singularly callous note. Of the two small children at work underground she notes:

> It must be owned to be not impossible that they may sometimes have exerted themselves even beyond their strength, which is now and then the case with little children, through the fault of those who exact the work from them; but since in this case the father had an eye on them during the hours of labour, while they had a prudent and tender mother also, to look after them at home, there is no particular reason to suppose, that at the time of which we are now speaking, they were ever much over-worked.[4]

Their performance of tasks is described as 'cheerful and contented diligence' and Mary's 'ready submission' is summarised warmly thus:

> Let my young readers recollect that in submission to the command of her father, or rather to that law of God which enjoins parental obedience, she cheerfully followed him down into the coal-pit, burying herself in the bowels of the earth, and there at a tender age, without excusing herself on account of her sex, she joined in the same work with the miners, a race of men rough indeed, but highly useful to the community, of whom I am happy to say that they have the character of being honest and faithful, as well as remarkably courageous, and that they have given moreover some striking instances of their readiness to receive religious instruction, when offered to them. Among these men, to their honour be it spoken, Mary's virtue was safe, and after the death of her father, she is even said to have received protection as well as assistance from them, her fatigue having been sometimes lessened, through their lending her a helping hand, with great feeling and kindness.[5]

This passage is noteworthy for its patronising tone and hints at dangers which, by recounting how Mary was protected from them, only draws our attention to their existence. Similarly, More's apparent glossing over of the realities of Mary's physical and mental sufferings seems smug and jars with the religious sentiments expressed in a passage like the following:

> I trust it is not superstitious to suppose that when sincere Christians come, as Mary now did, into very trying circumstances, they may hope, notwithstanding any appearances to the contrary, to experience still, in one way or another, the peculiar blessing of Heaven; I do not expect that such persons will be free from pain, poverty or sickness, or other worldly evils, for it is often quite the contrary, but then I believe that these very afflictions will be made the means of encreasing [sic] their trust in God, and prove in the end (I mean either here or hereafter) to have been entirely designed for their good.[6]

Although the religious didactic line is typical of the period and of More's other works, there is an awkwardness in this passage which suggests that the writer is to some extent already uneasily aware of the anomalies of such a view in the circumstances evoked.

In the late eighteenth century, many writers spoke approvingly of child labour for, at a period of widespread unemployment with the very real threat of starvation for an increasing population, the ability to work was seen as a question of survival.[7] Sarah Trimmer, for example, believed that pauper children should be trained, from as young as 5 years old, to perform manual tasks.[8] The following lines from *The Fleece*, a poem by John Dyer, present an optimistic picture of children working in textile factories:

> The younger hands
> Ply at the easy work of winding yarn
> On swiftly circling engines, and their notes
> Warble together, as a choir of larks:
> Such joy arises in the mind employed.[9]

Such saccharine sentiments were not borne out, however, by investigations of reality, as the Select Committee report on child labour for the first Factory Bill of 1802 indicated. Apart from the huge numbers of young children working alongside their parents or older siblings, there was a high demand for orphaned or abandoned children who were transported from London workhouses to drudgery as 'apprentices' in the mills and factories of the north of England where they learned no real trade and earned only their meagre food and lodgings. John Aikin's study, *A Description of the Country from Thirty to Forty Miles around Manchester* of 1795, for example, speaks of long working hours, the dirty and fetid air of the working environment and frequent epidemics of fever.[10] John Fielden, in his *The Curse of the Factory System* (1836), wrote of the heart-rending plight of the 'unoffending and friendless creatures' and 'the beautiful and romantic valleys of Derbyshire, Nottingham-shire and Lancashire [which], secluded from the public eye, became the dismal solitudes of torture, and of many a murder!'[11] Children of 7 commonly worked from 5.30 a.m. to 9.30 p.m., with an hour or less for dinner and were not allowed to talk or sit down during working hours. Since discipline was essential to the smooth running of the factories, punishments were swift, frequent and severe.[12] Although the 1802 Act restricted the weekly working hours for children to seventy-two and stipulated that they should receive religious and secular education, in the decades that followed, the employment of children increased alarmingly and became ever more problematic, such that by 1835 the cotton industry alone employed some 28,770 children under the age of 13 in conditions which amounted to slavery.[13] The 1819 and 1833 Factory Acts took further measures to protect children, stating that children under the age of 9 were not allowed to work in any mills (except, unaccountably, silk mills), and those between the ages of 9 and 13 could only work eight hours a day, with two hours schooling. Night work was also forbidden for young people under 18. (Children were subsequently replaced by women who were cheaper to employ than men and could, apparently, be more easily induced to undergo severe bodily fatigue.)[14]

In the mines, children as young as 4 worked as 'trappers', sitting alone in the dark, opening and closing the doors as the cartloads of coal passed, or from 6 upwards as 'drawers', pulling the carts from the workface to the foot of the shaft, often almost naked because of the heat, and with heavy chains around their waists. Compare this account from 1842 of the work of an 11-year-old girl employed as a coal bearer in Scotland with the portrayal of Mary's life in *The Lancashire Collier Girl*:

> She has first to descend a nine-ladder pit to the first rest, even to which a shaft is sunk, to draw up the baskets or tubs of coal filled by the bearers; she then takes her creel (a basket formed to the back, not unlike a cockle-shell flattened towards the neck, so as to allow lumps of coal to rest on the back of the neck and shoulders), and pursues her journey to the wall-face, or as it is called here, the room of work. She then lays down her basket, into which the coal is rolled, and it is frequently more than one man can do to lift the burden on her back. The tugs or straps are placed over her forehead, and the body bent in a semicircular form, in order to stiffen the arch. Large lumps of coal are then placed on her neck, and she then commences her journey with her burden to the pit bottom, first hanging her lamp to the cloth crossing her head . . . This one journey is designated a rake; the height ascended, and the distance along the roads added together, exceed the height of St Paul's Cathedral; and it not unfrequently happens that the tugs break, and the load falls upon those females who are following. However incredible it may be, yet I have taken evidence of fathers who have ruptured themselves from straining to lift coal on their children's backs.[15]

Children also worked long and hard in the sewing sweatshops, as chimney-sweeps (as Blake's famous poems revealed), in forges, brickfields and potteries as well as factories of all kinds. Of course, children had always worked in hard and sometimes injurious jobs, but it was the growing awareness of the particularly harsh conditions of the industrial workplace that brought the subject to the fore in the first half of the nineteenth century. The early Victorian conscience was stirred in the 1830s and 1840s when the consequences and controversies of the first reformist measures, the first Reform Act (1832), the Factory Act (1833), the Poor Law Amendment Act (1834) and, above all, the results of the Parliamentary Commissions' reports between 1830 and 1850 into conditions in the mines and factories, exacerbated by the manifestations of growing working-class discontent and the Chartist threats of the 1840s, began to open people's eyes to the real degree of hardship among the working classes. The fascination with progress and economic power gradually became tempered by an acute awareness of the enormous human price being paid, particularly by the nation's children.[16] Religious consciences were severely disturbed by the godless state of the poor and by their physical destitution, and by the realisation that old values of Christian charity, as exemplified in *Ministering Children*, were no longer viable nor effective among the multitudes of the urban sprawls.

Many writers seem to have been prompted by a sense of guilt on behalf of their class to expose these social ills and generate a questioning of values and a sense of individual responsibility in their readers. Although such a reorientation of approach became apparent in tract literature, the great social-problem novels of the 1840s also owed a considerable debt to the work of the Evangelicals, for their authors, products themselves of a period of intense religious fervour and an acute sense of mission, frequently brought the same values of duty, self-discipline, self-improvement and crusading piety to their portrayal of social questions. Once again, the figure of the child became central to their purpose, not only because here the iniquities of industrialisation were most apparent, but because what more effective stimulus could there be to guilt and the desire for reform than the pathos engendered by the spectacle of a starving, abandoned or exploited innocent. It was undoubtedly the success of Dickens which gave the impetus to the portrayal of the child in this respect. His *Oliver Twist, or, The Parish Boy's Progress* (1838) with its workhouse scenes is usually credited with being the first work to expose the evils of the industrial age, and the appearance of Little Nell in *The Old Curiosity Shop* (1840–41) coincided with the staggering revelations about the condition of working children. Dickens certainly developed the potential for pathos in his child figures, creating an intense emotional response in his readers which may indeed have derived from a latent collective sense of guilt about the plight of their real-life counterparts.[17] However, women writers were as quick to take up the challenge as Dickens and other reformer-writers like Charles Kingsley and Benjamin Disraeli, and, in fact, welcomed the opportunity afforded by literature to contribute their efforts to the great 'Condition of England' debate which came to a head in the 'Hungry Forties'.

In fact, the first writer to explore the conflict between capital and labour was Harriet Martineau, whose early industrial tales, like *The Rioters* (1827) about the machine-breakers and *The Turn-Out* (1829) about wage disputes, anticipated many of the concerns of mid-nineteenth-century fiction. Her imagination, like that of her contemporaries, was fired by these rapid changes, yet although she tended generally to respond more to the power, wonders and potential of what she saw and had a clear allegiance to the capitalist class, she was not unaware of or unconcerned about the soul-destroying implications of poverty and squalor in the everyday lives of people in urban communities.[18] She followed a different line from that of Dickens, however, preferring a rational stance and generally avoiding the temptation of sentimentality. The description in *A Manchester Strike* (1832), one of the *Illustrations of Political Economy*, of a back street full of rubbish and rooting pigs, the gutters brimming with muddy water and filth, equals those of Elizabeth Gaskell in *Mary Barton: A tale of Manchester life* (1848) and the scene at the cotton factory on the banks of the River Medlock where Martha, a lame child of 8, is subjected to the dust, smells, heat and 'incessant whizzing and whirling of the wheels' of the machinery which makes the pale children's heads ache, is an extremely affective one which even Gaskell did not attempt. When Martha has to allow her pet canary to be sold, the good sense which mingles with her grief prevents the moment from becoming the mawkish tear-jerker which it might have become in less able or differently motivated hands. Although the children are often seen as innocent victims of poverty, Martineau's approach also differs from Dickens in not criticising the fundamentally dehumanising nature of industrialised society but in stressing the need to inculcate in the working classes the importance of education, thrift, industriousness and clean living conditions. In *Cousin Marshall* (1832), for example, the underlying moral of the tale resides in the question 'What is Charity?' and her criticism is directed not only at the unthinking and arbitrary giving of financial aid, arguing that reliance on 'the parish' kills the urge to self-help, but also at the cynical exploitation of the system by such as the Bell family who continue to claim assistance for a sick child after its death. The moral of self-sufficiency, supplemented by judicious assistance for those unable to support themselves fully, is, as in Maria Edgeworth's tales, illustrated by contrast, in this case between a young brother and sister, Ned and Jane, both brought up in a workhouse. Ned is unhappy, fearful of pauperism and eager to work, and like his kind-hearted cousin Mrs Marshall, who willingly fosters two more of the orphaned family despite her own poverty, refuses to accept charity while he can shift for himself; Jane, who already has a tendency to be vain and giddy, becomes corrupted by the coarse talk and antisocial habits of some of the other inmates of the workhouse and eventually ruins her chances of independence by becoming pregnant.

Some of Martineau's attitudes and recommendations led to criticisms of harshness and insensitivity towards the plight of the truly poor and helpless and, in fact, led to a break with Dickens and the cessation of her contributions to his journal *Household Words*.[19] They also reflect some of the ironies and anomalies in contemporary responses and, indeed, in the situations themselves. Her rather surprising opposition to legislation to limit the employment of women and children in factories and mines, for example, is on the grounds that depriving workers of the free disposal of their own labour would steal from them their only possession, a view echoed by one of the characters in Gaskell's *Mary Barton* who laments that her young son can no longer be sent out to work to supplement the family income.[20] Although she argues against strike action and union activity, the leader in *A Manchester Strike* is seen as a hero (unlike Gaskell's John Barton, who is reduced to murder) and the manufacturer as a cruel, uncaring man who strikes the men's petition into the mud with his riding-whip. Nevertheless, her portrayal of the everyday life of children testifies to her powers of observation, compassion and skill in transmitting the flavour of the child's experience. In *A Manchester Strike*, for example, the long hours of the night shift and the events at dawn which herald the beginnings of the strike are seen through the aching eyes of Martha, and her envy of the freedom, fun and gaudy clothes of her friend Hannah Bray, who sings and dances in public houses with her father for a living, is realistically naive in its overlooking of the crude language and behaviour to which Hannah is constantly exposed and the beatings she receives from her frequently tipsy father.

The truth about the lives of children in the factories is explored in depth in Frances Trollope's much neglected novel *The Life and Adventures of Michael Armstrong: The factory boy* (1840) for which she drew on an original biography by John Brown published in 1832 and entitled *A Memoir of Robert Blincoe, an Orphan Boy; sent from the workhouse at St. Pancras, London, at seven years of age, to endure the horrors of a cotton mill, through his infancy and youth, with a minute detail of his sufferings, being the first memoir of the kind published*. Possibly influenced by *Oliver Twist*, which was then being widely read, Frances Trollope announced her intention of writing an industrial novel in 1839 and, like Dickens, travelled to Manchester by train to see conditions for herself. The memoir of Trollope written by her daughter-in-law relates that 'she spared no pains to acquaint herself with the real conditions of the people she intended writing about, and, with her son, visited many scenes of pitiable wretchedness and revolting squalor' such that 'every sense was sickened, and the very heartstrings wrung by what she had witnessed'.[21] Originally intending to write the novel in two parts, the first to expose 'the hideous mass of injustice and suffering to which thousands of infant labourers are subjected who toil in our monster spinning-mills' and the second to show the hero embarked upon 'perfectly constitutional struggles' for the amelioration of the miseries of his class, the author decided to limit the narrative to Michael's childhood because she had become aware that honest working men can be led astray to 'scenes of outrage and lawless violence' in the company of 'individuals whose doctrines are subversive of every species of social order'.[22] She thus demonstrates the same awareness of the potentially inflammatory nature of her novel at a time of industrial unrest and union activity as underpins *Mary Barton* and Charlotte Brontë's novel, *Shirley* (1849).[23]

Trollope's comment on the absence of factory children in literature highlights satirically the earlier tendency to romanticise certain categories of working-class child:

> Had he been a ragged sailor-boy, or a ragged plough-boy, or even a ragged chimney-sweeper, there might by possibility have been excited some feeling of curiosity or interest; but a ragged factory-boy was of all created beings the one least likely to give birth to such emotions, among his friends and neighbours, or indeed to any other emotion fit to be exhibited in good society.[24]

It is in her portrayal of Michael's childhood in the 'dark Satanic mills' of the north that the real power of the novel lies, and as one of the first to attempt a full description of the implications of factory work for children, Trollope deserves to be better known. As a small boy, Michael Armstrong is plucked from the obscurity of his factory by the owner as an object of charity for purely cynical reasons – to please an aristocratic lady friend and as a ploy to calm the rumblings of discontent among his workforce and to promote the view of himself as a great benefactor. Through a series of misadventures Michael ends up in a mill in the very heartland of the Industrial Revolution.

With the device of having her central female figure Mary Bretherton, an heiress to a factory fortune, flout social convention by visiting the factories to seek out the truth about child labour, Trollope employs both argument and direct description to paint the horrors of the situation. Implicit in the plot is the criticism that a brief guided tour of a factory only gives a cursory glimpse of the reality, inspiring admiration perhaps of the beauty of the complex, powerful machinery but obscuring the plight of the small operatives of the 'myriads of whirling spindles amidst which they breathe their groans, unheeded, and unheard'.[25] In the mills, children were greatly in demand because of their nimble fingers and small size which allowed them to work as 'scavengers', crawling beneath the machinery to free a tangled bobbin or collect cotton waste without the frame having to be brought to a halt. The horrific injuries which often resulted were just an additional hazard to the exhaustion of long hours spent standing at their work, the effects of poor food and lack of sleep, and the bronchial problems caused by the constant inhalation of lint from the atmosphere.[26] It is this reality of nineteenth-century childhood that Mary Bretherton sees: a multitude of pallid, feeble waifs

> lodged amidst stench and stunning, terrifying tumult – driven to and fro, till their little limbs bend under them – hour after hour, day after day – the repose of a moment to be purchased only by yielding their tender bodies to the fist, the heel, or the strap of the overlooker.[27]

The situation is portrayed even more potently through the eyes of Michael Armstrong in a scene in the Apprentice House attached to the infamous Deep Valley Mill, the activities of which are hidden from public view in an isolated valley by a river, where he glimpses that the 'filthy, half-starved wretches . . . were so many ghostly representations of what he himself was to be'.[28] Childhood, in every sense of the word, is denied to the children here. Trollope draws on the imagery of the slave trade, which with the work of William Wilberforce was an issue very much in the public eye, and one of which Trollope herself had personal experience during her sojourn in the United States, to comment incisively and with indignation on the source of trade which helped to build the British Empire, identifying it as 'slavery, probably the most tremendous that young children were ever exposed to in any part of the known world, civilised or uncivilised'.[29] It is not difficult to imagine the effect of such words for the early Victorians, flushed with pride and enthusiasm at their country's economic prowess.

In a chapter which is clearly a rather clumsy platform for the reformer, Mary is lectured by a clergyman on the 'plague' which threatens to 'poison the very life blood of our political existence' thus:

> 'Never, my dear young lady, did the avarice of man conceive a system so horribly destructive of human feeling, as that by which the low-priced agony of labouring infants is made to eke out and supply all that is wanting to enable the giant engines of our factories to outspin the world.'[30]

Apart from the deforming and stunting physical effects of the work, the worst long-term result of the juvenile suffering is seen to be the 'reckless, desperate despair, which by destroying hope, that beautiful mainspring of all our best actions, leaves the poor spiritless machine alive only to the wretched consciousness of its capacity for pain'. It is this bitter hopelessness and loss of autonomy which are the main cause of the deterioration of the moral character of the operatives: 'In no other situation, excepting only that of slaves purchased and paid for like an ox, or an ass, is the destiny of a human being so wholly and completely beyond reach of his own control.'[31]

Michael is saved from this dehumanising state by his affection for a fellow worker, Fanny Fletcher, who has fallen on hard times as an orphan, and by the memory of his mother's love, a popular motif in texts of this period. Trollope concedes to the sentimentality and pathos of the period in her portrait of Fanny whose lovely, though emaciated, features display a 'hopeless, yet enduring composure', inculcated by her early religious upbringing, and draws on the conventions of the novel of romantic adventure in her rather far-fetched resolution of the plot, for Michael becomes a hero and in the end is happily reunited with both Fanny and his crippled brother Edward who, improbably, marries Mary Bretherton. There is no sentimentality, however, in Trollope's indictment of a system which is the source of wealth to the few

and of physical, mental and spiritual destruction to so many. Unlike Elizabeth
Gaskell who also wished to open the eyes of her middle-class readers to the
'unparalleled destitution of the manufacturing classes' in Manchester,
Trollope is not reluctant to indict the masters and their supporters openly,
accusing them of inhumanity and cynical self-interest. There is blatant
hostility in her depiction of Sir Matthew Dowling as a monster of avaricious
cunning and duplicity, and of the overseers and millowners as suspicious,
defensive and sadistic. In a blasphemous parody of Evangelical fervour, one
owner harangues the half-asleep children at the Deep Valley Sunday school,
exhorting them to remember that only through obedience to their earthly
masters can they hope to be saved from 'eternal burning'. Thus, Trollope
argues, had the Evangelical values of determination, endeavour and self-
improvement become perverted by the implacable pursuit of wealth.[32]

Trollope leaves her readers in no doubt as to their individual, as well as
collective, duty, exemplified in the person of Mary Bretherton. In an authorial
intrusion full of rage and shame which follows a description of the Apprentice
House where the children, most of them sick or with atrophied limbs and all
with features pinched by famine, sleep like vermin, fifty to a room, she
addresses the sceptical directly:

> Let none dare to say this picture is exaggerated, till he has taken the trouble to
> ascertain by his own personal investigation, that it is so. It is a very fearful crime
> in a country where public opinion has been proved (as in the African Slave
> Trade), to be omnipotent, for any individual to sit down with a shadow of doubt
> respecting such statements on his mind. If they be true, let each in his own little
> circle, raise his voice against the horrors detailed by them, and THESE
> HORRORS WILL BE REMEDIED. But woe to those who supinely sit in
> contented ignorance of the facts, soothing their spirits and their easy
> consciences with the cuckoo note 'exaggeration', while thousands of helpless
> children pine away their unnoted, miserable lives, in labour and destitution.[33]

There is some exaggeration in her descriptions, nonetheless, both in the
extreme and uniform grimness and in the grotesque and vicious behaviour of
her 'villains', but this does not render the novel any less persuasive, although
it could be argued that the horrors of the factory system required no such
literary embellishment to be severely disturbing. Although a moving, painful,
outspoken yet often funny book, there is evidence to suggest, however, that
it was not particularly popular with either critics or the middle-class reading
public at the time, and that it appealed mainly to those already converted to
the fight for new legislation. Frances Trollope herself wrote, shortly after
publication, that 'I don't think any one cares much for *Michael Armstrong* –
except the Chartists. A new kind of patron for me.'[34]

A different approach is taken by Charlotte Elizabeth Tonna in *Helen
Fleetwood* (serialised in *The Christian Lady's Magazine* in 1839–40 and
published as a full-length novel in 1841) which also deals with the lives of

Manchester factory workers, for the novel was part of an active and sustained Evangelical campaign to alert public attention to the evils of child and female labour, a campaign which also involved a number of articles, a long poem on 'The English Factory' and four tales published together as *The Wrongs of Women* (1843–44).[35] Although she had personal experience of the problems through her philanthropic work in England and Ireland, Tonna based her novels, as did many of her contemporaries, on material from the Parliamentary Blue Book reports, including the first-hand accounts by witnesses. Indeed, she has been credited as the first of the social-problem novelists of the period to translate such living testimony into dialogue in her novels.[36] Though passionately and unequivocally critical of the evils of the factory system, her compassionate viewpoint succeeds in avoiding the tendency to sentimentality and melodrama to which other writers succumbed.

Apart from Frances Trollope, Tonna was the only novelist to describe in such detail the actual conditions of women and children in the factories and she even exceeds Trollope in her factual precision and close focus on her subject. *Helen Fleetwood* relates the rapid and inevitable decline of a family consisting of a grandmother, her four grandchildren and adopted grandchild, Helen, who move to Manchester from a rural area to escape from destitution. Like many people in reality, they are victims of one of the consequences of the New Poor Law, for they have been seduced by pamphlets issued by the parish guardians encouraging the poor to migrate to the city and thus ease the burden on local relief resources. In fact, the Green family are virtually destroyed. Drawing on many of the same images as Trollope, notably those of the slave trade, Tonna highlights the worst aspects of life for children in the cotton mills: exhaustion, injury to limbs and lungs, perpetual hunger and the effects of gin drinking. Her descriptions of the terrifying atmosphere in the mills, with the eternal deafening noise of the machines which dwarf and control the children, are dramatically visual as well as accurate: 'so you must step back, and run forward, and duck, and turn, and move as they do, or off goes a finger or an arm, or else you get a knock on the head, to remember all your lives'.[37] She is particularly sensitive to the dehumanising effects of the machinery which are all the more pernicious when the victims are small children, often under the age of 10, who are never able to develop their individuality. The following reflection is a chilling anticipation of a psychological danger still relevant in our own time:

> Seen at their work they are a community of automata. Nothing seems to animate them. The cold listlessness of their looks sends a chill to the heart of the spectator, who, if he feels rightly, must feel it a degradation to his species to be chained . . . to a parcel of machinery, confused by its din, and forced to obey its movements with scarcely an interval for thought or repose.[38]

Helen Fleetwood is concerned with exposing both the immediate and the long-term effects on the daily lives and morals of the workers, thus she highlights not only the gradual degeneration of her characters who, having more individuality and complexity that those of Trollope, are more akin to Elizabeth Gaskell's characters (indeed, Helen could be deemed to anticipate Mary Barton as the first working-class heroine in a full-length social-problem novel) but also the undermining of family loyalties and affection. She overtly condemns parents who send their children to work at a young age, colluding with an inhuman system through greed or ignorance, as cannibals 'sucking the young blood out of their veins'.[39] In *The Little Pin-Headers* and *The Lace-Runners* in *The Wrongs of Women*, the hazards to the health, eyesight and morale of the children because of long hours spent labouring over close, detailed work in airless, overcrowded rooms, are laid, implicitly, at the door of the fashionable women patrons, the implications of the oppression of children by the nation's wives and mothers providing a potent angle of attack on social complacency. After the detailed descriptions of the children's activities and sufferings at work and at home in *The Little Pin-Headers*, Tonna contrasts the passion of British women for evangelising missionary work abroad with their blindness to the realities of home in no uncertain terms:

> The miseries, the wretchedness, the sufferings, the degradation of young English girls, far exceed those of the little heathen abroad; nor is the foulest system of pagan demoralisation, cruelty or crime, second in atrocity to that which varnishes itself over with the name of Christianity, and seizes for its victims the free-born children of Britain, baptised into a faith of which they live and die in soul-destroying ignorance.[40]

In *The Little Pin-Headers*, Betsy and her brother Joe, ill-treated and neglected by their profligate stepmother who lives off their wages while their younger siblings are already in the workhouse and their older sister has found more congenial employment 'in another line', are both believable creations and representative of 'thousands upon thousands in this land'.[41] There is no tendency here to idealise or sentimentalise poverty and family relationships, the children she portrays have unwashed bodies and mud- and filth-encrusted rags, and far from dying exemplary deaths as in so many of the Evangelical tracts, they are seen to experience the real physical effects of malnutrition, beatings and exhaustion till they are 'thrown into the street, just as a broken wheel is thrown into the lumber room, to fall to pieces'.[42] Tonna's grasp of the psychological effects on the children is impressively conveyed. In the workshop, where the smells and closeness of the gas-lit darkness act like a narcotic and their mirth or manifestations of brotherly or sisterly feeling are punished, they sob and grow giddy, or fight and argue with an irritability induced by fatigue, hunger and the constant fear of the overseer's violence:

> The playfulness of childhood has utterly disappeared: mischief, before comparatively harmless, as a practical joke, has become the ebullition of

quarrelsome ill-humour, and the malice of a revenge that would fain wreak itself somewhere, and being unable to reach the tyrants who provoked it, finds vent on its fellow sufferers.[43]

At night, the 'frequent start, and half-uttered cry of imaginary torment betray how busily fancy is occupied with dreams of the future, grounded as they are, on bitter experience of the past'.[44] Joe has endured so many beatings that his spirit is completely broken and his childhood destroyed. He has become other, no longer a bright-eyed boy who

> even when tumbling among cinders or splashing in the liquid mud before his father's door, attracted notice by his energetic bearing and unflinching gaze, and merry, shouting tones, but a trembling, shrinking, hesitating whisperer, afraid, it would seem, of trusting his own step, or hearing his own voice, or encountering the look of any eye save Betsy's.[45]

When Joe is beaten with a heavy rod by the manager of the workshop, Betsy's terror and sense of impotence are painfully evoked:

> the effort by which she suppressed both the scream and the tears, and refrained from even moving to her brother's assistance, was a terrible one. It convulsed her tender frame, and made her hand tremble as with an ague. She now sits, apparently quiet, but with a film over her eyes, and a choking in her throat, and a pain in her side, often experienced by adults of a nervous temperament, but a strange concomitant of early childhood. All is outwardly still again, terror has paralysed the minds, but quickened the mechanical movements of those poor little slaves.[46]

The child is still seen from the viewpoint of the adult narrator, but with sympathy and admiration, rather than with the condescension of the earlier moral tales, the switch to the present tense effectively enjoining the reader to identify with Betsy's reaction. Like her contemporaries, Tonna was concerned about the degrading effects of industrialisation at all levels of society and argued for immediate and effective intervention in the regulation of conditions in the factories.[47] Many women writers used religious belief, particularly the Christian precepts of charity and compassion, as a weapon to attack their own class's obsession with the pursuit of self-interest, and Tonna, as an Evangelical polemicist, saw the only solution to the rapidly accelerating spiritual breakdown in both individuals and the nation to be the urgent recognition and re-establishment of the spirit of Christian brotherhood, a task in which the responsibility of the individual should be maximised.

Tonna's novels and tales of industrial life were more widely admired than Trollope's and possibly more influential: Harriet Beecher Stowe wrote an enthusiastic introduction to the American three-volume edition of her works published in 1844–45 and they may have inspired the poem by Elizabeth Barrett Browning at the head of this chapter. Although both Trollope and Tonna are generally accepted to have less literary talent than Gaskell or

Dickens, their willingness to expose social iniquities and indict the middle classes of perversion of the very religious values they professed to embody, demonstrates their significance in the development of the novel of the period. Both *Michael Armstrong* and *Helen Fleetwood* predate, after all, not only *Mary Barton*, but also Disraeli's *Sybil* (1845), Dickens' *Hard Times* (1854), Kingsley's *Alton Locke* (1850) and *Yeast* (1848), and Engels' *Condition of the Working Class in England in 1844*.[48]

The same kind of Christian interventionism is exemplified in Elizabeth Gaskell's work, although she refrains from depicting factory conditions, choosing to concentrate instead on what she herself had witnessed in her visits to the homes of the poor as the wife of a Unitarian minister in Manchester. It is perhaps this first-hand experience, readily acquired, since charity and philanthropic work were seen as a respectable and highly desirable occupation for middle-class females, which makes women's writings on the subject so compelling. In *Mary Barton*, begun as a form of therapy after the death of her own infant son, children are not central figures in the plot, for the story of industrial unrest and the murder of the millowner's son Harry Carson is blended with a conventional love story involving Mary, Carson and Jem Wilson, a mill-hand. Children do, however, play an important role for they are the innocent victims of the situation in which 'class distrusted class', and mismanagement and misunderstanding explode in hatred and violence. Gaskell in fact takes a curiously ambivalent stance to the problem, refusing on the one hand to indict directly the millowners of inhumanity (partly because she was convinced of the complexity of the situation and partly because she did not wish to alienate the very readers she sought to convince), yet on the other hand, painting such a persuasive and moving picture of poverty and hardship that a direct accusation would be superfluous.[49]

She does not, however, idealise the child as a symbol of exploited innocence and purity. Her child characters are voiceless in the text, simply the weakest and most vulnerable of the family unit in times of distress, their problems not spiritual or moral dilemmas, but physical survival. They do not mouth pious platitudes and carry sweetness and light wherever they go: they cry for food, and shiver, and die silently. It is the consciousness that they are unable to save their starving offspring that drives men mad with hatred. Thus, John Barton is consumed with a 'bitter spirit of wrath' when, standing outside a food shop unable to purchase a morsel for his small son who is dying of scarlet fever, he witnesses the departure of a wealthy woman laden with provisions for a party and returns home to see 'his only boy a corpse'.[50] When trade grows slack and work short, the manufacturers have more time to enjoy domestic pleasures while in the homes of the operatives

the family music was hungry wails, when week after week passed by, and there was no work to be had, and consequently no wages to pay for the bread the children cried aloud for in their young impatience of suffering ... Many a penny that would have gone little way enough in oatmeal or potatoes, bought opium to still the hungry little ones, and make them forget their uneasiness in troubled sleep. The evil and the good of our nature comes out strongly then.[51]

As in Tonna's work, the insidious effects on family life are lamented although Gaskell's picture of family life is a balanced one, the good qualities of compassion, fellowship, self-denial and charity among the workers springing from the same calamities which generate resentment and despair. There is also room for humour; for example, a delightful anecdote is recounted by one character of himself and a comrade trying to pacify a tired, hungry baby, one of them donning a woman's cap in an attempt to get the baby to respond to a 'female' presence.

Gaskell rejects the fictional stereotypes of angelic, dying children, basing her picture on reality. There is no morbid death-bed pathos in the description of the death of the Wilson twins:

> there sat Mrs Wilson in the old rocking-chair, with one sick, death-like boy on her knee, crying without let or pause, but softly, gently, as fearing to disturb the troubled, gasping child; while behind her, old Alice let her fast-dropping tears down fall on the dead body of the other twin, which she was laying out on a board, placed on a sort of sofa-settee in the corner of the room.[52]

The details are bare and factual, having no reference other than the natural grief of a mother and grandmother. Similarly, the authenticated realism of the description of the cellar dwelling of the Davenport family is all the more moving for its straightforwardness:

> You went down one step even from the foul area into the cellar in which a family of human beings lived. It was very dark inside. The window-panes were many of them broken and stuffed with rags, which was reason enough for the dusky light that pervaded the place even at mid-day. After the account I have given of the state of the street, no-one can be surprised that on going into the cellar inhabited by Davenport, the smell was so fetid as almost to knock the two men down. Quickly recovering themselves, as those inured to such things do, they began to penetrate the thick darkness of the place, and to see three or four little children rolling on the damp, nay wet, brick floor, through which the stagnant, filthy moisture of the street oozed up; the fireplace was empty and black; the wife sat on her husband's chair, and cried in the dark loneliness.[53]

Gaskell's recommendations echo those of the novels discussed earlier: knowing nothing, she claims, of political economy or the theories of trade, but, like other women writers, responding to what she saw about her as a Christian sensitive to the suffering of fellow human beings and alert to the need for increased social responsibility, she sees the only way forward as a matter of individual conscience, 'in short, to acknowledge the Spirit of Christ as the regulating law between both parties'.[54] This is enacted in the novel by the reconciliation of the manufacturer Mr Carson, who comes to realise, through his own suffering, his human responsibilities towards his workers, and John Barton, the disillusioned striker and Chartist delegate who shot Carson's son. In her preface, Gaskell claims that she tried to 'write truthfully', her aim being to 'give some utterance to the agony which, from time to time, convulses this dumb people', and it is this truthfulness, and the honesty and simplicity with which she conveys reality in the pages of *Mary Barton*, which account for its success, not only with her literary peers (Dickens, Carlyle and Maria Edgeworth voiced their approval) but with readers of both the middle and working classes.

The upsurge of interest in contemporary social issues in the 1840s also gave further impetus to the literary idealisation of the child, in which a sense of social responsibility converged with the taste for the sentimental. This tendency was apparent, for example, in Elizabeth Gaskell's short story *The Three Eras of Libbie Marsh* (1847), in which the spiritually impoverished life of the young seamstress protagonist is transformed by her friendship with a crippled child and his mother in the house opposite her lodgings. The 'most true and holy patience' of little Franky in his painful and tedious existence and the way in which his empty room becomes, after his death, a 'consecrated place' for those who loved him, are familiar echoes of earlier tract tales, but are here redeemed from mawkish sentimentality by Gaskell's characteristic-ally detailed evocation of slum life and the realities of grinding poverty and sickness. Once again, the child is the object of the adult narrator's pitying observation as well as of that of Libbie. Thus, Libbie is first moved by the sight of the 'little spectral shadow' of the bedridden child's arm on the window-blind:

> long, thin fingers hanging listlessly down from the wrist, while the arm moved up and down, as if keeping time to the heavy pulses of dull pain. She could not help hoping that sleep would soon come to still that incessant, feeble motion; and now and then it did cease, as if the little creature had dropped into a slumber from very weariness; but presently the arm jerked up with the fingers clenched, as if with a sudden start of agony.[55]

The close focus on detail in this passage induces the reader to share Libbie's response, just as Franky's delight in a bunch of Michaelmas daisies, a pet canary bought by Libbie to share his lonely hours and a rare day out in the countryside evoke a strong sense of the otherwise uniform bleakness of his existence. But Franky's main role in the narrative is that of instrument of spiritual regeneration. When he dies, the emphasis is on the end to his suffering and the consequences for the two women left behind, his stunned mother, who faints at the graveside but accepts that the next day 'she mun go washing, just as if nothing had happened', and Libbie, his only friend.[56] Gaskell writes: 'Out of the little grave, there sprang a hope and a resolution, which made life an object to each of the other two.'[57] One of the most interesting aspects of the story is the focus on the changing experience of the two women which foreshadows Gaskell's interest in her later novels in the fate of women in patriarchal society. Because of their shared affection for the dead child, the two lonely women make a home together, Libbie providing comfort and company to the bereaved mother and finding happiness herself in thus rendering the services of a daughter, 'no longer the desolate, lonely orphan, a stranger on earth'.[58] Out of the child's suffering existence has come, in almost Christ-like fashion, hope and the promise of peace and joy.

The virtual absence of the working child from Evangelical tract tales in the first half of the century seems to have been due to a range of factors, among them a kind of spiritual blinkering, despite their missionary zeal, to hardships close to home (as Charlotte Elizabeth Tonna complained) and a reluctance to criticise progress and the nation's pursuit of economic power by industrialists, many of them Evangelicals, whose values of energy, industry and enlightened self-interest were, in their unperverted form, supported by the tract writers.[59] As information about the condition of the working classes and the magnitude of the destitution in urban areas continued to be widely publicised in the 1850s and 1860s, however, and particularly after the publication of Mayhew's extraordinary work, *London Labour and the London Poor* in 1861–62, which documented the huge numbers and range of children surviving by their wits and labour on the streets as hawkers of all sorts of small goods such as matches, flowers, buttons and shoelaces, or as entertainers, crossing-sweepers, porters, shoeblacks and errand boys, the slums of the capital became increasingly popular settings for tract novels and the child-as-victim, or 'street-arab evangelist', became a favourite figure with readers of all classes.[60] Some of the most widely read tales were those written by Hesba Stretton and Mrs O. F. Walton, who depict different aspects of the phenomenon in a range of texts which were avidly read by juvenile and adult readers alike.

Hesba Stretton's tales are especially interesting because, like Elizabeth Gaskell's, they are firmly rooted in the grim reality of life in the city back streets, thus providing a very real insight into conditions and manners and breaking new ground in the Evangelical tract tale. Moreover, she writes from the viewpoint of the poor, rather than in a patronising way as a reformer, and when the protagonist is a child, this evokes a particularly poignant and persuasive view of the problems concerned. As a founder member of the London branch of the Royal Society for the Prevention of Cruelty to Children, she was actively committed to a number of very specific issues involving children and these, rather than a generalised picture of poverty, are tackled in an outspoken way in her works, notably the exploitation of children as beggars and entertainers, the lack of children's hospitals and rehabilitation institutions for young people in trouble, and the general lack of legal protection for women and children. The appearance of her tales coincided with the active work being carried out in the slums by such dedicated people as Dr Barnardo, Octavia Hill, William and Catherine Booth and Maria Rye, and was certainly influential in bringing more fully into the public eye the realities of the situation and the drastic need for action.[61]

Stretton's tales employ the same device used in earlier Evangelical tracts of placing a child figure at the centre of the text and there is a common pattern of a solitary, neglected child on whom a newly learned Bible text or prayer has an almost magical effect which sustains or transforms the life of the child who, in turn, transforms the lives of others. Her fundamental view of the child, characteristic of the later Evangelicals, was akin to the Romantic notion of the pure, innocent creature whose intuitive responses and simple piety light the way for their elders. As in Dickens' novels, adults are thus frequently seen as weak, greedy, cynical, neglectful, cruel and worse, an approach which would have been unthinkable in Mrs Sherwood's day.[62] Although her child protagonists are frequently both pathetic and sentimental, however, as has been seen in the discussion of *The Children of Cloverley*, this tendency is balanced in her slum tales by her willingness to portray the decidedly unsentimental aspects of their lives in relatively bold terms. For her settings she drew on her own experience in rural and industrial Shropshire, in Manchester where she lived in lodgings with her governess sister and in London, and the circumstantial detail is specific and graphically presented. However, since she wrote prolifically for the Religious Tract Society, she was, to a certain extent, constrained by their requirement that the sensibilities of their middle-class readers should not be so affected as to alienate them. Thus there are perceptible limitations to her portrayal which may puzzle a modern reader but which reflect the dichotomy of the supposed responses of a middle-class and a working-class readership.

Stretton's best-known work is *Jessica's First Prayer* (serialised in *Sunday at Home* in 1866 and published as a book in 1867) which was translated into many Asian and African languages, as well as every European language.[63] It tells the story of the friendship between a ragged slum child, Jessica, and Daniel, the miserly owner of a coffee-stall, through which she learns about God and becomes the instrument of redemption for the 'Christian' adult who has yet to learn the true meaning of charity and grace. Jessica is first seen externally, from Daniel's point of view and thus as an object of curiosity, as 'a pair of very bright dark eyes' watching him at his stall early in the morning. The sense of mystery is maintained by the contrast between her fancy name (derived from her mother's work as an actress) and the moving picture of hunger and neglect she presents, with her thin, meagre face half-hidden by a mass of matted hair, her tattered dress and 'gaze as hungry as that of a mouse which has been driven by famine into a trap', as she shifts from one bare foot to another on the damp pavement.[64] The destitution of her home (located, perhaps significantly, above a stable) and the violence of her life with her drunken mother mean that the warm coffee given to her by Daniel on a Wednesday morning becomes the focal point of her life. Her superiority to her surroundings and her potential for rising above them are demonstrated in a 'test' to which the still intrigued Daniel puts her, for she resists the instinctive temptation to steal a coin he deliberately drops, impressing and shaming him with her honesty and ability to reason, and, at the same time, proving her worth to the reader.

Stretton then shifts to Jessica's point of view to reveal new information about Daniel, for when she follows him one day we learn that he is a part-time chapel-keeper. Jessica knows nothing of religion and it is now her curiosity and wonder at his other life in the unfamiliar, dimly lighted building with its dark oak pews and glittering organ pipes which the reader shares. The title of the chapter, 'Peeps into Fairyland', in which she watches the well-dressed members of the congregation come and go from her hiding-place behind the door, expresses her wonder at this new shining world in terms of her only other experience of such glamour, as a 'fairy' in the theatre. Here the paradox on which the tale is built first emerges, for Daniel's religion is contaminated by misplaced snobbery (he tries to banish her from the door because the fine ladies and gentlemen of the congregation would be 'shocked to see a ragged little heathen like you'), while Jessica's whole being is moved by the 'sweet music' and, although she goes home with a heavy heart, she is drawn back every Sunday to the chapel. Such innate sensitivity and responsiveness are a common if somewhat implausible characteristic of many literary slum children of this period, notably in the works of Dickens, although in Jessica's case it is, at this stage, largely a matter of the senses, for the more tangible benefits of the warmth and light of the chapel are a major part of the 'secret and perilous pleasure' of her forbidden visits. Moreover she cannot articulate the attraction she feels, just as, when she is eventually allowed into the chapel to listen to the sermons, it is the tender pity of the minister's face and tones to which she responds with rapt attention rather than his words, of which she has little understanding.

It is the minister's children who find her hiding in the porch and, unlike the adults, acting spontaneously on the biblical injunction to treat rich and poor alike, take her to their father who reads 'the misery of her desolate life' at once and welcomes her into the chapel. A dubious light is shed on the Church's attitude towards the poor, however, for Jessica is made to sit apart by the pulpit steps and has to be clothed more suitably in a cloak and bonnet when she becomes a regular attender, so as to present a more respectable appearance to the congregation. Her first prayer, in which she unites her two most urgent desires – to know God and to have her friend Daniel paid for his coffee – moves all who hear it for its selflessness and simple piety.[65] Once Jessica begins to transcend her godless state, which contemporary readers might well have found even more shocking than her squalor, she becomes the prototype street-arab evangelist and the process of the re-education of Daniel begins. Her innocent questions awaken his conscience and force him, like Silas Marner, to question his motives in amassing the money he earns by selling coffee. It is revealed that he lives alone in a sparse house with only his bag of sovereigns for company and 'could not remember giving anything away, except the dregs of the coffee and the stale buns, for which Jessica was asking God to pay him'.[66] Thus, even before her own acquaintance with religion, she has been the unconscious medium of his salvation by presenting him with an opportunity to exercise charity. When Jessica is found ill and alone in her garret, Daniel experiences the revelation that he, in turn, has been tested by God who had sent her 'to see if I would do her a little good for His sake'.[67] He realises the error of his ways, and with the decision to take her home to nurse her himself, understands that he has been well repaid for his coffee by being given back his soul. In what threatens to be a conventional death-bed scene, Jessica lays her wasted hand on the man's bowed head and prays to live for his sake. At this point, however, Stretton subverts her readers' expectations by allowing Jessica to recover, become Daniel's adopted daughter and help him with his work at both coffee-stall and chapel.

Jessica's First Prayer is a genuinely touching little tale, for Stretton avoids mawkish idealisation of the ignorant child, ill-treated by her own world and looked down on by the middle-class one, and even in the final sentimental scenes rejects the anticipated form of closure in favour of a positive, dynamic and forward-looking ending with Jessica and Daniel leading full and happy lives. Although Jessica shows the way to the true meaning of Christian values, it is through the effect on Daniel of her example of patience, endurance and straightforwardness rather than through precocious religiosity. Indeed, it is clear that she herself initially responded to religion chiefly because it offered not only physical comfort but stimulus to her deprived and atrophied emotions. As in other tracts, though less patronisingly than in *Ministering Children*, for example, true charity is seen to bring benefits to both parties, a lesson which made more palatable the clear attack on Victorian materialism. The brevity and simple directness of the narrative, which do not harangue the reader but allow the moral to emerge through the events themselves, not only accounted for its phenomenal success but was the foundation stone for the 'street-arab' school of writing.

A more subtle text, which focuses more sharply on the experience of the child, who is seen by the narrator both from without and within, is Stretton's *Little Meg's Children* (1868). As their mother dies in the first chapter, and their father is away at sea, the tale is concerned with the day-to-day struggle for survival of three small children on their own in a slum attic in London. Like Jessica, Meg is described as a typical slum child with none of the sweet prettiness of many little 'tract' girls:

a small, spare, stunted girl of London growth whose age could not be more than ten years, though she wore the shrewd, anxious air of a woman upon her face, with deep lines wrinkling her forehead, and puckering about her keen eyes.[68]

Cast at an early age in the role of 'little mother' to her brother Robin, aged 6, and a baby, Meg has already lived a lifetime of hard work and deprivation. Yet, though typical of many real-life youngsters in many ways, Meg, like Jessica, is also exemplary, being honest, good-hearted, loyal and totally devoted to 'her' children. As a family they are also representative, yet apart, both morally and spatially, for they live in the top attic of a tenement which can only be reached by a ladder and do not mix with the 'bad crew' who live in the discordantly named Angel Court. This separateness is dramatised when Meg and Robin sit on the high window-sill, after their mother's death, and look down upon the squalid tumult of the yard below, the dirty, quarrelling children and drunken men and women, and find comfort in the 'white clouds floating slowly across the sky over their heads, which seemed to little Meg like the wings of the waiting angels hovering over the place where her mother lay dead'.[69] Although their poverty is considerable, the squalor of the surroundings is modified by Stretton's descriptions which, though accurate, are limited and do not linger on the full implications of the filth, smells, vermin and crudeness of language and behaviour of reality. A note of romance is added by the 'secret', a bag of sovereigns belonging, they believe, to a shipmate of their father's, which Meg's mother enjoins her to guard carefully, a device which alerts the reader to the probable outcome of the tale yet produces in itself an uncomfortable irony since it creates an additional focus of anxiety for Meg who, acting on her mother's instructions, will allow no one to enter the room, thus effectively cutting the little family off from any form of assistance. Meg becomes the embattled guardian of the family honour as she is reduced to pawning the very clothes from her mother's box beneath the bed which hide the sovereigns she is too honest to touch.

The tale can be read as a story of the development of the protagonist to emotional and spiritual womanhood based on a fairy-tale model, as Meg is left alone to fight against hardship and dangers, including the spectres of disease and starvation, in defence of her own space, the claustrophobic attic, which embodies her past (her dead mother), her present (Robin, the baby and her responsibility for the secret symbolised by the key to the chest she wears round her neck) and her future (the hope that her father will soon return and restore the stability of the family unit). Yet the tale focuses directly on the details of daily realities, just as Meg's qualities are demonstrated in their practical application so that she is never unrealistically idealised, unlike Dickens' 'little woman' figure in *The Old Curiosity Shop*, Little Nell, who is sentimentalised not least by being referred to constantly as simply 'the child'. The fact that events are seen largely through Meg's eyes hugely increases the impact of the narrative. She lives from day to day, her main concern to keep the children fed, warm and safe in constant anticipation of the arrival of their father's ship. She assumes a mother's pride as well as a mother's responsibilities, trying to teach Robin his letters and the wan, sickly baby with an old face and a sudden sweet smile which suggests that she is 'not long for this world', to walk a few steps. She scrubs and sweeps and keeps their only decent clothes neatly folded to present a respectable picture to their father. Her instinctive comforting of the others despite her own grief, her delight in being able to buy them the treat of a meat pie or a visit to the Temple Gardens, where the contrast between their life and that of the rich is everywhere apparent, and her visits to the docks to enquire after the ship display a self-effacing maturity, strength and independence far beyond her years. Indeed, Meg is treated as an equal by the few adults with whom she comes into contact. Yet Stretton does not divest her of the sensibilities and imagination of a child, revealing, by shifting the narration to Meg's point of view, her curiosity, uncertainty and vulnerability as she tries to keep awake to see if the angels will come for her mother, her worries about the logistics of negotiating a busy street with two small children, her anxiety and fear at the fog-bound docks with its strange sounds and looming shadows and her disappointment at her father's failure to appear, not least because she longs to lay down her responsibilities and 'be a child again':

> She drew back into a corner, and peered eagerly, with wistful eyes, into the thick yellow mist which hid everything from them, while she listened to the clank of iron cables, and the loud sing-song of the invisible sailors as they righted their vessels. If she could only hear her father's voice among them! She felt sure she should know it among a hundred others, and she was ready to cry aloud the moment it reached her ears – to call 'Father!' and he would be with her in an instant, and she in his arms, with her own clasped fast about his neck. Oh, if he would but speak out of the darkness![70]

The mixture of timidity, determination and an acute longing which allows her imagination to run ahead constructing the desired scene while her anxiety prompts a dawning suspicion that it might not materialise, is well captured here. Similarly, the children's awed delight at the unknown buildings in the Temple Gardens, the combination of apprehension and sorrow with which Robin approaches to kiss his dead mother's face, their 'sad but childish curiosity' at her funeral, and the baby's scream of 'mingled dread and delight' as she takes her first tottering steps are nicely observed and demonstrate the facility with which Stretton, at her best, can slip into the child's experience.

Meg's isolation is poignantly evoked as she sits alone on the window-sill after the others are asleep, feeling cut off from both the sky and the city of teeming thousands, 'none of whom had any knowledge of her loneliness, or any sympathy with her difficulties'.[71] It is significant that the Church as such plays no role whatsoever in the tale, but Meg, like the majority of Stretton's characters, draws her strength and comfort from her Bible, from prayer and from modelling her life on a simple text which she has discussed with her mother, and which becomes the moral of the tale: 'If ye then being evil, know how to give good gifts unto your children, how much more shall your father which is in heaven give good things to them that ask Him?'[72] Meg does eventually find help: a local shopkeeper, Mrs Blossom, takes pity on the family, giving both moral and modest material support by employing Meg as a charwoman, and Kitty, a young neighbour, helps to mind the children. Kitty's activities, including a six-week stint in a house of correction, suggest the nature of her employment more overtly than in most adult novels of the time, and hint at a possible fate for the likes of Meg too. The implications of this desperate prospect for young females are underlined when the baby is taken ill in Kitty's care after being given something (presumably opium or, possibly, gin, since Robin too is flushed, overwrought and bright-eyed) by one of Kitty's companions to stop her crying, and dies in Meg's arms. The shocking nature of this event gives a bitter taste to the climax of emotion preceding the dénouement which is not wholly dissipated by Meg's resignation and acceptance that it is better for the baby to have gone to her mother, sentiments which mingle with her wholly realistic and impotent grief at the loss of the life she has struggled so hard to preserve.

The tale ends on a double contrivance which ensures a happy ending for all involved. Kitty reveals herself to be the long-lost daughter whom Mrs Blossom has obsessively sought, and repents her ways, helped by Meg's explication of her favourite Bible text, and Meg's father finally returns on the very day that the baby is buried. Stretton presumably intends to be critical of the father's actions in concealing from his wife that the sovereigns were in reality their own in case she squandered them, but despite the fact that he subsequently sent a letter, ironically kept safe but unread by Meg, urging her to use them and saying that while in hospital on the other side of the world, he discovered Jesus and resolved to change his drunken ways, it is difficult not to feel that he is let off rather lightly in the narrative for the unnecessary suffering which has resulted. Moreover, the removal of Meg and Robin, together with Mrs Blossom and Kitty, from the London slums to a better life in another country by means of an emigration scheme, a device employed in other texts to solve the problem of creating the happy ending of fairy-tales in a context which by its very nature forbids such a resolution (see *Mary Barton*, for example), is a not wholly convincing form of closure.

Nevertheless, for her evocative settings, for tackling specific social problems and for treating openly and sympathetically the plight of the not-so-exemplary characters, Stretton deserves to be regarded as a significant figure in the history of popular literature. In *Pilgrim Street* (1867), for example, another tale set in industrial Manchester, she manifests her concern for children who are the victims of a criminal parent. Following a pattern not unlike that of Maria Edgeworth's tales, the elder of two brothers is helped to independence and an honest living by a benefactor who provides a donkey and cart, and the younger boy is sent to a decent school. *In Prison and Out* (1878) depicts a well-brought-up boy who, when his family falls on hard times through illness, is reduced to begging, falls into bad company and is subsequently unable to get a job. Stretton shows real perceptiveness in her portrayal of the shame and unhappiness he and his family experience in their double-bind situation, and puts forward the positive recommendation of a training-ship for such young offenders. In the same story a young woman is saved, like Kitty, from a possible fate as a streetwalker, a recurring theme in Stretton's work which illustrates her preoccupation with the moral consequences for women of life in the slums. (In *Jessica's Mother* (1867), a sequel to *Jessica's First Prayer*, it is revealed that her mother is in fact now a prostitute.) *Alone in London* (1869) is based, like *Silas Marner*, on the popular model of a relationship between an old man and a very young child, in this case his granddaughter, which brings about happy changes in the drab lives of several people. As in Eliot's story, there is a certain amount of humour as the elderly shopkeeper has to adapt his ways and fears that his failing memory will affect his ability to cope with his new situation, although the childlike qualities of the old man create an instinctive bond with the young child. The plot is complicated by the involvement of a young street urchin, Tony, who finds a purpose in life by devoting himself to helping the vulnerable pair. Besides the sentimentality generated by this situation, the tale also treats a very serious social problem: the lack of hospital beds for children in London hospitals. When the child, Dolly, dies, the traditional pathos of the calm, happy acceptance of the infant that she is only going home to the Lord where there is 'light brighter than the sun, and the streets are paved with gold' is contrasted with Tony's feeling, that 'a thick mist of darkness fell all about him' and that he is sinking into a horrible pit, and the dominating Evangelical tone of the scene does not obscure the implicit criticism that deaths like this need not and should not have happened.[73]

The best example, after *Little Meg's Children*, of the way in which Stretton mediates the good qualities of disinterested kindness, charity and self-sacrifice to be found in slum dwellers through the figure of a child is *A Thorny Path* (1879). The opening is a particularly alarming one for a young reader, because a desperate mother is seen to abandon her old, blind father and small daughter in Kensington Gardens in the fog and is almost immediately badly hurt and her baby killed when she is knocked down by a carriage. As in *Alone in London*, there is a reversal of gender roles, for it is a young boy, known only as Don, who befriends the pair and, after the death of the old man, takes on the role of 'mother', brother and provider for little Dot. The details of their life on the streets when Don runs away with the child to avoid the workhouse, sleeping in doorways and surviving on crusts and the little he can earn by odd jobs for over a year, are realistically portrayed. As in *Little Meg's Children*, the hardship is sweetened by a seed of primitive faith in Jesus as the saviour of the lost, the personal appeal of which sustains Don after it has been sown in his mind by a kindly old clothes-seller who gives Dot and her grandfather lodgings in her home. All the experiences of their wandering life are filtered through Don's perception, while the reader is enabled at the same time to grasp the effects on the boy to which he is oblivious. Thus, his concern about Dot's welfare and his anxious scrutiny of her sturdy form and rosy cheeks obscure from him the fact that he himself is growing progressively weaker, his difficulty in carrying her being attributed by him to her growth rather than to his own decline. When he ceases to feel the pangs of hunger, it is a relief to him rather than an ominous indication of the last stages of starvation. His all-consuming terror of the workhouse which would mean separation from Dot epitomises the depersonalisation which the institution embodied for the poor, but Don's eventual homesickness which draws him back to Mrs Clack's house reveals the dawning awareness of his weakened condition and his youthful vulnerability despite his assumption of adult responsibilities. Although he is reunited with Mrs Clack and Dot with her mother, who is humbled by the contrast between her own and Don's actions and trust in God as a friend who never abandons those He loves, Don pays the price of his instinctive self-sacrifice and dies of hunger and exhaustion. His death is seen in conventional religious terms by his grieving friends ('they thought of Don standing in the presence of the Saviour, whose footsteps he had followed so faithfully, though he had not known it') but Stretton also uses this scene to voice her outrage at the numbers dying thus in an age of plenty: 'There are charities enough provided for rescuing the perishing; but in the chain there is a link lost somewhere, which causes all the machinery of charity to fail in reaching the deep necessities of the poor.'[74] This tale is, in fact, one of Stretton's most outspoken stories, more uncomfortable for its attack on the insufficiencies of the Victorians' love of 'good works', and most effectively dramatising both the motif of the lost soul and the actuality of physical and social abandonment in the scenes in the fog-enclosed park.

The child as both a victim of contemporary society and an example to adults on both a spiritual and social level had, then, by the third quarter of the century, become a device widely used, though with differing emphases. While Dickens' rage about the victimisation of children, which was given increased impetus by his own childhood experience in a blacking factory, is effective because it is mediated through a powerful combination of satire and sentimentality, the comic, the grotesque and the pathetic, Stretton's appeal lies in the articulation of her deep concern through simple, down-to-earth statements about suffering. The superiority of Hesba Stretton to many of her contemporaries can be seen in the comparison of the realistic portrayal of her child protagonists, especially those like Meg or Don, with, for example, the angelic little girls and comic boys of a text like Silas Hocking's *Her Benny:*

A tale of Victorian Liverpool (1879). Although Hocking claims that his
characters are based on children he knew, the following randomly chosen
passage shows a heavy dependence on literary stereotypes:

> There was silence between them for a while, and Joe [a night-watchman] went
> out and heaped more fuel on the grate, while Nelly kept her eyes fixed on the
> fire. What did the child see as she gazed into its glowing depths? For ever and
> anon a sweet smile played around the corners of her mouth, and spread over
> her pale thoughtful face, lighting it up with a wonderful beauty, and smoothing
> out the lines of care that at other times were only too visible.
>
> 'What are 'e looking at, Nell?' said Benny, after a pause. 'You look as 'appy
> as a dead duck in a saucepan.'[75]

Women writers were much less likely to use the child as an object of humour
in this way which clearly is intended to arouse a patronising and indulgent
smile from a more sophisticated and materially as well as intellectually
privileged adult reader at the child's expense. The simple dignity Stretton
gives to her deprived children does not condescend to them in their misery,
nor does she seek to exploit them even further through her texts.

In the amazingly popular works of Mrs O. F. Walton, the last of the serious
Evangelical tract writers for the young, the 'street-arab evangelist' comes into
his or her own. Although she also highlighted social problems, Walton was
more concerned with the spiritual welfare of her characters and readers, and
presented her message with such a degree of sentimentality and pathos that
her tales are far less readable today than those of Hesba Stretton. Whereas
the protagonists in the latter's tales more commonly display a naive or
unconscious religiosity, affecting others by their behaviour, there is a very
conscious and relentless evangelising in Walton's texts which undermines the
credibility of the characters and, paradoxically, weakens the message. Yet, in
this respect, her work was symptomatic of the flood of sentimentality in fiction
which peaked in the 1880s and 1890s, and in a survey carried out in 1884 she
was one of the nine top favourite authors among girls of 11 and upwards,
together with Dickens, Charlotte Yonge, Charles Kingsley and Hesba
Stretton.[76]

Brief consideration of two tales will suffice to give the flavour of her
approach. *Christie's Old Organ* (1874), in which a child, in this case a young
boy, is once again teamed with a feeble old man who spends a large part of
the novel dying, is constructed around the maddeningly obsessive refrain of
'Home, Sweet Home', one of the four tunes played by Old Treffy on his
barrel-organ, and a synonym for the heavenly home to which the characters
aspire. Christie, an orphan, is moved by the song because, predictably, his
mother used to sing it to him, and begins eagerly to attend services at a
mission-room to learn how to get to heaven so that he can take the word to
his dying master. As in Stretton's tales, the relevant biblical text has an
intensely personal application to the characters' daily lives: thus, as Don and

Dot are 'lost' and 'rescued', so Christie and Old Treffy fear having no home and the sentimental attraction of the song fuses with the religious message to become an emotional prop.

Mrs Walton's best-seller was *A Peep behind the Scenes* which, like *Little Meg's Children*, has a structure and ingredients akin to the traditional fairy-tale and was still in print a hundred years after its publication in 1877.[77] The protagonist, Rosalie, is a girl of 12 who has been brought up in a fairground, loses her mother after a prolonged death-bed sequence, is exploited and ill-treated by her drunken father, acquires a cruel stepmother and a kind of fairy godmother in the shape of a circus dwarf, Mother Manikin, and eventually finds a home with her mother's long-lost sister's family in a country vicarage. Rosalie, to an even greater extent than Jessica or Meg, is distinguished as 'different', for not only have her innocence, integrity and simple faith remained unaffected by her grim environment, which is given a plausible explanation in that her mother, who ran away from her respectable family to become an actress, has shielded her as much as possible from the world outside their caravan, but she is also beautiful, a characteristic which was a standard concomitant of innocence and spirituality in much late Victorian fiction. Her individuality is thus subsumed in an intensified Romantic mythology of childhood which makes her far less representative than Stretton's waifs.

The tale is intended to highlight the evils of life in the fairground which, like the theatre, was regarded by the Evangelicals, in the light of Bunyan's 'Vanity Fair', as degenerate and harmful, and the plot concerns Rosalie's escape from a series of threats to her physical and moral well-being. Her journey through the fair in a chapter actually entitled 'Vanity Fair', in search of her friend Mother Manikin, is seen as a pilgrim's progress through hell from which she emerges, as she will ultimately and completely unscathed, and with a deeply felt disgust at what she has seen. Ironically, the descriptions of the show-ground folk and the sights, smells and sounds of the fair are so colourful that they must have been thrilling to Walton's young readers. The contrast between the appearance of glamour and glitter and the reality of such a life for a child is emphasised from the start when Rosalie appears on stage and is admired by the young girls, many of them domestic servants, in the audience:

They thought her life was much happier than theirs, and that her lot was greatly to be desired. They looked at the white dress and the pink roses, and contrasted them with their own warm but homely garments, they watched the pretty girl going through her part gracefully and easily, and they contrasted her work with theirs. How interesting, how delightful, they thought, to be doing this, instead of scrubbing floors, or washing clothes, or nursing children!

But they knew nothing of the life behind the scenes, of the sick mother, the wretched home, the poor and insufficient food, the dirty, ragged frock. They knew nothing of the bitter tears which had just been wiped away, nor of the weary aching of the little feet which were dancing so lightly over the stage.[78]

Walton does her best to demystify the enticing descriptions by insisting on the exhaustion and bewilderment Rosalie experiences, her fear of her father who forces her onto the stage and her desolation after her mother's death when she is left alone in the caravan at night on a windswept moor. Although her thoughts and reactions are explored, Rosalie is always seen from the viewpoint of the narrator as adult onlooker or through the eyes of the other admiring or pitying characters. Thus, her experience is interpreted rather than rendered directly:

> Oh, how glad she was to see her own caravan again! to get safely out of the restless, noisy multitude, out of the sound of the shouting of the show-people and the swearing of the drunken men and women, and out of the pushing and jostling of the crowd. She thought to herself, as she went up the caravan steps, that if she had her own way she would never go near a fair again; and oh, how she wondered that the people who *had* their own way came to it in such large numbers![79]

Yet, because her experiences are more varied and explored in greater detail than in *Christie's Old Organ*, her character has greater depth and her plight is more realistic and interesting. Her courage, dignity in grief, resignation and anxieties would have made her an attractive and sympathetic character to young readers and the religious message is integrated into a more complex framework. Rosalie's chief comfort is a picture of Jesus with a text about the Good Shepherd finding the lost sheep, which is a bond between the child and her mother and prompts a simple trust in Providence by means of which she is saved from her ordeals to live a happy life with her worldly and spiritual values well regulated. The individual thus becomes a symbol of redeemed mankind: 'She was not easily deceived by the world's glitter and glare and vain show, for Rosalie had been behind the scenes, and knew how empty and hollow and miserable everything worldly was.'[80] As in her other texts, Walton depends for effect on the hypnotic repetition of words ('little', 'old', 'poor'), an idea or refrain. Rosalie's habit of asking everyone she meets whether the Good Shepherd has found them yet certainly stretches the reader's patience and even at times verges on the comical, but is entirely typical of this kind of late Evangelical tale.

Poor, exploited and neglected children made a massive entry into literature in the course of the nineteenth century, responding to many of the social and spiritual concerns of the age and embodying a poignant and undoubtedly effective critique of contemporary values. Their more privileged counterparts also had an important part to play: as a vehicle for the promotion of an ideal which was at the heart of the Victorian consciousness – the family – and also in the questioning of some of the assumptions on which this ideal was based.

Chapter 4

Happy families:
The child at home

The Homes of England

The stately homes of England
  How beautiful they stand,
Amidst their tall ancestral trees,
  O'er all the pleasant land!
The deer across their greensward bound
  Through shade and sunny gleam;
And the swan glides past them with the sound
  Of some rejoicing stream.

The merry homes of England!
  Around their hearths by night
What gladsome looks of household love
  Meet in the ruddy light!
There woman's voice flows forth in song
  Or childhood's tale is told,
Or lips move tunefully along
  Some glorious page of old.

The blessed homes of England!
  How softly on their bowers
Is laid the holy quietness
  That breathes from Sabbath hours!
Solemn, yet sweet, the church-bell's chime
  Floats through their woods at morn;
All other sounds, in that still time,
  Of breeze and leaf are born.

The cottage homes of England!
  By thousands on her plains,
They are smiling o'er the silvery brooks,
  And round the hamlets' fanes.
Through glowing orchards forth they peep,
  Each from its nook of leaves;

And fearless there the lowly sleep,
  As the bird beneath the leaves.

The free fair homes of England!
  Long, long in hut and hall,
May hearts of native proof be reared
  To guard each hallowed wall!
And green forever be the groves
  And bright the flowery sod,
Where first the child's glad spirit loves
  Its country and its God!

                              Felicia Dorothea Hemans

The centrality of the family in middle-class Victorian society is, of course, well known. Its significance was both economic and spiritual, social and personal; it cut across the sectarian differences which thrived during the course of the century and united both men and women, although it involved clear gender roles:

> Anglicans, Congregationalists, Quakers and Unitarians could all agree that the home must be the basis for a proper moral order in the amoral world of the market, that the new world of political economy necessitated a new sphere of domestic economy, that men could operate in that amoral world only if they could be rescued by women's moral vigilance at home.[1]

With the rise of the middle classes and the Evangelical movement in the late eighteenth century there emerged strong ideologies of domesticity, dependent on a clear division between the public and private spheres, with the home seen as a haven of peace, a source of stability, security, virtue and piety, held together by moral and emotional bonds, a construct modelled on the heavenly home to which all who experienced personal conversion might aspire. This view was propagated by female and male writers alike at the turn of the century, notably in the much-loved poetry of William Cowper, with its celebration of rural domesticity and Hannah More's novel *Coelebs in Search of a Wife, Comprehending Observations of Domestic Habits and Manners, Religion and Morals* (1807). A spate of texts appeared, moreover, which attempted to establish ideal codes of behaviour, particularly for women, who were regarded as the cornerstone of the family. Mrs Sarah Stickney Ellis's books, *The Women of England* (1838), *The Daughters of England* (1842), *The Wives of England* (1843) and *The Mothers of England* (1843), which expounded the view that it was women's power for moral good in the domestic sphere which could revitalise and regenerate society, were widely read and recommended.[2]

In the unsettled times of the 1830s and 1840s, propaganda for the family as the repository of order and harmony amid the growing pressures and stresses of modern life were intensified, a trend bolstered by the emergence of women's magazines like the *Magazine of Domestic Economy*, founded in 1835, which fostered the notion of the vital importance of the home, on the levels of both personal fulfilment *and* of national stability and prosperity.[3] Home was the best context for moral and spiritual growth and a vehicle for the perpetuation of traditional ideas. In mid-century, the example of the Royal Family endorsed and advanced this ideology which became an increasingly sentimental one, with domestic emotions heightened and roles and relationships sanctified, notably the role of women as the 'angel in the house', a myth which was both fervently approved and attacked for many decades.[4] Religion was given a central place in the intellectual and moral framework of middle-class culture and in the ideology of the home, reflecting the idea of the congregation of believers as a family, with struggles in the domestic environment seen as equally important in spiritual terms as human conflicts in any other sphere. 'Every true Christian should make their home into a seminary,' wrote Ann Taylor in her *Reciprocal Duties of Parents and Children* (1818).[5]

In an age when religious controversies were rife, literature responded to the challenging climate and many of the family chronicle novels of the nineteenth century which satisfied the middle classes' desire to read about people like themselves, were firmly grounded in Evangelical, High Anglican or general Christian precepts. In fact, it could be argued that the best religious novels were those set against the background of domestic life where the conflict of different desires and needs and the weighing of different responsibilities could be explored in a context with which readers could identify. Significantly, Elizabeth Sewell chose the following lines from John Keble's poem 'Excursion' to stand at the head of her novel *Gertrude* of 1846:

> Turn to private life
> And social neighbourhood, look we to ourselves;
> A light of duty shines on every day
> For all.

Furthermore, the incorporation of a religious message in domestic fiction was seen as a fruitful way to influence a young readership, thus reinforcing and preserving traditional attitudes and beliefs.

Within the family, children played an essential role. Ann Taylor's view that 'the foundation-stone of public and private felicity should be laid in the nursery' was endorsed by the continuing debate on the responsibilities and duties of parents, particularly in the realm of religion and education, throughout the century.[6] As has been seen, Harriet Martineau, though unmarried herself, celebrated the domestic ideal of close parental involvement in the upbringing of children in her *Household Education* of 1848, although for Martineau the concept of the family is based on reason and the quest for individual fulfilment rather than on the religious precepts of Hannah More or Sarah Stickney Ellis.

Domestic novels not only explored the implications of parenthood but allowed for a close focus on the development of the child in the context of the daily minutiae of family life. The actual process of growing up became a matter of considerable interest, with children seen as emergent personalities ready to be shaped. In such novels, moreover, events could be worked out in detail, with physical and psychological dilemmas explored at a more leisurely pace in the different relationships. In her autobiography, Harriet Martineau remarks that 'self-analysis' was 'the spirit of the times', thus highlighting a consequence of the intense and varied religious climate of the mid-nineteenth century and indicating a tendency among writers to often painful introspection and self-examination, what was referred to as 'an ingenious invention of labyrinth meandering into the mazes of the mind', an observation which clearly foreshadows the preoccupations of the modern psychological novel.[7] Many writers, therefore, turned to the portrayal of the child and the child's experience of growing up as a means of interpreting themselves, of understanding their own origins, development and relationship to the world about them, especially after Darwin's theories on evolution rocked previously held beliefs. Apart from overtly autobiographical writings, the mid-nineteenth century was remarkable for the number of individualised moral and spiritual biographies in novel form which utilised ordinary domestic settings and everyday dilemmas. It is interesting to note, however, that the preoccupation with the developing personality was first developed in a simplified form in tales written for and about young people, although, once again, these were widely enjoyed by readers of all ages.

Women writers had considerable success with the domestic novel genre, too, for in the depiction of family life they were most fully operating in what was deemed their 'proper sphere'.[8] Confined as their lives were, for the most part, to the everyday problems of the private arena of the home, women were able to cultivate the very talents of close observation and analysis (as well as the tendency to introspection) which were demanded by the novel of domestic realism. Sensitive to the tensions of family life and more confident in their handling of children's problems, they also appeared more at their ease in depicting domestic settings than their male contemporaries. As early as 1777, Hannah More had commented upon the particular aptitude of women for writing about family life:

> The merit of this kind of writing consists in the *vraisemblance* to real life, as to the events themselves, with a certain elevation in the narrative, which places them if not above what is natural, yet above what is common. It further consists in the art of interesting the tender feelings by a pathetic representation of those minute, endearing, domestic circumstances, which take captive the soul before it has time to shield itself with an armour of reflection. To amuse rather than

to instruct, or to instruct indirectly by short inferences, drawn from a long concatenation of circumstances, is at once the business of this sort of composition, and one of the characteristics of female genius.[9]

In the nineteenth century, of course, the 'instruction' element was an important one, and by no means carried out 'indirectly', but the importance of amusement was also acknowledged, and copying from life was seen as an ideal way to achieve both ends. The increasing interest in exploring the developing personality within the framework of a full-length novel brought about a significant change in the course of the nineteenth century in the portrayal of children. No longer constrained by the demands of the simple moral tale or Evangelical tract, where detailed characterisation was subordinated to the need to make a point concisely and forcefully with the child as mouthpiece for the author's message, the child character as the focus of the text gradually became more plausibly realistic, more recognisably childlike, indulging in childish activities and childish thoughts at the same time as offering to the reader a morally and socially desirable model. They also, for the most part, revealed and reinforced traditionally sanctioned gender assumptions about how girls and boys are treated, develop, think and behave.

An interesting and relatively little-known writer of the early Victorian period who rose to the challenge of a more realistic portrayal of young children in a book *for* children was Catherine Sinclair (1800–64), who, while writing within the Evangelical tradition, has been described as the founder of the 'innocent mischief' school much in vogue in the later nineteenth century.[10] In *Frank Vansittart*, one of her *Common Sense Tracts* of 1853, she stated unequivocally her belief that high spirits should not be stamped out in children by excessive discipline or didacticism since they will be dampened soon enough by adulthood in any case, and that such rigours can be detrimental to both health and character:

> Many a vacant seat in many a nursery, and many a small tomb in the neighbouring churchyard, could testify against the calamitous assiduity with which a leaded weight of disproportioned learning is laid on diminutive heads, too young to bear it; while, meantime, the buoyant spirits and glowing affections of childhood have been extinguished beneath a deluge of lessons and a bushel of miscellaneous acquirements.[11]

In the preface to *Holiday House: A book for the young* (1839) she states that her aim is

> to paint that species of noisy, frolicsome, mischievous children, now almost extinct, wishing to preserve a sort of fabulous remembrance of days long past, when young people were like wild horses on the prairies rather than like well-broken hacks on the road; and when amidst many faults and eccentricities, there was still some individuality and character and feeling allowed to remain.[12]

While Mrs Sherwood's Fairchild children were also prone to high spirits and naughtiness, they were subject to the ever-present authority of their parents. In *Holiday House*, the mother of the two children, Laura and Harry Graham, is dead and the father ill abroad, the removal of both parents thus allowing the question of absolute obedience to parental authority to be conveniently sidestepped. In fact, the autonomy for children resulting from the absence of parents became a common device for stimulating and facilitating adventures in nineteenth- and twentieth-century children's fiction. The ideal of family life is still endorsed, however, for Laura and Harry live with their grandmother and Uncle David who are kind and caring with the only fault of being over indulgent and their home is a privileged, aristocratic one (Grandmamma is Lady Harriet). Significantly, throughout the century, naughtiness was seen as attractive in literary children as long as they came from the upper or middle classes – any suggestion of the approval of high-spirited disobedience in the lower classes might have been seen as socially subversive. The Graham children are boisterous and noisy, even destructive; they run and tumble, dirty and tear their clothes and at one point Harry sets the nursery on fire. As in *The History of the Fairchild Family*, there is a clear dividing line, however, between energetic mischief and unacceptable behaviour like cruelty or that most heinous of all childish crimes, lying. Laura, in particular, is an interesting character, defying the notion of feminine placidity and neatness to become a forerunner of later literary rebellious young females by spoiling her frocks, falling in the river and cutting off her carefully curled ringlets, asserting her equality with her brother who is busy at the same time setting the nursery alight. Harry is punished on this occasion in Rousseau-istic fashion, by being made to sleep in the burnt room, while Laura's cropped hair is deemed to be its own chastisement. The children are thus made to learn from the consequences of their actions, humiliation and discomfort being the most common punishment.

There is an uneasy feeling generated by such scenes, however, for the response of Uncle David seems complacent and inappropriate at times. When Harry is missing after the fire, Uncle David laughs at their nurse Mrs Crabtree's frantic efforts to find him, encouraging her to look up the chimney, and is reported to be hardly able to restrain his laughter as he chides them as 'two little torments', continually making excuses for them, almost, we are told, as if he had been the naughty person himself. This hints at a reason why the mischievous child became such a popular Victorian literary construct, for the repressed childhoods of many readers doubtless led to considerable vicarious enjoyment of such anarchy. In the fire episode, furthermore, the children are treated to a special cake by their grandmother for raising the alarm. Indeed, they are always rewarded for telling the truth, no matter what misdemeanour they are confessing. Lady Harriet's gentle chiding and advice occasionally bear fruit but are also quickly forgotten. Disturbingly, the strict and violent discipline of Mrs Crabtree, the dragon 'governor of the nursery', amuses Uncle David, who asserts that she should have been the drummer in a regiment, since she is so fond of beating. The 'old plan' of spare the rod and spoil the child is, in effect, endorsed in the first chapter, although Mrs Crabtree is clearly seen to exceed her brief and is eventually dismissed, not by the children's guardians, but by their father's order.

The portrayal of the children themselves is intriguing, because not only are they psychologically plausible in their impulsiveness and self-absorption and the dialogue between them believably natural and spontaneous ('"People at the shops should sell clothes that will never either dirty or tear"'), but Sinclair also attempts to capture their experience through their own perception.[13] Thus, when they are confronted by an enraged bull on one of their excursions, she slips fully into their viewpoint and we are made to share their terror as they gasp and stumble in their flight from the brute 'coming along, with his heels high in the air and his head down, like an enormous wheelbarrow'.[14] The fact that adults are not seen as infallible – the haughty Lord Rockville is reduced to ridicule when he too is chased by the bull after disbelieving the children – must also have been an attractive feature for young readers.

This promising approach is somewhat compromised, however, by Sinclair's resolution of the situation, effected by the return from sea of the children's older brother Frank and his subsequent death. In fact, the novel takes a different direction in the later chapters, with the increase in scenes more characteristic of Evangelical tales. When the children visit a poor boy and his dying mother, Sinclair asserts that their hovel is not like those in the tracts, but in fact the whole tone of the episode is very typical. The pious and ethereal Frank is also in the Evangelical mould. In contrast to Harry and Laura, he has already experienced personal conversion and has led an upright and godly life, admired and loved by all. On his death-bed, he demonstrates his religious principles by refusing to take laudanum to ease his pain because he is loath to enter the presence of his Creator in a state akin to that of intoxication. In his presence, Laura and Harry are forced to learn self-control and decorum and to subordinate their needs to his, and this effects the change in their characters and their own conversion. In what was to become good Victorian tradition, they are taught by suffering and learn to be quiet, gentle, self-sacrificing and unselfish. Laura remarks to Uncle David: '"Mrs Crabtree first endeavoured to lead us aright by severity, – you and grandmamma then tried what kindness would do, but nothing was effectual till now, when God Himself has laid his hand upon us."'[15] It should also be noted, in passing, that they are by now, in any case, older, and gender-stereotyped responses and attitudes have begun to manifest themselves in their behaviour. Such a shift in perspective suggests that Sinclair wished to please her child readers, but was also mindful of the need, as a woman writer for the young, to demonstrate that she also had a serious moral and didactic aim, and thus please the adult purchasers and readers of the book at the same time with the message that anarchic behaviour was no longer appropriate or attractive as the unthinking, carefree days of childhood were left behind.

By way of contrast, it is revealing to consider briefly a text in which criticism of the effect of an Evangelical home environment is mediated through child characters. In Harriet Mozley's *The Fairy Bower* (1841) and its sequel *The Lost Brooch* (1842), a spoilt young girl emerges from her Evangelical upbringing with her self-absorption and disregard for others untouched and with the arrogant assumption that anyone who does not share her views is *de facto* in the wrong. (The latter is, in fact, a characteristic attributed to Mrs Sherwood by one biographer.)[16] Constance Duff, in mouthing at the age of 16 the Evangelical tenet that faith in Christ alone brings salvation, rather than good deeds, is, in effect, defending her right to behave as she likes. Charlotte Yonge later wrote admiringly that Mozley's works 'did their part towards the Church movement by manifesting the unloveliness and unsatisfactoriness of this particular phase of suburban Evangelicalism'.[17] In *The Fairy Bower*, the Duff family and their strict religious principles (the children are not allowed to dance or play games with cards or dice and they have a horrendously severe governess) are contrasted with the lax, worldly Wards, whose children are allowed complete freedom. The Duffs' pretensions to spiritual and moral superiority are neatly overturned when a visiting child, the modest and unself-regarding Grace Leslie, aged 9, allows her idea of transforming a room into a fantastical bower with garlands of flowers for a Christmas party to be hijacked and passed off as her own by the unimaginative and domineering 12-year-old Mary Anne Duff who is always 'taking short cuts' to appearing good and clever. Grace's crisis of conscience as Mary Anne is overwhelmed with praise after lying about the bower and the web of deceit spreads, is nicely captured and the repercussions when the truth eventually emerges call into question the whole smug edifice of the family's righteousness. Mary Anne's punishment is to lie in bed late in the mornings to contemplate her sin!

In her preface, Mozley underlines the relevance of depicting moral trials and tribulations in a domestic setting, stating that her aim is 'rather to represent characters as they really are, than to exhibit moral portraitures for unreserved imitation or avoidance . . . it introduces young persons to those scenes and situations of life, which are their actual sphere and trial'.[18] Although the portrayal of Grace is open to the criticism that the author strives too hard to make her an admirable character (she is serious, scrupulous and worries about points of religious dogma), Mozley tempers this with a skilful depiction of her confusion and shows good sense in pointing out that her sensitivity runs the risk of becoming a painful and tiresome habit of self-effacing meekness, too ready to assume the burden of blame for other people's faults, attributes so often advocated as desirable in females in Victorian literature. The chatter of the youngsters, the cockiness of the boys, the self-righteousness of Constance and the childish egoism of Mary Anne are deftly portrayed and there is much interesting detail about their lessons, games and interests. The evident warping effects produced in the children by the rigid, self-regarding form of Evangelicalism to which they are exposed is a very effective indictment.

A very clearly defined myth of the ideal family began to emerge with the works of such writers for the young as Juliana Ewing, Louisa Molesworth, Elizabeth Sewell and Charlotte Yonge, in which certain motifs and assumptions were commonly employed. In their family novels, the mother is frequently an idealised creature, calm, lovely, caring, with great moral authority and endowed with an almost religious significance, although in upper middle-class settings she is often distanced from the children's everyday life which is in the hands of nurses and governesses, and wafts in and out of their days in a haze of sweetness and light. The father is a more remote, authoritarian figure, though kind and honourable, who can always be trusted by his children and is frequently idolised by his daughters. The children are lively but basically serious-minded. Girls are diligent, thoughtful and obedient, quietly religious and eager to please, devoted to the family, especially their brothers, unself-regarding and submissive, ready to suppress their own desires and ambitions for the sake of others. When naughty or rebellious girls appear in books for the young, it is usually so that the reader can follow their progress to goodness, appreciation of the family, and assumption of the correct female role in the domestic context.[19] Boys are dutiful and honourable like their father, whose approval they crave despite displays of bravado, keen to do well, protective of their sisters though given to the mocking banter of the consciously superior, and frequently subdued by their adoration of their mothers. Sisters are often represented as the source of social or moral salvation for their erring brothers, although it can be argued that they are less likely, in women's novels as a whole, to be merely the embodiments of a sickly, disinterested goodness that they are in some novels by men (Dickens, for example) where their role is as catalysts of the development of a male protagonist.[20]

Charlotte M. Yonge (1823–1901) was the doyenne of family chronicle novelists. An Anglican who as a young woman fell under the influence of the Oxford movement and the Tractarian ideals of John Keble, and spent the whole of her life in the Hampshire village where she was born with the church and parish school as focal points of her interests, she produced a vast quantity of fiction which embodies in many ways the values of the Victorian age. Thoroughly critical of the Evangelical tracts in which 'little children amaze their elders, and sometimes perfect strangers, by sudden enquiries whether they are Christians', she approved and cultivated in both historical stories and lengthy contemporary novels the realistic depiction of life 'as it really is seen by Christian eyes'.[21] Her portrayal of the everyday lives and dilemmas of her fictional families, members of which link different novels thus creating the illusion of a comfortingly familiar world, shows extraordinary insight and still makes engaging reading. Her focus of interest is the development of the children, and the detailed exposition of the tensions and frustrations, as well as the delights and compensations, of growing up in a large family is nowhere better seen than in one of her most popular novels, *The Daisy Chain or, Aspirations: A family chronicle* (1856). In her preface, she describes the book as 'a domestic record of home events, large and small, during those years of early life when the character is chiefly formed, and . . . an endeavour to trace the effects of those aspirations which are a part of every youthful nature'. She also leaves no doubt as to her moral intention: 'That the young should take one hint, to think whether their hopes and upward breathings are truly upwards, and founded in lowliness.'[22]

The May family belong to the comfortable middle class (father is a doctor) and there is a great deal of period interest in the descriptions of the habits and activities of the various members of the large household of eleven children, the 'daisy chain' of the title. The novel opens arrestingly with the sudden death of Mrs May in a carriage accident, the drastic early removal of her 'gentle power' as guide, comforter and peacemaker thus thrusting many of the responsibilities of adulthood onto the older children of her brood, who are now left in the care of their loving and respected, but sometimes preoccupied, father. Interestingly, Dr May, though 'superior' in many ways, is not seen as the infallible parent, for he is capable of rashness and imprudence: he is regrettably harsh towards his oldest son who has disappointed with his lack of academic prowess and it is his insistence on driving a nervous horse that causes the accident which kills his wife and cripples his oldest daughter, Margaret. She, in fact, morally takes the place of her mother, in another popular female literary role, the cherished and revered invalid whose sick-bed is the centre of the home. The bustle and tumult of family life and the claustrophobic feeling of the home with its lack of privacy and inevitable clashes as the children compete for attention and attempt to establish their roles in the household are energetically depicted. All the May children have clearly defined personalities which are consistently maintained so that each always acts in character and the crises afflicting the family grow credibly out of the interaction of the different temperaments with each other and with the world around them. In effect, apart from school for the boys and the girls' charitable activities in the vicinity, their home is their world, for their closest friendships are with each other. The cultivation of outside friends is seen as risky and may lead to moral dangers as Harry, who is easily influenced at 12 years old, discovers.

The rather clumsy device of the mother's unsent letter which describes each child in turn, outlining their faults, is in fact redundant, so well does Yonge bring out the essential characteristics of each member of the family.

For example, the agitation of the frightened and stunned children when they hear of the accident is admirably conveyed and their reactions reveal the difference in their characters at once: Flora (17) is quietly capable despite her great grief, Norman (16) is faint and fearful, Ethel (15) is too devastated to be of any real help, while the younger ones are merely fractious, not fully comprehending the reason for the chaos which has invaded their orderly lives. The novel's concern is, thereafter, to chart the process of the characters' recognition and overcoming of their various faults, especially the liking of 'being first', the central theme on which all the different dilemmas converge. All the youngsters are lively, enthusiastic and impulsive, but share a fundamental seriousness which allows them to admit their errors speedily and make efforts to change. They are by no means idealised, however, for their good resolutions are not always kept and conversions to desirable behaviour and attitudes do not happen overnight. The variety and complexity of character 'flaws' show considerable psychological perception, and some are comparatively unusual in fiction of this type. For example, Yonge rejects the literary stereotype of the winsome, babyishly pretty little girl in the suggestion that 5-year-old Blanche's coquettish ways are a symptom of an expectation of attention and praise which is not wholesome. Tom and Mary, who together with Harry are known collectively as 'the boys', exhibit reversed gender behaviour, for Tom is timid and girlish and Mary rough and noisy. Norman too suffers from an acute sensitivity and is prone to nervous attacks. Although they reveal themselves through their actions and conversations, which are far from the stilted dialogues of earlier texts and often ramble or proceed in fits and starts in a highly realistic manner, with a range of vocabulary appropriate to each child's age, the perspective is still that of the omniscient, observing narrator who offers comments on the characters' attitudes. Indeed, Yonge has frequently been accused of being *too* watchful and critical, speaking, especially in her works for younger children, with the moral superiority of a governess, such that no child could identify with her heroines.[23]

The text focuses in greatest detail on the trials of Ethel, a thin, sallow, self-conscious girl, excitable and impatient, who is rebuked in the opening lines for her impetuosity. Seen as an exaggeration of her father's 'peculiarities', she is short-sighted and clumsy, which, together with her strong intellectual leanings, make her the frequent object of ridicule and disapprobation, such that, as is often the case with nineteenth-century literary females, studying becomes a clandestine, almost shameful activity. The idealised picture of Mrs May is, in fact, undermined somewhat in modern eyes by her refusal to allow Ethel to wear glasses and by her disapproval of her desire to read Greek to keep up with her brother Norman. Ethel's aspirations are gently mocked and patronised by the author too, however, for Ethel's development is based on her realisation that caring for intellectual endeavour is 'a wrong kind of ambition' for a girl, and on her sacrifice of her academic interests to redirect her energies (though not without a struggle) into becoming the mainstay of the family and her father's companion. There is a tension, however, between Yonge's evident approval of the sacrifice of 'improper' ambition ('wanting to be first rather than wanting to do one's best') and the vivid portrayal of the mental conflicts Ethel undergoes as an intelligent girl thwarted by convention, which inevitably creates sympathy for her frustrations.[24] In this respect, Yonge, like several of her contemporaries, is demonstrating her awareness of the day-to-day frustrations of young females with the cultural and gendered influences on their lives, while doing her best to reconcile her young readers to their situation and encouraging them by depicting fulfilling channels for their energies. The area in which Ethel is allowed to fulfil her ambitions is that of activities generated by the family's deep religious principles, the only outlet, in fact, for efforts outside the home for the girls. Her aspirations, like those of her creator, are to have a school and build a church in a spiritually deprived area, obsessions which dominate many of the family discussions.

The dilemmas of the boys relate to school as well as the home and here Yonge may be compared with Harriet Martineau in her lively depiction of the problems of bullying, breaking bounds and trust, tale-telling and keeping up with work. Norman suffers acute anxieties about maintaining the coveted place of head of the class for, like Ethel, and indeed Flora, he is afflicted with the desire to excel and all have to learn to revise their estimations of themselves and the importance of humility and duty. Duty, as Yonge wrote in the first of her family chronicles, *Scenes and Characters* (1847) is 'love doing unpleasant work'.[25] Thus, ultimately, all the children find their true role in life in and through the family context, in accordance with Yonge's High Anglican principles. The most impressive quality of her writing is undoubtedly the sensitivity and perceptiveness with which she explores the physical and psychological stresses, for girls and boys alike, of family life and learning to adapt to a gendered domestic and social identity. Though immensely popular with adult and teenage readers, the majority of them female, for forty years, her inevitable endorsement of traditional gender roles (in her imaging of young girls in particular), the parochial atmosphere of her settings and the emphasis on ecclesiastical matters as a chief source of interest and enjoyment for young people make her works very dated, despite their many merits, and unlikely to find an audience among younger readers of the twentieth century.

Charlotte Yonge's views were shared to a considerable extent by her friend Elizabeth Sewell (1815–1906) whose novels, directed chiefly at educated young girls and women, are all based on some point of the Anglican faith. More overtly didactic than Yonge, she nevertheless created believable family settings in which domestic and religious duties and dilemmas are freely discussed. *Laneton Parsonage* (1846), a book for young readers, is predicated on the precepts of the catechism, while *Margaret Percival* (1847) is a warning against the dangers of Roman Catholicism. She too promoted the ideal of home life and many of her young female characters approximate to the ideal early Victorian girl outlined above. In *The Experience of Life or Aunt Sarah* (1853), which has a partial grounding in her own experience as one of a large family, a more complex and revealing portrait of a young girl's growth to womanhood appears, however, despite the view of the self as only significant as part of a whole, the family, underlined at the start in the self-effacing assertion that 'my history is to be found in the history of others' and of the typicality of her experience, 'what must be the lot of hundreds similarly placed'.[26] Written as a first-person narrative, the novel is a reconstruction of the past from memories, letters and journals, by the protagonist Sarah, now an elderly spinster (intriguingly, we only learn the sex of the narrator after several pages) and the narrative, particularly in the first part, employs an interesting counterpoint of the child's view of events and adult discursive comment.

Sarah, aged 13 when the narrative opens, displays many of the quintessential preoccupations and troubles of early adolescence. A delicate, plain girl, thoughtful for her years and sensitive to nuances of mood and character in those around her, she suffers through being the middle child and feels herself to be the ugly duckling of the family, destined to be a spinster. Frustrated with the muddle and hectic pace of their family life, she suffers frequent headaches and other debilitating ailments. A hint of self-dramatisation emerges, however, in the narrator's image of her past self as one of those 'set apart from their earliest childhood for patient endurance'.[27] In many respects, this 'self-portrait' is close to that of Sewell herself which emerges in her autobiography, for she also emphasises her moodiness, self-consciousness, sudden outbursts of temper and a sense of being the 'black sheep' of the family with a low sense of self-esteem.[28] In her case, too, frequent bouts of illness may have been a symptom of her psychological malaise. In this respect, bearing in mind the narrator's comment on her lot quoted above, the experience of author and character could be seen to reflect the experience of many young girls, just as illness became a common metaphor in literature for female frustration and dissatisfaction. Sarah has hard lessons to learn, about human nature, money and religion and most of her outstanding memories are traumatic ones, including finding her forbidding grandfather dead in his chair. Indeed all her memories, we are told, have been selected because, 'though trifling in themselves, they stamped a definite impression upon my, as yet, unformed character, which I can trace to this hour', thus signalling the subjective status of the text as an exercise in retrospective self-analysis.[29]

Sewell's portrayal of the parents in this novel is far from uncritical – the father is indolent and lives beyond his means which eventually leads to financial disaster for the family, and the mother is kindly but compliant and ineffectual in practical matters. An interesting aspect of the first-person narrative is that the father is overtly judged by his daughter, both in retrospect and, implicitly, as a child, for the earliest event recorded and seen by the narrator as one of the most important in her family history is Sarah's awareness that something is amiss when her uncle Ralph arrives, 'bringing the November mist with him', and his dispute with her father, despite her inability to comprehend its content, evokes a first awareness of family troubles and grave misgivings associated with her father's conduct in their affairs.[30] Although her mother is seen in conventional literary terms as an 'angel of goodness and beauty who blended with it the charms of a higher existence', she also comes under scrutiny for her 'unconscious superiority' and well-bred reserve 'not calculated to guide a family through the toils of life'.[31] Furthermore, although home is deemed 'the Paradise of my brightest joys and holiest affections', Sarah's actual experience of family life tends to modify the ideal picture thus evoked.[32]

Sarah's main support comes from her elderly spinster aunt, also Sarah, who, independent and strong-willed, but content and at peace with herself and the world, becomes her secular and religious teacher and comforter, helping her to overcome her religious doubts and tendencies to self-pity and hypochondria, just as she soothes her crippling headaches. Aunt Sarah is a surprising role model for a young girl at a time when marriage was the ultimate goal for women, but the significance of her influence reflects not only the narrator's self-image, for Sarah grows up to be the devoted spinster aunt to her nieces and nephews, but also that of the author, who never married and devoted her life to teaching and writing and the care of her brothers' children. The influence on the children of Aunt Sarah's presence ('I do not remember that even a scramble for caraway comfits or a game of ball with oranges, ever led us beyond the bounds of sober satisfaction') is nicely contrasted with the young Sarah's feeling of guilt when they are praised for being good and her urge to confess that they are noisy and naughty at home.[33] Her home is first evoked through the details which fascinate the children: the barometer in the form of a monk, the Indian-rubber pig on the mantelpiece and the wax dolls on the strings of the wires of the harpsichord.

Although Sarah enjoys the fun of visits and shopping, she finds stressful the constant animation and tumult of family life, of which Sewell paints an absorbing picture. Most affecting are the moments when Sarah feels isolated and alone even when surrounded by those she loves. On her confirmation day, her serious approach is contrasted with the family's delight in the social aspect of the occasion. When she is left at home because she feels it is her duty to be quiet while the others go to a ball, the unhappiness which steals over her with a presentiment of a solitary future as she sits in the cold, dark room with aching head is dispelled in a touching scene with her younger sister in which she realises that there is no 'must be miserable'. Aunt Sarah's lessons in strength, self-reliance, trust in God and satisfaction in doing her duty bear fruit and her namesake eventually becomes radiant and content in her turn, the Aunt Sarah of the next generation.

A fascinating portrait of young Victorian girlhood which goes a long way to modify the picture of a restricted, passive existence that emerges from Charlotte Yonge's works, is presented by Juliana Ewing (1841–85), one of the most successful writers for juveniles, in *Six to Sixteen* (1875), a story for teenage readers narrated by the 16-year-old protagonist herself. Margery Vandaleur writes down her past life and memories to please her friend Eleanor during a Yorkshire winter, and in doing so, comes to understand a lot about herself and others. The writing of a 'simple and truthful history of a single mind from childhood' is thus seen to have a personal and public value, and although Margery begins by declaring that her account will be only a 'record of small facts important to no one but myself', her narrative does, in fact, through its very self-consciousness, reveal a great deal about her mind in the process of growing up.[34] Her account has both the freshness of perception of the child she has lately been and the critical and analytical viewpoint of the reflective teenager. Thus, her early memory of her mother, appearing in her child's room like a 'fairy dream' in her rustling silks and glittering jewels, is juxtaposed with the recognition that her mother failed her emotionally:

> and yet, O Mother, Mother! better than all the triumphs of your loveliness in its too short prime would it have been to have left a memory of your beautiful face with some devout or earnest look upon it – 'as if it had been the face of an angel' – to your only child.[35]

In adopting a first-person narrative of this type, Ewing was more successful than many of her contemporaries in avoiding the danger of talking down to her young readers, allowing a narrator nearer their own age to appear to be sharing confidences with them, as Margery is with Eleanor, rather than instructing them from a superior adult position.

Although Ewing draws on her own experiences in her portrayal of interests and activities in the later Yorkshire scenes, as her dedication to a childhood friend makes clear, Margery's life is otherwise unlike her own, for while Ewing was one of the eight surviving children of Margaret Gatty, author of *Aunt Judy's Tales* (1859) and editor of the popular *Aunt Judy's Magazine*, to which Ewing was also a contributor, Margery is born in India and loses both her parents at a very young age. As has been seen elsewhere, the absence of the parents implies an altered context to growing up and different criteria for portraying it. Margery, as an orphan, experiences radically differing approaches to upbringing in the households of her relatives, the Bullers, and her great-grandparents, at school, and at the home of her friend Eleanor. She reconstructs her very early days largely from hearsay, but there are certain memories which plunge the reader directly into the child's experience, like the death of her father in a cholera epidemic on her sixth birthday, when she is preoccupied by the thought of the angels coming to fetch him and the loss of the promised birthday dinner, and the highly naturalistic 'war of words' over dresses in which she engages with the tyrannical Matilda Buller.

Memories of her boarding school are dominated by the familiar complaints of ill-health and exasperation generated by a sedentary and over-supervised regime, and Ewing reveals, particularly in the depiction of the physical sufferings, 'follies and fancies' of the unfortunate Matilda, considerable insight into the problems of adolescent girls: 'What quaint, pale, grave little maids we were! As full of aches and pains, and small anxieties, and self-repression, and tender sympathy, as any other daughters of Mother Eve.'[36] Her schooldays are not devoid of fun and interest, however, and the girls' preoccupations and chatter and their delight in mimicking and outwitting the teachers are conveyed in a lively manner. One of the strengths of the book is, in fact, that it focuses on relationships between young people, and with one or two exceptions, the adults remain on the sidelines. It is at Eleanor's vicarage home in Yorkshire that Margery blossoms and learns to live in a happy family, holding her own against the friendly torments of Eleanor's brothers and benefiting from Mrs Arkwright's enlightened advice. In a life 'free . . . from the trammels of conventionality' (symbolised by the shedding of her high-heeled boots, veil and crinoline) for the first time, she can give full rein to the enthusiasms of youth and walk, climb walls, paddle in streams, exercise dogs, draw and botanise and indulge in amateur theatricals. Unlike Charlotte Yonge, Ewing writes warmly of intellectual pleasures which, when enthusi-astically and spontaneously enjoyed, 'have this in common with the consolations of religion, that they are such as the world can neither give nor take away'.[37] The beneficial effects of such mental and physical stimuli in an isolated natural environment in the heart of a family are contrasted implicitly with the socially conscious Bullers' obsessive concern with dress and etiquette in contact with which Margery risks becoming vain and preoccupied with appearances. The development in her intellect, artistic talent and self-confidence is such that she is able to write her life up to this point with a calm and clear-eyed analytical stance, confronting even those memories which cause her most pain, and promises to be a happy and fulfilled young woman. For its perception of the process of growing up, for its vivid detail of the period and settings and its lack of didactic authorial intrusions, *Six to Sixteen* remains a most enjoyable and illuminating read.

Ewing is equally good at writing about the problems of growing up for boys. In *We and the World*, which appeared in *Aunt Judy's Magazine* between 1877 and 1879, she portrays both the light and dark sides of a Victorian childhood. Like Margery and her friends, Jack and his brother are neither idealised with overscrupulous consciences nor winsome scamps – their enjoyment of life, their often wild behaviour and lively talk are entirely natural and the presentation of their fun through the eyes of Jack as narrator is fresh and irreverent. Thus Jem is so enraptured with a sentence in his reading-book ('I had my bat, and I hit him as he lay on the mat') that he whacks the family cat, sleeping peacefully nearby, with the book so hard that she 'bounced up in the air like a sky-rocket'.[38] Encouraged by a local funeral, the boys decide to bury their dead puppy with full pomp and ceremony, and Jack, exercised by the fact that he cannot be both mourner and undertaker, places a wheelbarrow by the grave with a note to the effect that he has sent his carriage as a mark of respect.

The novel is also noteworthy for its criticism of adults, particularly the father's handling of his sons. When the boys are sent to a private academy where they endure hypocrisy, corruption, bad teaching and severe physical discomfort at the hands of a man with a 'passion for cruelty' who would have felt at home at Dickens' Dotheboys Hall, such that they eventually run away, he refuses to believe them. Favouring Jem, the eldest, whom he hopes will take after him, his father sends him to school at a more expensive establishment elsewhere, but Jack is made to return to Mr Crayshaw's. His deflection of responsibility when his mistake is discovered and he accuses Jack of not confiding in him is criticised severely as a gross injustice to the boy which, Jack admits, breeds resentment. He is indicted too for his desire to make Jack what *he* wants him to be, rather than allowing the boy's individuality to flourish, mocking him for his intellectual interests and forcing him into an uncongenial career, so that once more Jack decides to run away and seek his fortune in the world. The filtering of these events both through the boy's perception of them and through that of the older Jack looking back, creates a powerful attack on parental authority, but Ewing ultimately confirms her allegiance to the values of home and the family by modifying her criticism in Jack's reflection that 'parental blunders and injustices are the mistakes and tyrannies of a special love that one may go many a mile on one's own wilful way and not meet a second time'.[39]

In the second half of the nineteenth century, the wave of enthusiasm for the convention of the sentimentalised, innocent child who effects a change in adults, which reached its apogee in *Little Lord Fauntleroy* as discussed in Chapter 2, also invaded the family novel, frequently to facilitate the condemnation of heedless (or even downright wicked) parents. An important influence on this vogue was Florence Montgomery's novel *Misunderstood* (1869), which was written primarily for adults, but was soon widely read by children too.[40] It has all the ingredients of a sentimental novel – two motherless boys left in the care of servants and their French governess while their father, a Member of Parliament, is absent all week, and a protracted, heart-tugging death-bed scene which lasts for some sixty-six pages. Yet *Misunderstood* is superior to its successors in its humorous and perceptive portrayal of the relationship between the brothers, Humphrey, aged 7, and

Miles, 4, and remarkable for its attempt to enter a child's mind to portray his experience, including the experience of dying.

The plot is a simple one: Humphrey, being an extremely active, devil-may-care child, always running and climbing and exploring, is deemed heartless by his father because he *seems* not to care much about the death of his mother and incorrigibly disobedient because he ignores repeated warnings about not leading his delicate brother into mischief. Tragedy strikes because of his thoughtlessness and Humphrey himself is the child who is fatally injured. Yet it is clear that his naughtiness is the result of liveliness and fascination with the world around him, and he cannot remember warnings for long because of his avid thirst for experience. Moreover, far from being heartless, he deeply mourns his mother in secret and misses her daily with a grief which his high spirits merely disguise. Thus he is 'misunderstood' by his loving but emotionally short-sighted father. The real strength of the book lies in the scenes between the two boys on their own, without an observing adult, as they get into the various scrapes resulting from Humphrey's good ideas. His hyperactive enthusiasm for mushroom-picking, climbing trees and exploring ponds is effectively conveyed, as is Miles' fervent, though sometimes doubtful, faith in his brother which causes him to repeat his words and follow his lead, despite the frequent discomfort, trouble and, on one occasion, illness which result. The following scene in which Humphrey offers to carry the tired Miles across a large field is typical in its humorous rendition of a situation from both points of view:

How shall I describe the intense discomfort of the circumstances under which Miles now found himself?

One of Humphrey's arms was so tightly round his neck that he almost felt as if he were choking, and the hand of the other grasped one of his legs with a gripe which amounted almost to pain; and *still* there was a feeling of insecurity about his position which, already very strong while Humphrey was standing still, did not diminish when he began to move.

Humphrey started with a run, but his speed soon slackened, and grave doubts began to rise even in his own mind as to the accomplishment of the task he had undertaken.[41]

The episode in which they get up early to pick mushrooms is interesting in several respects. The chapter opens with Miles dreaming of falling down a hill clutching his brother, which is seen to be induced by Humphrey attempting to drag him out of bed. His urgency and Miles' reluctance to get up are realistically conveyed, and Humphrey's efforts to cope with the complexities of the sleepy younger boy's clothing, with the inevitable result of 'strings all knotted together, buttons forced into the wrong holes, and hooks clinging to outlets that were never intended for them' are genuinely amusing.[42] As the expedition finally gets under way, the novel sight of the house in the early morning is evoked through the children's eyes, 'as if the unwonted appearance of the familiar apartments threw something of the supernatural round about them'.[43] Although their reactions are interpreted by the author, she succeeds admirably in conveying their sense of wonder, tinged with slight alarm. The boys' speech, both when they talk alone or with adults, is convincingly childlike and frequently amusing in an unpatronising way. Thus Miles surprises the housemaid by his knowledge of death: "'I know all about it. When people die they are packed up in a box and put into the ground, and then, if they've been good, God will come some day and unpack them."'[44] Many of the scenes between the boys and adults are hugely enjoyable, often resulting in toe-curling embarrassment for the adult, like his father's utter dismay when Humphrey arrives in the drawing-room to see the 'Wild Men' after an incautious joke about his constituents, and his increasing discomfort and foreboding as to what the child might say as he insists on going round and shaking every hand. Similarly, Humphrey's vociferous and persistent reminders to his father, at dinner, that it is the footman's birthday, leave both adults squirming with red-faced discomfiture. Such scenes reveal the origins of the novel as a book for adults since a child reader would probably see nothing amiss in the situation and identify with the child's insistence. Nevertheless, the humour is at the expense of the socially constrained adult rather than at that of the child. In more serious vein, the reader alone is privy to Humphrey's sensitivity, manifested in his thoughts rather than his actions, particularly his yearning for his mother, activated by the sight of the mustard and cress he was growing for her and by his fear as he crouches outside his sick brother's door.

Some sentimentality does intrude in the first part, notably in the tragic significance attached to the absent mother, an idealised portrait of whom haunts Humphrey, but it fairly explodes in a torrent of emotions in the second part of the novel when Humphrey lies gravely injured after both boys fall from a rotten branch into a pond. Montgomery's effective manipulation of point of view maintains the suspense about the outcome of the accident until we discover, with Sir Everard, who is all set to blame Humphrey, which boy has been hurt. The likelihood that his son may be a cripple awakens Sir Everard to the boy's true nature, that his energy and mobility are 'all that went to make up the sum of his existence' and his grief is exacerbated by the guilt of having failed to understand him.[45] It is revealing to contrast Humphrey's own attitude to the prospect of being crippled with that of Harry in *The Crofton Boys*, for he becomes hysterical and eventually announces that he prefers to die and be happy with his mother in heaven. His slow decline is not just portrayed through the eyes of the watching adults as is the usual strategy, but insight into his semi-coherent, rambling thoughts are conveyed in passages approaching stream-of-consciousness, confusing memories of Miles' earlier illness, of the excursion to the pond and of his mother, and images of a lame bird and a crippled village boy, which foreshadow his own plight, recognition of which is suppressed but hovering fatally on the fringes of his consciousness:

> She is in Heaven. She got there by being ill and dying. Why should he not get ill, and die too? Miles is dying, mother is dead – he should so like to die too. But it's no use. He never is ill – not even a cold. Miles caught cold going to the pond – the pond where the water-lilies are. How quiet it is! how cool! How gently they dance upon the water, those lovely water-lilies! How the birds and the rat splashed . . . Come up, Miles – it's as safe as safe can be! . . . Stop! . . . Miles is dying – how could he come up? Miles came into the room, and talked about the – jackdaw – wasn't it? the poor lame jackdaw . . . Miles is dying . . . How did he come in? . . . Hop! hop! comes the jackdaw, poor old fellow! What did Miles say about the jackdaw?[46]

Though self-consciously introduced ('We will follow his thoughts for a moment') and employing the third-person pronoun 'he' to refer to the thinker, this attempt at subjective narrative is remarkably modern for its time.

The Wordsworthian view of the child is evoked in Sir Everard's amazed contemplation of Humphrey's calm, even joyous attitude towards his approaching death. Because a child always looks with eager anticipation to the unknown future and their world is so full of mystery and new things that they can easily accept the inexplicable, the afterlife, it is suggested, is no more incomprehensible than any temporal prospect. Father and son are brought close together in mutual comprehension, with Sir Everard humbled and chastened by Humphrey's fortitude, generosity and lack of jealousy of his once more favoured brother. Humphrey's death, the 'turning and whirling' of his anxieties about 'the sound as of rushing waters' which throbs in his head, soothed by the childish prayer Miles repeats by his side, is radiant, his eyes lifted to the portrait of his mother. Significantly, there is no longer the emphasis on repentance for sin which was an essential part of earlier death-bed scenes and Humphrey's anticipation of heaven is clearly associated with his desire for reunion with his mother.

Though undeniably lurching into treacly sentiment, *Misunderstood*, as a portrait of a twofold family tragedy (not only the death of the delightful Humphrey but the fact that he has never been understood, and has even been resented for his buoyancy by his remaining parent) has considerable merit and interest. It illustrates the move towards greater interest in the individual child and the exploration of his or her psychology which was characteristic of the domestic novel, rather than the simple use of the child figure as a vehicle for a single message. In two novels by Marie Corelli, a more virulent attack on the insidious effects of harmful parental authority is mediated through children who embody the full flowering of late Victorian Romantic sentimentality, including some of its worst aspects.[47] *Boy: A sketch* (1900) charts the fortunes of the child of a drunken, bestial ex-army officer and his fat, slatternly, self-absorbed wife, who changes from an angelic, blue-eyed, golden-haired infant to a world-weary, cynical, dishonest youth. His indifferent parents nevertheless obstruct his only chance of salvation, the attempts by a wealthy spinster, Miss Letty, to adopt and educate him. Ironically, the elderly Miss Letty is seen as potentially a better parent than Boy's own, who incur the full weight of Corelli's disapprobation for their failure in their moral obligation to nurture their son.

The promising device at the beginning of the novel of the uncomprehending anxiety of the small child in his high chair, as his 'large, angelic blue eyes' follow his drunken father staggering about the room, is rendered almost nauseating by Corelli's attempt to convey the infant's lisping speech: '"Oh Poo Sing! Does 'oo feels ill? Does 'oo feels bad? Oh, Poo Sing!"'[48] Such an imitation of childish language which is clearly constructed to amuse or stimulate saccharine sentiment in the adult reader succeeds only in patronising child and adult alike. (Contrast the simple dignity of Humphrey's speech or that of Meg and Jessica in Hesba Stretton's works.) The Wordsworthian notion that children have memories of a previous celestial 'home', vague recollections of which cause them to contemplate wistfully their altered condition, is pressed into service overtly to comment on the 'lovely far-away look' in Boy's eyes and the 'whole serene and wise expression on his fair and chubby countenance'.[49] In a highly implausible scene, Boy's recollections of 'rainbow eternities' are invoked as he pounces on a picture of heaven in a copy of Dante, surprising the adults present with the assertion that '"Boy 'members it; – pitty p'ace, – pitty f'owers, all bwight, – awfoo' bwight! – 'ess! me 'members it!"'[50] At 4 years old, we are told, 'the halo of divine things was still about him . . . and it remained for the coming years to witness how long the brightness would last in the hands of the untrustworthy individuals who had it in their possession'.[51]

As Boy moves further away from Miss Letty's influence through his mother's jealous determination to 'educate' him according to her own ideas, he goes steadily to the bad, gets expelled from Sandhurst for drinking, is lured into gambling debts through his naivety and liking for an easy life, and tries to steal from Miss Letty by forging a cheque. Rejected by his parents, who have made him what he is, when he gets into trouble, he is redeemed by Miss Letty's kindness and forgiveness and enlists for the Boer War, where, predictably, he is killed. To reinforce her point, Corelli contrasts another boy, Alistair, who befriends Boy in Scotland; an active, natural child, close to his mother and brought up to be fearless and honest (a lie is, in fact, one of the first signs of Boy's moral degeneration) and who, as a 'warm-blooded, courageous man', turns up again to care for Boy on his soldier's death-bed. Corelli pulls no punches in attributing all Boy's crimes to his upbringing, for he is, in her view, merely typical of many such victims of family life:

> young men and women who owe their mistakes and miseries to the blind tyranny and selfishness of the parents who brought them into existence . . . From the

earliest beginnings of childhood, all the seeds of his present misery had been sown – by neglect, by carelessness, by bad example, by uncomfortable home surroundings, by domestic quarrellings, – by the want of all the grace, repose, freedom, courtesy, kindness and sympathy, which should give every man's house the hallmark of 'Home'.[52]

She demystifies the ideal of family life from a different angle in *The Mighty Atom* of 1896, uniting, as many earlier writers had done, the Romantic child with the theme of religion. The dedication sets out the ground on which her battle is to be fought:

> To those self-styled 'progressivists' who by precept and example assist the infamous cause of Education without Religion and who, by promoting the idea, borrowed from French Atheism, of denying to the children in board-schools and elsewhere, the Knowledge and Love of God, as the true foundation of noble living, are guilty of a worse crime than murder.[53]

The innocent child in this novel, Lionel Valliscourt, is the victim of his atheist, rationalist father's educational principles. Mr Valliscourt is a harsh, distant father, soured by the departure of his wife with another man and determined to mould his son in his own image. Made to study all day, Lionel has 'an almost appalling look of premature wisdom on his pale, wistful features' and a 'methodical patience and resignation' odd in a young child.[54] His nerves, emotions and strength taxed by the lack of fresh air, company and childish recreation, Lionel is bothered by questions of the why and wherefore of existence. Brought up to believe that a Mighty Atom created the world, he finds this concept of an abstract, indifferent, mechanical agent increasingly difficult to accept, especially after the death of the little girl, Jessamine, whom he meets one day when he plays truant from his lessons.

In Jessamine, Corelli has taken the Romantic, pious child to an extreme: with her 'heavenly' blue eyes and tumbling chestnut curls, she is always likened to flowers and enjoys talking to Lionel of her mother who is with the angels. Although the pleasure Lionel gets from playing with his new friend is conveyed convincingly enough, there is something distinctly unwholesome in the mixture of innocence and sensual titillation which informs descriptions of Jessamine's behaviour. Like the infant Boy, she lisps in baby talk (as well as Devonshire dialect): '"What boy be you? You be prutty – all th' boys roond 'ere be oogly."' Corelli comments frequently on the 'winsome, provocative, innocent allurement of her manner', however, and applies feminine stereotypes to the child: 'Jessamine, like all female things, condescended to be caught at last and to look shyly in the face of her youthful captor.'[55] Such a blatant attempt to sexualise the child while emphasising its innocence is, in fact, rare in the work of women writers, although it is frequently encountered in nineteenth-century paintings and male-authored fiction in varying forms (Dickens' 'womanly' little girls are manifestations of the same phenomenon) and perhaps testifies to Corelli's implacable pursuit of the ingredients of commercial success.

When Jessamine dies, though witnessing and envying her father's simple faith, Lionel remains severely disturbed by the enigma of human life ('in wicked oblivion of the grand truth proclaimed with such a grand simplicity – "God is Love"') and, bereft of comfort and guidance, hangs himself with his baby sash, left in his care by his mother.[56] His suicide is without doubt a shocking scene, although Corelli somewhat undermines its effect by juxtaposing it with statistics on child suicides. The force of her thesis is made clear, however, with characteristic panache: 'this mere child, nerved to sternest resolution, calmly confronted the vast Infinite, and went forth on his voyage of discovery to find the God denied him by the cruelty and arrogance of man!'[57] Even more shockingly, and running entirely contrary to literary tradition, his father remains unconverted, vowing to marry again and replace the child, and is only persuaded to allow Lionel to be buried next to Jessamine by the threat of the elderly tutor, moved to unaccustomed tears, that he will tell the story of the 'poor, murdered boy' if his last wishes are not carried out.

What emerges strongly here, and is implicit in many such narratives where the death of a child forms a sentimental climax, is the extent to which the idea of innocence and purity had been distorted by the love of pathos. Nevertheless, for all their faults (and they are indeed full of cliché, overblown sentiment and near-hysterical prejudices) Corelli's novels are significant in that they admit that there was a serious disparity between the Victorian ideal of the family and the situation in real life, and openly castigate her contemporaries through the very image, the figure of the child, which was at the heart of that ideal.

Chapter 5

'The one I knew the best of all':
The childhood self

I kept the life thrust on me, on the outside
Of the inner life with all its ample room
For heart and lungs, for will and intellect
Inviolable by conventions.

Elizabeth Barrett Browning, from *Aurora Leigh* (1856)

It is revealing to compare the portrayal of family life in nineteenth-century novels with the recollections of their own childhoods in the autobiographical works of women writers. They not only provide many revealing insights into the real child's experience, but illuminate the writer's view of that experience and their sense of the connection between the child and the adult. For women, the impulse to write an autobiography presented special problems, for writing about and thus displaying the private self to the public gaze was directly contrary to conventional prescriptions of female modesty and reticence.[1] Unlike male authors, who, for the most part, wish to emphasise their public and professional life, those women who had a professional life tend to play down their successes because of the very real risk of courting accusations of egotism and neglect of home duties.[2] Writing about their childhood experiences was, however, less controversial and more consistent with a woman's supposed sphere of interest, and, if handled tactfully, could serve as an important means of predisposing the reader's sympathy to the descriptions of later achievements. In fact, in some cases, there is a strong tendency to interpret childhood experience in the light of the writer's later life in order to explain and justify the latter. It must therefore be borne in mind that the accounts are frequently coloured, even manipulated, by the adult author's attitudes and motivations in writing about her past and by the kind of image she wishes to emerge from the text. This, of course, may also be true of male-authored works, but the many strategies of self-justification and evasion in women's autobiographical writings reveal, through their self-consciousness,

114

particular anxieties about the act of writing about the self, resulting in what Valerie Sanders has described as 'a split between the desire to attract notice and a deep-seated consciousness that this is wrong and must be atoned for'.[3]

Whereas nineteenth-century male autobiographers tend to attach importance chiefly to their intellectual or social development, women, who were encouraged to be reflective and introspective, are frequently more interested in the general psychological effects of ordinary everyday experience and, in this respect, provide a subtle and detailed picture of the formative influences on the young child.[4] Many women also saw the portrayal of their childhood experience as an opportunity to articulate their protest against the restrictions that their society imposed on young females. In many cases this criticism emerges more through a sub-text readily discernible to the modern eye than through what is openly stated. In autobiographical memoirs, writers were faced with the same kind of problems as in their fiction of adequately representing childhood experience, and some of the strategies used to cope with this are considered here. Some view their past selves with the detachment of an omniscient narrator, while others make a real attempt to capture the quality of reality as the child experienced it. Even then, however, the memories recounted tend to be of isolated experiences which can only suggest the flavour of the daily life of childhood, which, as many writers show themselves to be aware, is so difficult for the adult to recapture despite it being their own history and an intimate part of themselves. Occasionally, moreover, autobiographical accounts are recognisably influenced by literary conventions and prevailing mythologies of childhood, so that the distinction between the two genres of autobiography and novel is blurred in a fascinating way. Out of the large field of autobiographical writing by women, I have limited myself, for the most part, to the works of the writers considered in this study, both in the interests of conciseness and to enable comparisons to be made between the autobiographical self and the fictional children in their works.

The Life and Times of Mrs Sherwood (1910) is an interesting work in many respects. Compiled from the diaries she kept for most of her life, it proceeds methodically year by year and gives a very vivid portrait of the times, covering a phenomenal range of people, places and events. Indeed, for the most part, displaying the typical female reticence about self-exposure, she is more concerned in this very long work with portraits of others rather than with her inner self. Surprisingly, given the tenor of her fictional work, there is comparatively little about religion. Although her father was a clergyman in the Midlands, she was not brought up as an Evangelical (she came to this in India through the influence of a young missionary called Henry Martyn) and perhaps omits significant reference to the influence of religion in her upbringing for this reason. Her childhood is presented overtly as a very happy one, although some of the elements she chronicles might be deemed to conflict with the authorial commentary. Thus she records 'sweet remembrances of parental kindness', and the first recollection of her mother, singing and playing sweetly on the guitar in the beautiful drawing-room at the Stanford vicarage, corresponds to a conventional literary image. She goes on to recount, however, that her mother was the source of discipline in the household and paints a rather grim picture of the 'undeviating strictness' of her regime:

> It was the fashion then for children to wear iron collars round the neck, with back-boards strapped over their shoulders. To one of these I was subjected from my sixth to my thirteenth year . . . At the same time I had the plainest possible food; dry bread and cold milk were my principal food, and I never sat on a chair in my mother's presence.[5]

Though telling us that before the age of 12 she was 'obliged to translate fifty lines of Virgil every morning, standing in stocks, with my collar on' (p. 51), she says of her mother that 'it might have appeared that no other person in the world could have been so well fitted to bring a mere child of many imaginations under regulation' (p. 34), thus, apparently, deflecting criticism onto herself and, mindful of the need to endorse her own fictional portrayal of parental infallibility, adds that 'I have many times thanked God and my beloved mother' for such early discipline (p. 35). Although she insists that she was a very happy, though shy, child, she also indicates, like many women autobiographers, that she suffered agonies of self-consciousness over her appearance, in this case her height in her early teens, seeing herself as looking 'a very extraordinary sort of personage', teased by others 'as one that was to be a giantess' (p. 50). Moreover, her confessed tendency to seek refuge in the woods near her home, communing with nature or playing with a large wooden doll which she had to hide under her pinafore to avoid ridicule, suggests a tension running in counterpoint to the surface narrative. In her fiction, nature is only appreciated insofar as it reflects the hand of God, but here it appears that for Sherwood herself as a child, nature was a liberating force and a retreat from restriction, as it is for many literary heroines in the nineteenth century: '[I was] never so happy as when I was in my own beloved woods . . .' (p. 50). Significantly, her shyness was dissipated only when she recounted interminable, rambling stories to her sister and cousin or played at fairy-tales with her brother and his friend. Indeed, she promotes the view of herself from the start as a sensitive and reflecting child whose tendency to let her mind always 'run upon an imaginary world' was increased by being kept severely ignorant of the real one. The acknowledgement of a dual life of outward conformity and an inner fantasy world is, in fact, common in autobiographies written by women who frequently seem to have found comfort and security in a private world of their own making and over which they had more control.

Although there is some direct, mild criticism of her parents (her mother is seen later as being old before her time: 'she could bear no noise, she could endure no derangement of her plans, she never suffered any ebullitions of gaiety in her presence', p. 49), this is generally thinly varnished over. Thus of her father, preoccupied with his work and loving good society, she writes 'Influence and money were pleasant to him, because they increased his power of manifesting his benevolence' (p. 53) and in her description of her 'dear brother' who was her constant companion before he was sent away to school, there is a curious duality which serves only to draw attention to itself:

> he used to put me in a drawer, and kick me down the nursery stairs; he also used to heap chairs and tables one on the other, and set me on the top of them, and then throw them all down; he used to put a bridle round my neck, and drive me about with a whip. I was a very hardy child, and, I suppose, not easily hurt, and he was very, very kind to me, and I loved him very much. It was wonderful how many . . . tender feelings were called out by him in my infancy. (p. 29)

Her overview of her childhood seems to put a romantic gloss on events which perhaps testifies to a wish to see herself as special, even as the 'genius' her father told her and her brother they might become.[6] Throughout the narrative of her early years, Sherwood is at pains to pick out omens of her later life and it is easy to identify elements which are reworked in her fictional work, although, of course, they may be emphasised here as memories because of their prominence in the novels, suggesting a two-way influence.[7] Interestingly, she expresses her dislike of a child who was 'the sort of boy whom the old story-books call a good boy', opining that 'a few blows would have been . . . salubrious' (p. 64), a reaction which perhaps explains her willingness to allow her own literary children to display a carefully controlled amount of naughtiness.

A far more self-conscious, even defensive, narrative is Charlotte Elizabeth Tonna's *Personal Recollections* (1841), for the author is intent from the start on presenting an appropriate image. She was prompted to write her own story, she claims, by her awareness of herself as 'public property' and the fear of 'indecent exposure' in a biography by which she might be made the 'heroine of some strange romance' after her death.[8] This elaborate apology for a deliberate act of self-display clearly reflects her anxiety about her role as a writer and as a woman who risks attracting criticism for pretentiousness and self-conceit. The romance she writes for herself is of an imaginative but serious-minded and intensely religious child with the clear purpose of emphasising her worthiness in later life as a purveyor of Christian beliefs. The autobiography is thus directed towards a very specific end, that of suggesting that her whole life was a preparation for her 'mission' as an Evangelical writer. It is, she writes,

> a record of that mental and spiritual discipline by which it has pleased the Lord to prepare me for the very humble, yet not very narrow, sphere of literary usefulness, in which it was his good purpose to bid me move. (p. 4)

The daughter of a Protestant clergyman, she later converted to Evangelicalism and she reads her early experiences in this light, selecting such episodes as may confirm and illustrate her Evangelical views. Among the first recollections of her home in Norwich is the house opposite, where the 'glorious martyrs of Mary's day' were imprisoned, which she claims in retrospect made a huge impression on her imagination, as indeed it might on that of any sensitive child, but her bias is revealed in the reflection which follows: 'Are any of the prayers of those glorified saints fulfilled in the poor child who was brought into the world on that particular spot, though at the distance of some ages?' (p. 6). We learn that her father took her to see the pits where the martyrs were burned (an excursion of which Mr Fairchild would heartily have approved) and that when she asked him if she would ever be a martyr, she took great pleasure in his reply that if the Papists ever got power again, she might well become one. Her love of the Bible is attributed to hearing her father read it in the cathedral such that at 6 years old 'the foundation of a truly Scriptural Protest was laid in my character' (p. 15), and her pledge to fight the 'diabolical iniquity' of Roman Catholicism must be read in the light of her later obsessive concerns. She illustrates the ambiguous influence of early religious training on children by describing how she and her brother would urge each other to confession and, after a fault, go hand-in-hand to their mother, where 'the one who stood clear of the offence acknowledged it in the name of the transgressor, while both asked pardon' (p. 18). Moreover they felt bound together by the discovery of 'laxity' in other children, 'we would shrink into a corner by ourselves, and whisper: "Do they think God does not hear that?"' (pp. 18–19). As though anticipating the reader's reaction to such preternaturally good childish behaviour, she adds that they developed a high degree of self-righteousness, becoming like 'baby Pharisees', but that the habitual regard for truth helped her to avoid many snares in later life.

Though willing to confess her rejection of traditional female activities, having a 'natural antipathy to all that did not engage the intellectual powers' (p. 72) and the desire to share the pursuits of her father and brother (which led to a 'habit of deference to man's judgement and submission to man's authority', p. 67), Tonna is aware that she is on dangerous ground in writing of the development of her imaginative powers, for, while wishing to suggest that she was endowed with imagination to a considerable degree, as an Evangelical she is at pains to condemn improper indulgence in it. In this, Tonna also resembles many women writers who express guilt about their childhood fantasies, particularly those imaginary exploits which suggest a craving for success and power.[9] Thus she shows how her early love of silence was conducive to the 'positive evil' of a habit of 'dreamy excursiveness into imaginary scenes, and among unreal personages, which is alike inimical to rational pursuits, and opposed to spiritual-mindedness' (p. 7). The dangers of literature are repeatedly stressed, particularly in her description of her early teens, when it seems that she was very vulnerable to her imagination. A history of recurrent illness threw her back onto reading as a pastime which with hindsight she condemns as 'diverting the young spirit from a sacred path' (p. 64), and which led her so far astray that she became the heroine of improbable adventures in her mind. The 'pernicious study' of fairy-tales in which she took 'unutterable delight' (although she is quick to add that she never really believed in them) is condemned as a snare of the devil

> to mislead, by wild, unholy fiction, such as should come within the range of its influence. To God be all the praise that I am not now pandering with this pen to the most grovelling or the most impious of man's perverted feelings. (pp. 8–9)

She also believes herself saved by the direct intervention of God from other intellectual and spiritual snares: of her love of music she writes that 'the Lord broke it in time, by taking away my hearing' (p. 9) and the temporary blindness she suffered, at 6 years old, is attributed to eyestrain through studying a French book, thus checking her desire for 'mere acquirements, which I believe to be a bad tendency, particularly in a female' (p. 11). Such extreme self-disparagement in fact reveals more than it conceals her intellectual and spiritual ambitions which she wishes to stress were channelled, with God's help, into the acceptable domain of religious writing.

Even in her attractive descriptions of the childish recreations of exploring fields and building snowmen in the countryside where her health gradually improved (she was made to inhale the breath of cows, whereas she had previously been treated with mercury which caused an 'exciteability' leading to the deafness at 10), she emphasises her awareness of the presence of Satan everywhere. Her adult endorsement of the Evangelical view of severe discipline for children clearly colours her description of a beating administered by her father when she had been led into a lie by a servant-girl:

> I took the punishment in a most extraordinary spirit; I wished every stroke had been a stab; I wept because the pain was not great enough, and I loved my father at that moment better than even I, who almost idolised him, had ever loved him before. I thanked him, and I thank him still, for I never transgressed in that way again. (p. 26)

It seems likely that this is not so much the child's actual reaction at the time as a gloss put on the situation by the adult to render it exemplary, especially as she goes on to affirm that no punishment is too great for such an 'infamous vice' in a child and extrapolates a condemnation of the spirit of the present age for 'the blind indulgence that passes by, with a slight reprimand only, a wilful offence' (p. 20). Like Mrs Sherwood, she is keen to express her recognition of the long-term benefits of a discipline which she appears to suspect contemporary and subsequent readers of her memoirs might view with alarm. Unlike Sherwood, however, the whole tone of her recollections is intensely personal and self-orientated; we learn virtually nothing of her mother, her father is held up as a model of religious and parental virtue in relation to herself and her brother makes his most vivid appearance in the memory of a regiment of children they formed at the time of the threatened invasion by the French, resolving to kill Napoleon who, they were convinced, would attack their house. Such moments in the text, which evoke a revealing picture of life at the time, are embedded, however, in a narrative designed to show a clearly delineated spiritual trajectory and are always presented from the standpoint of the reflective, self-conscious adult.

Elizabeth Sewell, in her autobiography, shows a similar desire to trace the characteristics of her adult self in early habits, but she is not so intent, as befits her more restrained Anglican beliefs, on emphasising anything like a religious mission. Like Tonna and Sherwood, she comments on her past self from the outside and with hindsight, but is at much greater pains to criticise herself, highlighting what she regards as her serious faults as a child. The recurrence of similar patterns of denial, self-reproach and reluctance to admit to being clever, talented and ambitious in women's autobiographies clearly reflects the adult's sense of a need for such evasionary strategies in order to preserve the reader's sympathy and not make themselves vulnerable to the charge of unfeminine boasting.[10] As seen in the discussion of her novel *The Experience of Life*, Sewell depicts herself as an unpleasant child, moody, troublesome, vain, ignorant and naughty. Like many women writers, she sees her childhood self as solitary, despite being part of a large family, and suffered from low self-esteem and lack of attention. She also recounts that she was criticised and laughed at a lot by her family (her brothers called her 'Blighted Betty' because she was small for her age) and suffered from 'longings for something better, and vague dreams of distinction, kept under from the sense of being a girl'.[11] Although she attributes her longing to be noticed to vanity, she reveals an awareness of her early strong sense of individuality and reaction against a repressed childhood. Her account of her early religious education throws some light on her approach and, indeed, on the effects of such a rigid training on an impressionable young person. As a very small child, she relates, she had a taste for religion, comforting herself in her cot with little hymns and prayers, but it had little effect on her everyday life and conduct. At the local school of a Miss Crooke, in Newport on the Isle of Wight, however, she came into contact, between the ages of 4 and 13, with strict Evangelical beliefs and blames the overseverity of the regime for the 'fidgety self-worrying state of mind' and 'strange scrupulous fancies' which began to afflict her. The children routinely had to accuse themselves of faults and Sewell admits to experiencing obsessive anxieties and guilt about her thoughts. She was reduced to 'great wretchedness of mind' because

> I imagined that every time the thought of making a vow came into my head I
> had actually made it, and was bound to keep it. I even went so far as to worry

myself with the question whether I was not bound to kill my mother because I thought I had vowed that I would. (p. 25)

The urge to confess became compulsive, till she alarmed her teachers by begging to be allowed to confess her faults every day, among them, to the incredulity of her friends, the fact that she called Miss Crooke an old witch. 'I can scarcely forbear a smile now when I think of the scene', she writes, 'but the moment was one of terrible agony to me' (p. 26).

She is able at this distance to present a humorous view of her spiritual troubles at that time:

> the climax must have been reached when having received an order in common with my companions to mention if we saw any black beetles in the schoolroom, I made it a subject of confession that I had seen a black beetle crawl out from under a large bureau, and had not told of it. (p. 27)

Yet, though aware of the dangers for a sensitive child of excessive emphasis on sin and conscience, Sewell stresses the far-reaching effects on adult character of childhood experience, for although she learned not to distress herself about imaginary shortcomings after the comforting intervention of her mother, she acknowledges that

> the greatest difficulties that have come in my way since, as regards self-discipline, have arisen from the fatal necessity of using in those early years my commonsense as a defence against the working of a morbid and overstrained conscience. It laid the foundation of a sophistical habit of mind; and some of the actions of my life for which I most condemn myself can be traced to it. (pp. 27–8)

Moreover, the tone of her autobiographical account itself is clearly coloured by the same tendencies to introspection and self-condemnation which she recognises in herself as a child and which became a habit of self-repression. She continued in fact to indulge in excessive self-examination and, like her protagonist in *The Experience of Life*, was plagued, at the time of her confirmation, with religious doubts which seem to have been largely involuntary in nature and were exacerbated by a sense of guilt at her sceptical thoughts. Once again, she identifies this as a seminal influence in her life for 'there was a tender spot in my mind for years after – a wound healed which might be reopened, and would not bear being touched' (p. 38). Unlike Tonna, who wished to stress an unswerving spiritual correctness, Sewell admits that it was only in middle life that she was able to confront these 'phantom doubts' fully.

Significantly, it was her brother William who proved to be her mentor in religious matters. Brothers frequently loom large as an influence in the lives and writings of nineteenth-century women, and Sewell idolised William to the extent that, by her own admission, it became a source of further nervous trouble to her for she feared her over-engrossing love would displease him. Although her account of being humiliated by his patronising view of her intellectual ability is an implied criticism of his affected superiority, it appears nevertheless that she internalised his attitude, unable to admit for years her enjoyment of the book they were discussing, and submitted to having her literary efforts edited by him before publication.

There is comparatively little about her parents in her autobiography, because, like Tonna, she is more concerned with the development of the self. The assertion that it was begun at her mother's dying request that she should finish an account she herself had begun of the family circumstances, would appear to be another strategy of self-justification, for she remarks that 'the history of a family, told by one of its members, must, in a certain degree, resolve itself into the history of the person who writes' (p. 1). Her mother is represented as kind, clever and popular, 'the support and comfort' of the whole family through many trials and associated with the happiest moments in her early life. Her confession of 'unswerving faith and joy' on her death-bed inspired her daughter throughout her life and informed the portrayal of the last hours of Aunt Sarah in *The Experience of Life*.[12] Her father, a solicitor, was more distant to his children, a fact reflected by his relatively few appearances in the text. Her description of him is a mixture of praise and implied criticism, a duality not uncommon in autobiographical writings where the adult is forced to submit a parent to judgement in a way which would be unthinkable for a child. Thus he is seen as 'irritable and cold-mannered, but most benevolent and really tender-hearted' and his kindness as almost a fault, because 'it led him into imprudence, and he would sometimes do what might really be an injury to his own family, rather than favour them against the interests of others' (p. 9). Unlike the autobiographies of Sherwood and Tonna, there is a notable lack of emphasis on severe parental discipline which reflects the family's more relaxed religious views. Home is, in fact, contrasted with school as a paradise of freedom (p. 4).

The self-deprecating tone that Sewell adopts throughout extends to her development as a writer: 'no one certainly could have had less perception in childhood or youth of possessing any power of imagination, or indeed of having any talent of any kind than I had' (p. 54). Unlike Tonna, who underlines the liveliness of her early imaginative faculties through her severe criticism of them, Sewell does not comment upon this aspect at all until her first literary efforts, inspired by her parish work, are discussed. Interestingly, although the books of Mrs Sherwood were part of her childhood, she felt that their portrayal of children was unnatural and herself favoured the reserve of expression she found in the works of the Tractarians and developed in her own full-length family novels.

Unlike Sewell, Charlotte Yonge's preoccupation with large families stemmed from her longing as a child to belong to one. In her autobiography, which covers only her childhood and early adolescence, she recalls her joy, as an only child up to the age of 6½, at visiting her numerous cousins in Devon:

> I was happy at home, but it was with calm, solitary happiness; there no one but myself was a native of the land of childhood. The dear home people gave me all they could, but they could not be children themselves, and oh, the bliss of that cousinland to me.[13]

She recounts that, when alone at home, 'my great world was indoors with my dolls, who were my children and my sisters; out of doors with an imaginary family of ten boys and eleven girls' (p. 59). In the adventures she wove mentally and subsequently wrote about to her cousins and as an exercise given to her by a French master, these children became the prototypes of the members of the fictional families like the Mays whose lives fill so many novels. Interestingly, she makes no attempt to apologise for, or disguise, her imaginative activities, rather dismissing other children who saw 'pretending games' as falsehood as not 'perfect playmates' (p. 95). Her desire to see herself as part of an extended family is also revealed in the fact that one-third of her short autobiography is concerned wholly with family history.[14]

Her self-portrait as an eager, high-spirited child, 'very excitable, shrill-voiced, and with a great capacity for screaming' (p. 82) and the lively descriptions of the boisterous games in which she and her cousins indulged (skating and playing hockey in the hall, making spider's webs of thread on the stairs and rearranging the furniture to play at shops) defy the image of placid, sedentary childhood. Yet Christabel Coleridge, who develops Yonge's autobiography with extracts from her letters and evidence from relatives and friends, suggests that her upbringing was, in fact, very strict: 'Her father was her ideal and her mother her closest friend, but a less loyal and loving nature might have found the criticism and repression hard' (p. 122). Yonge herself claims that she was brought up by the 'Edgeworth method . . . modified by religion and good sense': 'There was nothing to make me think myself important; I was repressed when I was troublesome, made to be obedient or to suffer for it, and was allowed few mere indulgences in eating and drinking, and no holidays' (p. 56). She quickly learned habits of self-denial and self-repression, especially as she was frequently criticised as a chatterbox and hence unfeminine in being too noticeable in company. Like many of her young female characters, her life was essentially tied to the house, and although she reiterates that her childhood was happy and uneventful, she adds that she felt 'a dull yearning at times for something to look forward to' (pp. 94–5). Clearly the relaxing of strict and exclusive parental supervision and the congenial companionship of other children in the homes of her relatives acted as a welcome release for her energies.

Like other women writers, she admits to anxieties and all-consuming irrational night terrors involving violence or annihilation of the self which conflicted with her usual common sense, but which she does not see as exceptional in any way:

> just like what other solitary and imaginative children have – horrors of darkness, fancies of wolves, one most gratuitous alarm recurring every night of being smothered like the Princes in the Tower, or blown up with gunpowder. In the daylight, I knew it was nonsense, I would have spoken of it to no one, but the fears at night always came back. (p. 60)

Her dread of the end of the world, inculcated by her religion, when 'having understood "Watch lest He cometh" to mean that He would come when no one was awake, I used to try to keep awake by means of pulling hair out of my mattress' (p. 96), provides an interesting insight into the influence of familiar names:

> All the little Sunday books in those days were Mrs Sherwood's, Mrs Cameron's and Charlotte Elizabeth's, and little did my mother guess how much Calvinism one could suck out of them, even while diligently reading the story and ignoring the lesson. (pp. 96–7)

Though denying that she was precociously devout, even if 'forward in religious knowledge', her sense of religion being largely based on fear, she loved the teaching of other children in Sunday and day schools, an activity she carried out throughout her life, and, like the May children in *The Daisy Chain*, was enthralled by her father's plans to build a church. In common with many women writers, she continues to look up to the male influences in her life – her exacting but affectionate father, who nursed her himself through measles and who during their arithmetic and writing lessons frequently 'thundered' at her but whose 'approbation was so delightful that it was a delicious stimulus' (p. 108), and, in adolescence, John Keble, whom she is keen to acknowledge as 'the chief spiritual influence of my life' (p. 116).

Coleridge writes that 'the story of childhood is specially important in her case, because the child was so entirely the mother of the woman: what she was at fifteen that she was with modifications at fifty' (p. 120). Indeed, the picture Coleridge paints closely resembles the Victorian ideal of womanhood, claiming that Yonge accepted social, intellectual and practical limitations, regarding them as 'safeguards, rather than hindrances' (p. 130) and that 'authority, family ties, faculty, and aspiration all flowed in the same and powerful stream, and for her the newest *youngest* thing was to do home and family duties more perfectly' (p. 145). Her recognition of the 'atmosphere of mingled ardour and submission in which she lived all her life' suggests one of Yonge's own female characters, but in the light of the conflicts undergone by such as Ethel May, her view that 'all other contemporary and contending aspirations were so entirely outside her ken that she did not so much oppose them as remain in ignorance almost of their existence, and certainly of their

force' (p. 145) seems a singularly inadequate assessment of Yonge's sensitivity to the pressures on young girls growing up in Victorian society. While
Coleridge's suggestion that Yonge's life remained one of extended childish
happiness, since she never married and remained all her life in the same
village of her childhood with the same activities and interests, though
conceivably motivated by a desire to promote a wholly desirable image of her
recently deceased subject, tends implicitly to diminish her adult achievements, it is nevertheless true that the values she imbibed in childhood,
especially her sense of duty, decorum, love of Church and family, informed
her fiction to a considerable extent.

The development of the imagination and the embryonic creative talent so
often denied or obscured by women autobiographers is at the heart of Frances
Hodgson Burnett's fascinating autobiographical work, *The One I Knew the Best
of All* (1893). As the subtitle, *A memory of the mind of a child* indicates, her aim
is to explore a child's experience from the child's viewpoint. Motivated by the
wish to 'see the minds of young things with a sight stronger than of very
interested eyes, which can only see from the outside', for they all too soon go
off to an 'undiscoverable far-away land', she writes of 'the one I knew the best
of all', herself.[15] The overt presentation of this statement as a justification
for her courting accusations of 'bad taste' in producing such an overtly
autobiographical account, reveals once again the uneasiness about hostile
reader reaction so characteristic of female autobiographers while, paradoxically, asserting the importance of the individual self.

In order to both reproduce and analyse her experience, she becomes
'other', distancing herself from her childhood self by the use of 'she' or 'the
Small Person'. Although the account is highly personal and subjective, she
insists that it is the 'Story of any Child with an Imagination', thus emphasising
rather the universal validity of what she writes, and the memories recounted
do indeed reveal areas of experience common to many young children of any
period. The impetus for the book was, she claims, her observation of her own
children which prompted recollections of her past in which she found

> interest and instruction, and the most serious cause for tender, deep reflection
> on her as a thing touching on that strange, awful problem of a little soul standing
> in its newness in the great, busy, tragic world, touched for the first time by
> everything that passes it, and never touched without some sign of the contact
> being left upon it. (pp. 2–3)

As is frequently found in accounts of early childhood, her very first memory
of this contact with the world is one of pain, as her nursemaid drags a comb
through her hair. The second, an equally common one, of the arrival of her
baby sister, is utilised to portray the child's dawning awareness of herself in
relation to adults, for when she is not allowed to hold the new baby on her
knees without the nurse supporting it, she understands that 'grown-ups could

do as they chose, and that there was no appeal against their omnipotence' (p. 9). Burnett insists that the senselessness of a 'Struggle against the Fixed' (p. 10) was grasped by the child although she had not the words to articulate it, and that she soon acquired the habit of adjusting the self to the inevitable. This passage is characteristic of Burnett's technique of attempting to convey in adult language the emotions deeply felt by the child but which she lacked the language to express. Thus she evokes the 'impressionable sensitiveness which it seems so tragic that we do not always remember' in her agonies over her 'first society problem' when she cannot force herself to agree that a neighbour's new baby's name is pretty and her terror that she might fall from a park bench and be arrested by a policeman for trespassing on the grass. This last example exemplifies the insensitivity of adults to a child's fears for both the nursemaid who tells her this is the policeman's job and the policeman who jokingly confirms it fail to understand her anxiety. The nightmares resulting from this trivial episode, exacerbated by her fear of being separated from her mother, made it more traumatic even than the death of her father, 'a thing of mystery of which there was so little explanation that it was not terrible' (p. 21).

The incomprehensible nature of death for a child is articulated by Burnett as 'the Strange Thing', the 'impossible', which, when a delicate classmate dies, she finds impossible to relate to herself. Allowing herself to be taken to see his body by her friends, she cannot reconcile the 'indescribable awed dreariness' (p. 166) with literary representations of death and cannot adjust her imagination to encompass the fact that the boy who shared the same day-to-day school life as herself has undergone this awesome experience. The subsequent unexpected death of a pretty, petted little girl at school who does look beautiful lying on a flower-strewn bed makes the young onlookers less afraid because this is more easily assimilated into the conventional image. Burnett's portrayal is one of the most thoughtful and full descriptions of a child's response to death in nineteenth-century autobiographical writing. Charlotte Yonge, a number of whose relatives, including several of her young cousins, died when she was a child, gives a similarly honest description of her reactions which earned her the criticism of being unfeeling. Her account of the death in their house of her 18-year-old cousin James when everything seemed a 'dull dreary dream' and 'I could not cry, and I was ready for any distraction. It was a great satisfaction to run down the kitchen garden, and recollect the cats must be fed whatever happened' suggests not so much indifference as a characteristically childish inability to grasp fully the import of what has happened and the desire to cling to normality in the face of the unimaginable.[16] Curiously, in the autobiography of Mrs Sherwood, who in her fiction is obsessed with death, there is very little discussion of the subject until the adult sections, although she does, predictably, admit to a fascination with funerals.[17]

A memory Burnett clearly regards as seminal is learning to read at 3 years old. Her 'First Book', an alphabet book with coloured pictures of flowers and moral rhymes, is remembered for its brilliant beauty rather than its didactic value. The following comment is clearly the adult narrator's reflection on instructional literature, despite her imputing it to the child: 'I think one rather had a feeling of having been born an innately vicious little person who needed labouring with constantly that one might be made merely endurable' (p. 25). More convincing are the guilt she claims to have felt at her dislike of tract literature ('The Small Person suffered keen pangs of conscience, and thought she was a wicked child, because she did not like those books and had a vague feeling of disbelief in the children', pp. 111–12) and her feelings of inadequacy in not matching up to the pious standards of the literary models, her inability to remember sermons and spout texts seen as a 'fatal flaw in her nature' (p. 189). These sentiments are compounded by her all-consuming love of reading, telling and, eventually, writing stories, for which she imagines being chided by an 'ideal child' for being addicted to lies.

Her imagination is, in effect, the true protagonist of this narrative, transforming reality and hence her existence at will into a world of endless possibility. Such a talent is not seen as a sign of superiority in herself, however, for the capacity to 'pretend' and be fascinated by new experiences is, she claims, the province of every child. Of the exotic possibilities of a garden, of a lamp-post in a rain-washed Manchester square, or of furniture in a familiar room, seen through a child's eyes, she writes nostalgically:

> As one looks back across the thousand years of one's life, to a time when one saw all things like this – recognising how far beyond the power of maturer years it is to see them again – one says with half a smile, and more than half a sigh: 'Ah, does not one wish one could'. (p. 69)

Such an acknowledgement that a child's experience is different in quality as well as in kind from that of an adult points forward to the efforts of many twentieth-century writers to convey its flavour adequately. The adult can, in Burnett's view, only make an attempt to recapture the magic in words, although 'words are always poor things. One only uses them when one has nothing else' (p. 251). Her description of an episode when her imagination was a source of suffering rather than pleasure is, in fact, very effective in capturing the child's unarticulated response to a situation. When persuaded by a cottage girl to purchase a piece of parkin 'on trust' when she has no money, she so fears the disgrace of discovery that she cannot bring herself to eat it, hiding it away in a drawer (like a murderer hiding a body, comments the adult narrator) and is amazed that she is still treated normally by her family and allowed to play with the baby or in the garden as though 'her presence would not blight the gooseberries, and the red currants would not shrivel beneath her evil eye' (p. 42). In contrast, the disillusionment engendered by the failure of reality to live up to a child's expectations, in this case the excitement of a party, is evoked from the viewpoint of the sadder and wiser adult: 'One does it all one's life. Everybody dances, everybody hears the music, everybody sometime wears a sash and a necklace and watches the other White Frocks whirling by – but was there ever any one who really went to the party?' (p. 141).

Her discovery of literature stimulates her imagination to the invention of long, rambling, highly coloured fantastic narratives, which, as for many young females, fulfil the need for a sense of adventure and power as an escape from the monotony of everyday life. This talent is revealed as a source of power over others (she is courted and bribed by her friends, hungry for the continuing adventures of some beautiful heroine with long golden curls and languorous eyes) but also, paradoxically, as a source of obscure shame: she is so teased by her brothers when she begins to write that she is driven to indulge in it, like her omnivorous reading, clandestinely, 'secretly afraid that it was a ridiculous thing for a little girl to do' (p. 212). The gentle approval of her mother, who with her sweetness, kindness, simple faith, class-consciousness and unworldliness, embodies and promotes to her daughters the Victorian ideal of the 'lady', sustains and encourages her after her first attempt at writing a poem. The family's move to America because of financial difficulties is the turning point for her development as an artist. In the glorious rural environment, she experiences what she calls her 'Dryad days', 'something she must have been waiting for all through her young years of exile' (p. 264), all her senses coming alive in the intoxication of solitary communion with nature, no longer having to 'pretend' but finally living '*in* the Story' (p. 261). Coinciding with her early teens, this change is seen to be associated with all kinds of indecipherable urges. The climax of the book is her decision to try to get one of her stories published, the family's financial straits being the factor which urges her to 'go public'. Thus her imagination, 'her best beloved, who had stood by her all her vivid short life making dull things bright and bright things brilliant' (p. 320), becomes the foundation on which the whole of her future life as a writer is built.

The overall tone of Burnett's narrative is a positive and reassuring one, in which alarming or distressing elements are few and the child's development takes place against the background of a secure and loving home. In the autobiography of Harriet Martineau, which tells of her extraordinary rise to literary fame, we find one of the most open and sensitive accounts of the more painful and disturbing aspects of real-life nineteenth-century childhood to be found anywhere in writing of the period.[18] The first part, which describes her life up to the age of eight, is perhaps the most interesting for, instead of bare biographical facts or selected important moments, it attempts to recapture her early impressions, including those of pre-verbal experience. Always a sickly child, she recalls being sent into the country and standing on the threshold of a cottage, holding fast by the doorpost and putting my foot down, in repeated attempts to reach the ground. Having accomplished this step, I toddled (I remember the uncertain feeling) to a tree before the door, and tried to clasp and get round it; but the rough bark hurt my hands.[19]

Most of her earliest memories are sensory, especially, as might be expected in infancy, tactile ones: the coarse feel of the sheets on her bed and her delight, at the age of 2, in the velvet button on her sister's bonnet, 'the rapture of the sensation was really monstrous, as I remember it now' (p. 13). Thus she evokes the child's experience of reality by using adult language to verbalise a sensation which, as a child, was only felt, not analysed, and the memory of which has endured in the adult's consciousness. Because she never had a sense of smell and only imperfect taste, the tactile, visual and auditory were all the more vivid and important to her, and all the more devastating was her gradual loss of hearing.

Martineau is clearly fascinated by the process of memory: 'I know nothing more strange than this power of re-entering, as it were, into the narrow mind of an infant, so as to compare it with that of maturity' (pp. 14–15) and is constantly at pains to establish the continuity between childhood and adulthood. In fact, she sees her whole life as an outcome of her childhood experience. Her wonderfully immediate and perceptive descriptions of the irrational fears and panics, especially night terrors, to which, like Charlotte Yonge, she was prone, testify to the universal nature of some childhood experiences and are unusual only in their number and frequency:

Sometimes the dim light of the window in the night seemed to advance till it pressed upon my eyeballs, and then the windows would seem to recede to an infinite distance. If I laid my hand under my head on a pillow, the hand seemed to vanish almost to a point, while the head grew as big as a mountain. Sometimes I was panic-struck at the head of the stairs, and was sure I could never get down; and I could never cross the yard to the garden without flying and panting, and fearing to look behind, because a wild beast was after me. The starlight sky was worst; it was always coming down, to stifle and crush me, and rest upon my head. I do not remember any dread of thieves or ghosts in particular; but things as I actually saw them were dreadful to me, and it now appears to me that I had scarcely any respite from the terror. (pp. 10–11)[20]

Among her many fears – of people, of unseen sounds (notably the muffled noise of featherbeds being beaten), of a tangle of long grass around the base of a tree and of the sea seen through the holes of the jetty at Yarmouth – all of which reveal the child's sense of vulnerability in a world of unknown phenomena, her most constant and severe panic attacks are associated with light. She evokes her horror at a magic lantern show, where the white circle on the wall and the moving slides brought on 'bowel complaint', even at the age of 13, and recounts the moment when, on entering the drawing-room, she once screamed with terror, for the drops of the lustres on the mantel-piece, on which the sun was shining, were somehow set in motion, and the prismatic colours danced vehemently on the walls. I thought they were alive – imps of some sort; and I never dared go into that room alone in the morning from that time forward. (p. 16)

Thus, what to one child might be enchantment, to another is sheer terror. Martineau insists that the trauma of childhood persist into later years, despite the ability of the adult to rationalise the situation: 'I am afraid I must own that my heart has beat, all my life long, at the dancing of prismatic colours on the wall' (p. 16). She is conscious that the terrors were 'a matter of pure sensation, without any intellectual justification whatsoever, even of the wildest kind' (p. 15) but, because of this very irrationality, were all the harder to bear. In this respect she clearly feels that her parents' attitude was blameworthy:

It seems to me now that a little closer observation would have shown them the causes of the bad health and fitful temper which gave them so much anxiety on my account, and I am sure that a little more of the cheerful tenderness which was in those days thought bad for children, would have saved me from my worst faults, and from a world of suffering. (p. 11)

In fact, she was seen by her family, she tells us, as a 'dull, unobservant, slow, awkward child' (p. 23). This suggests that, as with Elizabeth Sewell, some of her frequent illnesses and alarming imaginings may have been symptoms of psychological malaise. Certainly her increasing deafness exacerbated her sense of isolation and difference. An unusually explicit indictment of the rule of severity which prevailed in the house, the general mismanagement and flouting of justice ('least understood in our house in regard to servants and children', p. 18), and the 'grievous mistake' of lack of sympathy and support, is her insistence on her almost constant misery which manifested itself as a habit of crying, perpetual obstinacy and crossness. A disturbing example of her state of mind is her determination at the age of 5 to commit suicide by cutting her throat with a carving-knife, a plan which was fortunately thwarted by the presence of the servants in the kitchen.[21] The duality she diagnoses in her childhood self between bad temper and unhappiness and the longing to be loved ('I had no self-respect, and an unbounded need of approbation and affection', p. 19) prefigures that of many literary heroines, as will be seen in the next chapter. Despite her dogged wilfulness, disagreeableness and jealousy (she hated all red books because her sister was given one), she admits that she was melted instantly by a word of kindness. That these were few and far between is evidenced by her singling out of two examples, one a lady who understood her fear of the magic lantern and took her on her knee, and the other an occasion when her mother comforted her during a bout of earache. Generally there was a lack of the 'slightest indulgence shown to my natural affections, and any rational dealing with my faults' (p. 19). Although she does not gloss over these faults, the blame for her unhappiness and temperament is squarely laid at the door of her upbringing: 'I must have been an intolerable child: but I need not have been so' (p. 21). Thus, self-analysis is directed specifically towards criticism of her parents and traditional methods of rearing children, rather than to the self-condemnation of Elizabeth Sewell or Charlotte Elizabeth Tonna.

Though galled by the doctrine of 'passive obedience', she clearly repressed her rebellious instincts in traditional manner, remaining 'abundantly obedient in act; for I never dreamed of being otherwise', always seeing herself as wrong but refusing to admit it: 'My moral discernment was almost wholly obscured by fear and mortification' (p. 22). Only one instance of open rebellion is recorded in these early sections, when Harriet accused her mother of favouritism to her sister Rachel, an occasion when she felt, for once, entirely in the right. Her greatest regret is her mother's failure to talk to her which she intuits as a source of much unnecessary and unspoken conflict between them: 'I believe this would have wrought in a moment that cure which it took years to effect, amidst reserve and silence' (p. 87).

What emerges from these pages is a portrait of a young girl very like those in a number of nineteenth-century novels of self-development which portray the pain of growing up female. It is, of course, possible to argue that she is, to some extent, consciously constructing an image of herself as a misunderstood heroine in the literary tradition. In the second volume of her autobiography, Martineau reveals that Charlotte Brontë had recognised in some of the autobiographical passages of *Household Education* (1849) the same kind of childhood terrors as she herself recounted in *Jane Eyre* (1847), notably the fear of the moving gleam of light on the wall.[22] Indeed, the bitter resentments, the sense of isolation and estrangement, the furious miseries and brief outbreaks of rebellion against the oppressor are common not only to Harriet Martineau and Jane Eyre but all the young females in the texts discussed in the next chapter.[23]

Like Maggie Tulliver in George Eliot's *The Mill on the Floss*, Harriet's main consolation, as a young girl, was found in religion, her depiction of her early encounter with which brings humorously to life the literary convention of the pious child, for she returned from the cottage family with whom she had lived between the ages of 2 and 3 'the absurdest little preacher', quoting maxims at every opportunity and later, like Elizabeth Sewell, suffering agonies of remorse for her behaviour. When she was older, her piety became a kind of placebo ('I pampered my vain-glorious propensities by dreams of divine favour, to make up for my utter deficiency in self-respect', p. 12) and her 'only support and comfort' in times of misery. In fact, her autobiography is the story of her eventual deconversion from the family's Unitarianism and her spiritual growth as a 'free rover on the broad, bright, breezy common of the universe' (p. 116). Significantly, although a rift between herself and her idolised brother James resulted from his harsh review of one of her books favouring atheism, she refrains from discussing their estrangement in the autobiography, remarking only on her early dependence on him.

Her reflections on her education are unusual in that they are extremely positive. Although her early education at home was marred by her utter dread of the singing-master, her 'delectable schooling' from the age of 11 at a mixed day school is acknowledged not only as an entry to the intellectual life, but as a 'refuge from moral suffering, and an always inexhausted spring of moral strength and enjoyment' (p. 65). This is in refreshing contrast to the picture of Miss Crooke's school, painted by Elizabeth Sewell, where the education seemed 'strange beyond belief' although the 'limited and mechanical' lessons were thoroughly inculcated, and the spartan conditions confirmed many literary portraits of the cold and hunger endured by young children in such establishments.[24] Sewell's account of her subsequent school at Bath corresponds quite closely to Mrs Sherwood's description of the school she attended for a while at Reading. While Sewell portrays this period as 'years of rapid growth for good and evil', detailing her relationships with the other girls and their activities and, predictably, accusing herself of the bad habit of working too hard, Sherwood is more concerned with discussing the privileges she enjoyed, the social activities and amusements (an outstanding moment is her depiction of a visit to a museum, when the boys frightened the girls in the gloom by pursuing them with a large stuffed crocodile on wheels).[25] Martineau's return to education 'en famille' when the schoolteacher left is described, in contrast, as a 'desperate and wrangling life' (p. 70), aggravated by lethargy and ill-health, although it heralded her interest in social, political and economic problems through her reading of books and newspapers. Her love of private study increased later at boarding school in Bristol, where, despite typically adolescent anxieties about her hair, handwriting and deafness, and, paradoxically, homesickness, she became less fearful and more confident. Interestingly, although, unlike many of her female contemporaries, Martineau is prepared to proclaim her enthusiasm and aptitude for intellectual effort, her awareness of the censure and ridicule to which any hint of 'blue-stockingism' could expose her caused her to do her own work early in the morning and late at night, and her comment on the advantage of being brought up to be industrious in traditional female occupations ('Thus I was saved from being a literary lady who could not sew', p. 27) is by no means tongue in cheek, as her praise of Charlotte Brontë's domestic talents in her obituary of her friend demonstrates.[26]

There are a number of pleasant memories in this autobiographical account (of Harriet's enjoyment in watching seeds grow and a holiday in the countryside, the birth of her little sister and the stimulation of learning Latin and writing verses) and some humorous ones (her delight in seeing the sea at Cromer after being unable to 'see' it at Tynemouth earlier, despite the vast expanse before her, paralleled by her failure to 'see' the comet of 1811).[27] So vividly does she evoke her miseries and resentments, however, that this narrative of repression, startling in a woman's autobiography of the mid-nineteenth century, although her experience was by no means unique, presents a stark contrast to the rosy family settings promoted by so many of her contemporaries.

The most vitriolic denunciation of a Victorian family upbringing must surely be Hannah Lynch's *Autobiography of a Child* (1899) in which she portrays her *alter ego*, Angela, as a victim of an 'unloved and illtreated childhood' from the start. Her approach is not unlike Harriet Martineau's in that she recognises the difference in the way a child experiences reality and aims to recreate this in her narrative, the title of which itself suggests an immersion in the child's viewpoint, although the narrative voice is clearly that of the adult:

> I have always marvelled at the roll of reminiscences and experiences of childhood told consecutively and with coherence. Children live more in pictures, in broken effects, in unaccountable impulses that lend an unmeasured significance to odd trifles to the exclusion of momentous facts, than in story. This alone prevents the harmonious fluency of biography in an honest account of our childhood. Memory is a random vagabond, and plays queer tricks with proportion. It dwells on pictures of relative unimportance, and revives incidents of no practical value in the shaping of our lives . . .[28]

Thus, in the early chapters she evokes random memories of passing sensations – an engine ride with its feeling of rushing through the air, the noisy shouting of the men and the sting of smuts on her eyelids – and impressions – of her friend Mary Jane's oily ringlets and her conviction that America lay on the other side of the village pond – which demonstrate that experience can be memorable even if the cause is trivial. The age of 7, she claims, is 'the age of continuous reminiscence' when 'life begins to be a story' and from that point her narrative also acquires more structure and linear coherence.[29]

Significantly her earliest memory, of taking her first steps (self-consciously recreated with the words 'I shut my eyes and I am back in the little parlour . . .', p. 1), is associated with one of the central and most extraordinary themes of the book, her terror of her mother. When the infant totters and falls, the tears are not of pain or frustration but because she is near her mother. For the first seven years of her life, Angela lives with a nurse in the country, visited only very occasionally by the 'handsome, cold-eyed woman, who did not love me' (p. 1). Lynch's portrayal of her mother and of their relationship subverts all literary stereotypes. Though aware of the reader's probable distaste, she insists that 'to suppress the most passionate instinct of my nature, would be to suppress the greater part of my mental and physical sufferings' (p. 14) and graphically depicts her physical antipathy to her mother, so strong that, as a baby, she had convulsions when placed in her mother's arms, feared her touch when ill and felt her glance 'as though someone were walking over my grave' (p. 15). Although her stepfather is portrayed positively because he is kind and attempts to champion and protect her, her mother is seen as having the

> implacable passion to wound, to strike the smile from the little faces around her, to silence a child's laughter with fears of herself. She was a curious woman, my mother. Children seemed to inspire her with a vindictive animosity, with a fury for beating and banging them, against walls, against chairs, upon the ground, in a way that it seems miraculous to me now that they were saved from the grave and she from the dock. (pp. 3–4)

Her violence and vindictiveness (she eggs Angela's sisters to treat her as a slave) are incomprehensible to the child and are not explained by the adult narrator, although there are clues which suggest that her mother may have been a deeply insecure person, perhaps resentful of her repeated pregnancies and of rivalry from her attractive daughters. Examples of her physical abuse reveal them to be triggered by attention paid to the children by other people, any deviation from her wishes or orders, or unwanted intrusion on her presence: 'She was simply exasperated by their inconceivable incapacity to efface themselves and "lie low"' (p. 53).

This remarkable picture of a mother, worse than 'the traditional stepmother of fairy-tales' (p. 4), is only part of Lynch's portrayal of her Dublin home as a 'land of ogres and witches' (p. 45) and a family life which left her 'permanently maimed for the battle of life' (p. 51): 'Could any possible future paradise make up to us for infancy in hell?' (p. 51). Her account is, in fact, very conscious of literary models – her description of herself as a 'desperate little spitfire, full of uncontrollable passion' (p. 26) completely subverts the angelic image which her blonde, blue-eyed beauty evokes. Her description of her crippled little brother Stevie, whose spine was broken when a tipsy town nurse dropped him down the stairs, is partially informed by literary stereotypes of the dying child but his 'beautiful unearthly eyes of the deepest brown' are 'full of passionate pain and revolt' (p. 20) and he 'did not bear his sorrow patiently . . . but with sullen courage and with a corrosive silent fretting' (p. 21), his querulous, demanding manner and the 'vindictive clutch of his bloodless fingers' which gave her 'the first draught of the soul's bitters' seen in retrospect as the frustration of the 'poor little fellow with the soul of a buccaneer' (p. 23). Her uncomprehending uneasiness at the atmosphere in the nurse's cottage where Stevie dies is vividly evoked through the child's eyes: coming across his coffin she is appalled at what has been done to him ('Worse than wicked fairies did in stories', p. 35) and in her rage tries to pull him out. This potentially macabre scene is, in fact, a poignant criticism of the behaviour of the adults who are too busy and too insensitive to explain the situation to her.

She also admits to a strong tendency, as a child, to self-dramatisation which, like her passions, derives from her sense of rejection and displacement. When she is sent away to school in England she sees herself as a literary heroine, braving the seas 'to be snubbed by and to subdue a haughty people' (p. 121), and rejoices in being seen as glamorous by the village people on her return, even revelling in transforming her woes 'into dramatic entertainment' for the sake of admiration and pity. Just as much of her childhood is seen as 'unconscious acting', so her narrative itself undeniably works to construct a romantic, dramatic image of herself as an unhappy outcast, the tragic heroine. The tone of the following passages has clear echoes of Romantic and sentimental literature: of her stepfather she writes

> what did he know of the inward bruise, the hunger for love and sympathy, the malady of life that had begun to gnaw at my soul at an age when other little girls are out racing among the flowers in a universe bounded and heated and beautified by the love of mother and father? (p. 93)

and at school she feels 'cast out of a warm circle where my empty place would not be felt, where no word of regret would ever be uttered for the unwelcome waif that called them sister' (p. 128). In fact, home life seems grim for all the sisters who, left to themselves with little emotional support or moral guidance, have established relationships and games from which Angela, the outsider, is excluded when she is not subjected to their rough and contemptuous treatment, because of her frequent exiles. There is no sentimentality in the merciless exposure of the cruelty of children in oppressing the already weak and vulnerable.

Lynch's portrayal of her convent school gives an equally grim picture of institutionalised religion, for not only does Angela suffer from loneliness and the sense of rejection, but also becomes the object of sadistic treatment by the nuns. After rebelling against an unjust punishment by barricading herself in the room in which she has been locked by one of the nuns and throwing a stool at the 'exquisite monster', she is beaten, naked, by another of these 'ladies, devoted to the worship of mercy and of Mary . . . the mild mother of humanity' (p. 159) and has to stay in the infirmary till the wounds on her back heal. It is a very carefully constructed, cynical portrait of religious life – the nuns confiscate the contents of the hampers the girls receive from home and begin to behave better to Angela when she is singled out for notice by the bishop at her confirmation. At 11, in common with many impressionable young girls (as contemporary and twentieth-century accounts confirm), she delights in feeling saintly, her emotions 'nourished upon incense, music, taper lit gloom and a mysterious sense of the intangible' (pp. 294–5), although she subsequently faints with fear in the confessional. There is humour too, however, in the children's ponderings over which sins they can confess (can adultery be safely added to the list?) and despite the 'incompetence, ignorance, cruel stupidity and futile vexation' (p. 144), they are a 'merry lot of little savages' for whom life is full of 'quaint surprises and thrilling terrors' (p. 146).

To her school life she attributes the completion of her transformation from a pallid, pathetic figure to a 'hardened reprobate', an 'active and abominable little fiend' who saw all adults as the implacable enemy and became a fighter for herself and others, a kind of rebirth as a new person. Like Harriet Martineau, Hannah Lynch's narrator is conscious that her character as a child was formed largely by the way she was treated and, although she can, as an adult, view some aspects with an objectivity impossible in childhood, she acknowledges the long-lasting effects of childhood experience. Paradoxically, these are frequently seen as positive. Thus, she can comment that her mother's harsh treatment 'has answered better than that of many a tender or self-sacrificing mother' for it taught her self-reliance, silent strength and honesty: 'bleak as the start was, I would not have had it otherwise at the cost of these great and virile virtues' (p. 262). Here, even more than in other works, it is impossible not to wonder at the impulse to exculpate parents. Even Lynch's gloss on her childhood terror of her mother ('I wonder that the woman who inspired it should in middle life appear to me a woman of large and liberal and generous character, whose foibles and rough temper in perspective have acquired rather a humorous than an antipathetic aspect', p. 15) which, stated early in the narrative, suggests that the subsequent picture has been distorted by the child's viewpoint motivated perhaps by her sense of abandonment, is not a convincing antidote to the sustained portrait of mental and physical cruelty she evokes. Nor is this cruelty restricted to her mother: she recounts an episode in which her grandmother gets her uncle to punish her for a slight misdemeanour by threatening to place a heated knife-sharpener in her mouth. It is revealing that, contrary to the conventional imaging of women in literature, it is the women who are the oppressors and torturers in this narrative. Moreover, Lynch continues to insist on her dislike of large families because 'every large family holds a victim' and on the enduring psychological effects of her upbringing: 'The heart that has been broken in childhood can never be sound again, whatever the sequel the years may bring . . . the muffled apprehension of ache, the rooted mistrust bred by early injustice, can never be effaced' (p. 256).

Few women writers portray their childhood as a time of unqualified happiness. Even when it is viewed with nostalgia, there is frequently a sub-text of unhappiness and resentment. The boredom of inactivity, frustration at restrictions and, above all, a sense of isolation, are recurring elements which are commonly seen to manifest themselves in physical ailments, nervous complaints, bad temper and irrational fears, or drive the child inwards into a life of the imagination. The writing of their own childhood was, then, a potent means for women of articulating their response to a society that marginalised and repressed them by creating an image with which readers would readily identify – a suffering child – although their awareness of the possible dangers of this caused some to invent strategies of concealment and denial. It was also a means of expressing their early sense of the importance of the self, although here too they often recognised the need for disguise, appearing simultaneously to emphasise and condemn the very aspects of their childhood characters which made them special.

The following chapter will consider how four women novelists translated their views on the real-life complexities of growing up female in Victorian society into fictional works which were at once controversial and inspiring, and which attacked as openly as Harriet Martineau and Hannah Lynch the image of family and upbringing which many of their contemporaries were labouring so hard to perpetuate.

Chapter 6
'Growing up wrong':
The child of conflict

Unloved – I love; unwept – I weep;
Grief I restrain – hope I repress:
Vain is the anguish – fixed and deep;
Vainer, desires and dreams of bliss –

My love awakes no love again,
My tears collect, or fall unfelt;
My sorrow touches none with pain,
My humble hopes to nothing melt.

For me the universe is dumb,
Stone-deaf, and blank, and wholly blind;
Life I must bound, existence sum
In the strait limits of one mind;

That mind my own. Oh! narrow cell;
Dark – imageless – a living tomb!
There must I sleep; there wake and dwell
Content, with palsy, pain and gloom.

Charlotte Brontë

The effects on the child of the harsher aspects of nineteenth-century social, religious and educational precepts are exemplified in a number of fictional texts which derive from real lived experience and demonstrate that children could be the victims of the family context in life as in fairy-tales. Rudyard Kipling, John Stuart Mill and John Ruskin, for example, survived the rigours of a strict religious upbringing to, literally, tell the tale. Two texts which always find their way into studies of nineteenth-century childhood are Samuel Butler's *The Way of All Flesh* (written sporadically between 1872 and 1884 but not published till 1903), the story of a son trapped in a repressive, religious milieu from which he eventually emancipates himself, and Edmond Gosse's *Father and Son* (1907), a record of a struggle between two temperaments (his father was an extreme Calvinist) and of a lonely, imprisoned childhood.

For young females, the sheer logistics of rebellion and escape were much more problematic, given the fewer opportunities for financial and social independence. Nevertheless, the values and assumptions discussed in the previous chapters are challenged and even openly rejected in a number of female-authored texts of the period, particularly in novels of self-development in which the female protagonist is seen to grow, from a difficult or deprived childhood, through a tormented adolescence to womanhood. Such an approach became common in the latter years of the century as every aspect of society's attitudes towards women was questioned in the 'New Woman' novels, two of which are included here. Significantly, the fate of these literary females is frequently an uneasy or resentful conformity, a state of continuing alienation or even death, thereby acknowledging the difficulties of triumphing over circumstances. Such novels of rage and rebellion also frequently have a strong autobiographical basis, thus confirming that, despite their popularity, the imaging of females in the domestic and religious novels did not correspond to the real truth of female experience. This chapter considers in detail the portrayal of childhood in five novels, three of which are now considered as among the 'greats' of Victorian literature. All of these novels are informed by the awareness that childhood is where the self is shaped and the experiences of the protagonists as children are communicated through images and narrative patterns which both encapsulate and pervade their succeeding conflicts in life.

In Charlotte Brontë's *Jane Eyre* (1847), the quintessential novel of young female rage and rebellion, for example, the detailed portrayal of Jane's childhood at the age of 10 in nearly as many chapters is explicitly presented by the narrator (the adult Jane) as a seminal period, for this is not to be a regular autobiography. 'I am only bound to invoke memory where I know her responses will possess some degree of interest.'[1] The following eight years are passed over 'almost in silence', a period during which her life was 'uniform: but not unhappy, because it was not inactive' (p. 115).[2] Jane's childhood is the exact opposite of this: the opening pages capture the oppressive state of misery and inactivity of her life in the Reed household with images of slavery and entrapment. An orphan who is both poor and plain, Jane is victimised and excluded from this parody of a family circle because she constitutionally and mentally cannot match up to the role of docile, placid female. The theme of the orphaned or motherless child is, of course, a central one in the works of all the Brontës, testifying to their acute awareness of the loss of their own mother when they were very young.[3] Jane's sense of resentment at injustice is apparent in the first words she speaks in the text: to Mrs Reed's injunction that

> until she heard from Bessie, and could discover by her own observation that I was endeavouring in good earnest to acquire a more sociable and childlike disposition, a more attractive and sprightly manner – something lighter, franker, more natural as it were – she really must exclude me from privileges intended only for contented, happy little children

her instinctive response is to bluntly question: 'What does Bessie say I have done?' (p. 39). Her subsequent retreat into the window-seat behind a heavy curtain is emblematic of Jane's inability, in adult life as in childhood, to accommodate herself to polite, drawing-room society which rewards and privileges those who conform to its requirements and isolates and punishes those who are unable or unwilling to do so.

The treatment Jane receives at Gateshead Hall is in fact largely responsible for her failure to be a happy, contented child. Regarded as an interloper by her cousins and an anomaly by the whole household ('less than a servant, for you do nothing for your keep', p. 44), Jane is abused physically and mentally. The loathsome John Reed, a brutal, flabby, overindulged schoolboy of 14, exploits her impotence as an inferior and outsider, bullying her continually, such that 'every nerve I had feared him and every morsel of flesh on my bones shrank when he came near' (p. 42), and dehumanising her by calling her 'rat' or 'bad animal'. The motif of imprisonment is introduced in the split between what the narrator-Jane describes as her habitual shrinking obedience and her inner self which assesses and despises the character of the tyrant as he prepares to strike her, a self which, perhaps significantly, when her blood is shed by an act of violence by John Reed, rebels in an outburst of rage against her 'slave-driver' which transforms her into 'a desperate thing' (p. 43). This moment when Jane allows her pent-up rage to become visible, revealing herself as 'a picture of passion', is a transitional one, as the narrator recognises:

> The fact is, I was a trifle beside myself; or rather *out* of myself, as the French would say: I was conscious that a moment's mutiny had already rendered me liable to strange penalties, and like any other rebel slave, I felt resolved, in my desperation, to go all lengths. (p. 44)

Her punishment, the much-commented-upon scene of imprisonment in the red-room, establishes images which foreshadow much of Jane's later life. Her resistance (like a 'mad cat'), which causes Bessie and Mrs Abbot to doubt her sanity, thus establishes the correlation of female rebelliousness and refusal with madness, a clear presaging of the plight of Mr Rochester's wife, Bertha, just as being 'useful and pleasant' is postulated by Bessie as the acceptable female norm in opposition to being 'passionate and rude' which leads to rejection and expulsion. Jane's terror in the red-room, which, with its contrasting colours of fire and ice, heavy dark furniture and massive bed 'like a tabernacle' in which Jane's uncle, Mr Reed, had died, is clearly associated with the notions of an avenging deity, patriarchy and death of the self, is powerfully portrayed by contrasting the older Jane's comment with a direct evocation of the frightened child's responses. Her vision of herself in the great looking-glass is of an alien being, not quite human:

> All looked colder and darker in that visionary hollow than in reality: and the

strange little figure there gazing at me, with a white face and arms specking the gloom, and glittering eyes of fear moving where all else was still, had the effect of a real spirit: I thought it like one of the tiny phantoms, half fairy, half imp, Bessie's evening stories represented as coming up out of the lone ferny dells in moors, and appearing before the eyes of belated travellers. (p. 46)

Although the older Jane acknowledges that 'superstition was with me at that moment', the image recurs, for she is later accused of being a bewitching spirit by Mr Rochester on their first meeting in the evening light in the deserted lane near Thornfield Hall. Still absorbed in the 'mood of the revolted slave', Jane's thoughts in this scene are a tumult of insurrection, no longer those of a passive victim, her reason, 'forced by the agonising stimulus into precocious though transitory power', questioning the injustice of her situation: 'Why was I always suffering, always browbeaten, always accused, for ever condemned? Why could I never please?' (p. 46). The adult Jane supplies the answer the child only intuits, objectifying herself to underline the smug, self-orientated hypocrisy of her relations:

I was a discord in Gateshead Hall . . . They were not bound to regard with affection a thing that could not sympathise with one amongst them; a heterogeneous thing, opposed to them in temperament, in capacity, in propensities; a useless thing, incapable of serving their interests, or adding to their pleasure; a noxious thing, cherishing the germs of indignation at their treatment, of contempt of their judgement. I know that had I been a sanguine, brilliant, careless, exacting, handsome, romping child – though equally dependent and friendless – Mrs Reed would have endured my presence more complacently. (p. 47)

Her sense of 'wrongness' culminates in the contemplation of achieving escape from oppression either by running away, or by starving herself to death, alternatives which, as Gilbert and Gubar point out, recur not only in *Jane Eyre* but in many nineteenth- and twentieth-century female-authored texts.[4] Her escape, on this occasion, however, takes the form of loss of consciousness. As the light fades, Jane's mood changes as 'my habitual mood of humiliation, self-doubt, forlorn depression, fell damp on the embers of my decaying ire' (p. 48) to the extent that the internalisation of her 'wrongness' allows her to attempt to exculpate Mrs Reed of conscious injustice. It is of course significant that in this novel the chief oppressor in Jane's childhood is, in fact, the 'mother' substitute, for in other novels too the woman is seen as the cultural oppressor of her daughters or female charges. Though moved by the conviction that her dead uncle would have defended her, her simultaneous terror at the prospect of his spectral return, couched in terms which suggest a rejection of patriarchal patronage ('fearful lest any sign of violent grief might waken a preternatural voice to comfort me, or elicit from the gloom some haloed face, bending over me with strange pity', p. 48), is exacerbated by a light from a lantern outside quivering on the ceiling above her head like a 'herald of some coming vision from another world' (p. 49). Her fear-induced panic as she attempts to shake the door is rendered in vivid terms: 'My heart beat thick, my head grew hot, a sound filled my ears, which I deemed the rushing of wings: something seemed near me; I was oppressed, suffocated: endurance broke down . . .' (p. 49). When her evident terror is dismissed by her aunt as 'repulsive violence' (although Jane once more modifies her spite by a further attempt to see the situation from Mrs Reed's point of view: 'she sincerely looked on me as a compound of virulent passion, mean spirit and dangerous duplicity', pp. 49–50) and she is locked up once more in the red-room, 'a species of fit' brings the lamentable scene to a close. Her first sensation, on waking up in bed, is the sight of the 'terrible red glare, crossed with thick, black bars' of the nursery fire, an image which clearly foreshadows even more terrible fires later at Thornfield, the work of female 'madness', of desperation out of control, although here the flames, like Jane's rage, are contained by the imprisoning bars.

The more gentle and privileged treatment she receives during her illness is seen by the reader to be the consequence of her tormentors' guilt and fear lest she should die, although Jane's nerves are too strained by the servants' talk of ghosts which keeps her awake in 'such dread as children only can feel' and an 'unutterable wretchedness of mind' (p. 52), to derive any pleasure from it. Although she claims that she suffered no severe bodily illness after this episode of the red-room, the adult narrator acknowledges the enduring consequences in psychological terms:

> it only gave my nerves a shock, of which I feel the reverberation to this day. Yes, Mrs Reed, to you I owe some fearful pangs of mental suffering. But I ought to forgive you, for you knew not what you did: while rending my heartstrings, you thought you were only up-rooting my bad propensities. (p. 52)

The latter is a most effective indictment of the notions of absolute parental authority and infallibility and passive obedience on the part of the child.

Jane's replies to the questioning of the apothecary, Mr Lloyd, about the causes of her unhappiness, illustrate the author's awareness of the difficulty of portraying children's perceptions of their situation: 'Children can feel but they cannot analyse their feelings; and if the analysis is partially effected in thought, they know not how to express the result of the process in words' (p. 56). Her meagre attempts to articulate her feelings, including her instinctive rejection of the prospect of the degradation of living with poor relations, certainly do not adequately convey the depth of her misery as it has been revealed. It is, indeed, their obliviousness to the causes and extent of her pain and rage which prevents the servants from sympathising with her plight. The discussion between Bessie and Mrs Abbot of Jane's sad family background clearly illustrates the way in which attitudes can become conditioned by superficial and stereotypical assumptions:

'if she were a nice, pretty child one might compassionate her forlornness; but one really cannot care for such a little toad as that'. 'Not a great deal, to be sure' agreed Bessie: 'at any rate, a beauty like Miss Georgina would be more moving in the same condition.' (p. 58)

Like many rebellious females in nineteenth-century novels, Jane's plainness is contrasted with the stereotypical and inherently 'unnatural' prettiness of her cousin Georgina '"with her long curls, her blue eyes, and such a sweet colour as she has; just as if she were painted"' (p. 58). It is clear that her lack of the 'right' physical attributes contributes to the view of her as an '"ill conditioned child who always looked as if she were watching everybody and scheming plots underhand"' (p. 58). One suspects that it was a not dissimilar process of discrimination which aggravated the shock that many nineteenth-century readers and reviewers felt at Jane's manifest anger, resentment and refusal to accord respect to Christian society, crystallising in such responses as the famous one of Mrs Rigby in the *Quarterly Review*, accusing Jane of ingratitude in terms which, to the modern reader, seem stunningly inappropriate:

It pleased God to make her an orphan, friendless and penniless – yet she thanks nobody, and least of all Him, for the food and raiment, the friends, companions and instructors of her helpless youth . . . on the contrary, she looks upon all that has been done for her not only as her undoubted right, but as falling far short of it.[5]

It is, indeed, Jane's outspokenness which caused the book to be seen as dangerous and revolutionary, an 'anti-Christian composition'.[6] Jane subverts all the myths by becoming the Cinderella who refuses to accept the treatment meted out to her as an inferior. After the red-room experience, following upon her first outburst of passion, her passivity gives way to physical and violent responses to John Reed's bullying and her aunt's ostracism. Significantly, when she confronts Mrs Reed with her cruelty, it is as if 'my tongue pronounced words without my consenting to their utterance: something spoke out of me over which I had no control' (p. 60). At this point Jane herself seems half-afraid of this newly emerging angry self, the bad feelings within her seeming to confirm Bessie's view of her as 'the most wicked and abandoned child ever reared under a roof' (p. 60), but her second confrontation with Mrs Reed, when she openly accuses her of hard-heartedness and deceit with the uncompromising honesty which is the hallmark of Jane's character, completes the process of liberation from the slavery of her position and is seen as a kind of rebirth:

Ere I had finished this reply, my soul began to expand, to exult with the strangest sense of freedom, of triumph, I ever felt. It seemed as if an invisible bond had burst, and that I had struggled out into unhoped-for liberty. (p. 69)

Her sense of triumph, however, is succeeded by a reaction expressed in terms which admirably convey the author's understanding of the child's psyche and further foreshadows Jane's experience of destructive, but purifying, fire:

> A child cannot quarrel with its elders, as I had done, cannot give its furious feelings uncontrolled play, as I had given mine, without experiencing afterwards the pang of remorse and the chill of reaction. A ridge of lighted heath, alive, glancing, devouring, would have been a meet emblem of my mind when I accused and menaced Mrs Reed: the same ridge, black and blasted after the flames are dead, would have represented as meetly my subsequent condition, when half an hour's silence and reflection had shown me the madness of my conduct, and the dreariness of my hated and hating position. (pp. 69–70)

The sweetness of vengeance turned to poison because of the impotence of her position, Jane's existential dilemma ('what shall I do?', p. 70) is solved for her when she is sent to Lowood school. It is, in fact, her first encounter with Mr Brocklehurst, the headmaster, during which Jane is humiliated by Mrs Reed's depiction of her as a naughty child, given to deceit, that prompts her outburst of truth-telling (it will be remembered that the lie was deemed the worst of faults). Seen through the child's eyes, the whole scene is a sinister one. Jane helplessly watches Mrs Reed create an identity which she knows she does not possess and intuits that her aunt is deliberately poisoning her future:

> I dimly perceived that she was already obliterating hope from the new phase of existence which she destined me to enter; I felt, though I could not have expressed the feeling that she was sowing aversion and unkindness along my future path; I saw myself transformed under Mr Brocklehurst's eye into an artful, obnoxious child, and what could I do to remedy the injury? (p. 66)

Her first glimpse of Mr Brocklehurst, as she looks up at him from a low curtsey, conveys not only the child's impression of his size and grimness, but embodies his role as stony-hearted pillar of repressive patriarchy:

> I looked up at a black pillar! – such at least, appeared to me, at first sight, the straight, sable-clad shape standing erect on the rug: the grim face at the top was like a carved mask, placed above the shaft by way of capital. (p. 63)

Yet there is also a strong suggestion of animalism in the description of his large features and great prominent teeth, just as his religion appears to be a mixture of sterile puritanism and worldliness.[7]

It is well known that Charlotte Brontë's experience of the Cowan Bridge school of the Evangelical minister William Carus Wilson informed her portrayal of Lowood and Mr Brocklehurst, and here, as in later scenes, she is at pains to reveal the anomalies and hypocrisies of institutionalised Evangelicalism seen through the child's eyes but plainly endorsed by the adult's narrative.[8] Many of the harsher Evangelical beliefs described in Chapter 2 of this study are introduced here to reveal their potentially cold, repressive nature: the view of the child as natural hell-bait, the likelihood of early death and hence the need for constant self-vigilance to avoid the 'pit full of fire' and the emphasis on the mortification of the individual will in the name of humility.[9] Jane's considered answer when he asks her what she must do to avoid hell ('I must keep in good health, and not die', p. 64) does not endear her to him from the start. Brontë also satirises the extreme Evangelical position to highlight its potential absurdities and cynicism: Mr Brocklehurst's homily about the child who, when offered a gingerbread nut to eat or a verse of a Psalm to learn, chooses the Psalm and gets *two* gingernuts for his piety, subtly illuminates the tendency, already noted in Evangelical and in rationalist writers, to suggest that material rewards can also be the fruits of virtue, and his personal anecdote, recounted as proof of his success in mortifying the worldly sentiment of pride, is made to rebound on him, unnoticed, significantly, by himself or Mrs Reed:

> 'My second daughter, Augusta, went with her mama to visit the school, and on her return she exclaimed "Oh, dear papa, how quiet and plain all the girls at Lowood look; with their hair combed behind their ears, and their long pinafores, and those holland pockets outside their frocks – they are almost like poor people's children! and", said she, "they looked at my dress and mama's as if they had never seen a silk gown before."' (p. 66)

His description of Lowood school – '"plain fare, simple attire, unsophisticated accommodations, hardy and active habits"' (p. 66) – is a cynical glossing of the truth and illustrates an early Evangelical tendency to approve as a simple Christian duty a puritanical way of life for those less materially fortunate than themselves.

The 'consistency' on which Mr Brocklehurst prides himself ('"the first of Christian duties"', p. 66) is indeed apparent at Lowood, for cold, hunger, spartan conditions and rigorous self-regulation are the order of the day. The girls are starved with burnt porridge and rancid meat and humiliated into submission as befitting their status as orphans.[10] Jane's first months at Lowood coincide with winter, the bitter cold aggravating the physical suffering. In such conditions of deprivation the younger children are oppressed also by the older girls who coax or bully them to share their meagre rations or give up their place by the fire. Jane's fear of failure with new rules and tasks is superseded by her dread of the arrival of Mr Brocklehurst – ironically referred to by the narrator as the 'Coming Man', for he is no saviour – but once again, the child's fear is juxtaposed with a satirical portrait of rigid Evangelical precept in action. His criticism of his assistant Miss Temple's provision of a lunch, when the breakfast is inedible ('"Oh madam, when you put your bread and cheese, instead of burnt porridge, into those children's

mouths, you may indeed feed their vile bodies, but you little think how you
starve their immortal souls!"', p. 95), and his affected horror at the sight of
a pupil's naturally curly hair ('"Yes, but we are not to conform to nature. I
wish these girls to be the children of Grace . . ."', p. 96) effectively convey
the illogical and inhuman nature of such beliefs. His insistence that the girls'
'topknots' of plaited hair must be cut off directly because '"my mission is to
mortify in these girls the lusts of the flesh"' (p. 96) plainly endorses the
mutilation of female attributes because of the fear of sexuality (one cannot
help but wonder whose lusts he fears). Moreover, the girls' grimacing
reactions when they turn their backs suggest that 'the inside was farther
beyond his interference than he imagined' (p. 96). The ironical indictment
of Mr Brocklehurst's hypocrisy is crowned by the juxtaposition with this scene
of the arrival of his family, clad in rich velvets and furs, their hair elaborately
arranged in long tresses. Like the false economy of his housekeeping methods
which advocate the cheapest and worst-quality goods, the perverted notion
of virtue and cynical abuse of Christian values are everywhere apparent.

When Jane's presence is brought to his notice by the crashing to the floor
of her 'treacherous slate', the reader endures with her the torment of Mr
Brocklehurst's public denunciation of her as a 'marked character', a servant
of the Evil One, 'a little castaway', 'an interloper and an alien', culminating
in the worst of all accusations, 'a liar!' (p. 98). His description of Jane's history
not only plainly perverts the truth, reconstructing the past to endorse his
image of Jane as a vicious example, but, in itself, is deeply ironical in its
assertion that Jane has been sent to the school to 'be healed'. It is when Jane
is submitted to the most severe of tortures for a child so shrinking from notice,
forced to remain standing on a stool before the whole school, that she receives
a glimpse of the strength and comfort which can come from another human
being. Helen Burns, who makes an excuse to come near her and gives a smile
'of fine intellect, of true courage', a smile 'like a reflection from the aspect of
an angel' (p. 99), has already been noticed by Jane as an unusual, solemn child
who, despite the constant chidings and punishments she receives for her
daydreaming and untidiness, especially from the harsh mistress Miss
Scatchard, evinces a quiet stoicism beyond Jane's understanding: 'I could not
comprehend this doctrine of endurance; and still less could I understand or
sympathise with the forbearance she expressed for her chastiser' (p. 88).[11]
Her calm spirituality is alien to Jane's passionate nature which openly
questions the Christian precept of turning the other cheek and finding
comfort in loving one's enemies.[12] Helen's explanation of her feelings
inspires Jane's admiration for her fortitude and wonder at her eloquence, but
cannot overcome her scepticism and instinctive resistance to injustice. Yet
Helen Burns, too, as her name suggests, suffers from repressed resentment
which manifests itself in her inability to fulfil the school's basic requirements
of tidiness and order, and, of course, is symbolised by the sickness which,

already apparent in her hollow cough and pain in her chest, literally consumes her.

It is Helen who, with her friendship, affection and common sense, makes Jane's life bearable at Lowood, for it is clear that, like many literary female rebels, Jane desperately needs love and support to develop her own identity. The otherworldly goodness of Helen and her perpetual looking to eternity are consistent with portrayals of such angelic creatures in the religious tracts and novels but here the overt sentimentality is counterbalanced by Jane's fundamental inability to share her attitude. 'Helen had calmed me; but in the tranquility she imparted there was an alloy of inexpressible sadness' (p. 101) and the spectacle of her resignation gives Jane 'an intolerable pain at the heart' (p. 106).[13] Helen, it would seem, represents an ideal 'other' to whom Jane is attracted but whom she cannot ultimately ever emulate. Yet Jane does learn from Helen to control her rage such that when called upon by Miss Temple to defend herself against the charge of falsehood, her narrative, containing 'less gall and wormwood than ordinarily' becomes more convincing and credible, and leads to her exoneration before the school. The reader is thoroughly prepared for Helen's inevitable death by the description of the unhealthy site of the school, 'a cradle of fog and fog-bred pestilence' (p. 108), producing the typhus epidemic which affects a large number of the pupils, already weakened by semi-starvation and neglected coughs. The horrific and factual juxtaposition of images – the arrival of early summer with its sunny days contrasting with the gloom and fear inside and with its fragrant flowers whose only use is to decorate coffins – stems from Charlotte Brontë's own experience at Cowan Bridge of the death of her sisters Maria and Elizabeth.[14]

The description of the decline and death of Helen Burns from consumption thus contains the emotiveness of personal sorrow as well as the sense of impotent and baffled grief of the child's first experience of death. Unlike Helen, Jane imagines only 'an unfathomed gulf' of 'formless cloud and vacant depth' as her mind 'shuddered at the thought of tottering and plunging amid that chaos' (pp. 110–11). The dread she feels, mixed with determination, as she approaches Helen's bedside is well realised and Helen's death in Jane's arms as they lie asleep together, though externally a sentimental scene, is redeemed from becoming maudlin by the matter-of-fact tone of the narrative (Jane is carried back to her own bed and only discovers the truth a day or two later) and the traditional, pious dialogue of a death-bed scene is undermined by her questioning response to Helen's view of death as a welcome escape and to her certainty of the existence of heaven.[15]

The other female role model offered to Jane at Lowood is that of Miss Temple, a model of refinement and stately elegance, whose kindness and compassionate nature help to mitigate some of the hardships the pupils undergo. Although she remains coldly respectful in the face of

Mr Brocklehurst's criticisms and injunctions, her features ('especially her mouth, closed as if it would have required a sculptor's chisel to open it, and her brow settled gradually into petrified severity', p. 95) suggest that she too is full of suppressed rage and contempt. Her kind deeds take place in private, her subordinate position not permitting any more public defiance of authority. Her approval of Jane rests on present conduct and refuses the prejudices endorsed by Mr Brocklehurst. Though subject, too, to the deprivations of Lowood, she treats Jane and Helen, her favourite, to a feast of seedcake and conversation in her own parlour. Yet, although Jane both 'derived a child's pleasure' from her attractive physical presence and is soothed and encouraged to be herself by the serenity and gentleness of Miss Temple's manner, her model of coldly controlled, ever-courteous deference to evil is not one which Jane can readily assume, any more than is Helen's pious resignation.

Jane does, however, derive some positive benefits from her experiences at Lowood: not only does she gain an education which fits her to seek work as a governess, but she learns to curb her temper and become more self-possessed and confident. In the wake of the typhus epidemic, when an enquiry generates public indignation at conditions at Lowood, the school undergoes radical changes combining 'reason with strictness, comfort with economy, compassion with uprightness' (p. 115).[16] Jane remains a further eight years as pupil and teacher, with Miss Temple filling the role of mother, governess and companion, under whose calming influence Jane appears 'a disciplined and subdued character' (p. 116). When Miss Temple leaves to be married, Jane becomes conscious that she has undergone a rite of passage, but the transformation is in fact a reversion to her old self with the stirrings of her old feelings. Jane's adolescence seems to end at this moment, a transition marked by the symbolic throwing open wide of her window and the longing for new horizons and new experiences, even though her awareness of the limitations of her prospects forces her to express her yearning for liberty and stimulus as the desire for 'a new servitude'.

Thus Brontë establishes in the portrayal of Jane's childhood the seminal images and themes of the novel as a whole: slavery, the anomalous position of the orphan/governess in other people's homes, the longing for love, the arousing of anger and passion and the failure of social forces to contain them, just as the attic at Thornfield cannot contain the fury of Bertha Mason Rochester. These are communicated all the more effectively by immersing the reader in the child's perspective on her experience which is controlled and interpreted by the adult narrator. The novel goes on to chart Jane's struggle to escape from the imprisoning servitude of her childhood to an eventual self-determined identity and existence.

Jane Eyre is clearly only partly autobiographical, for Charlotte Brontë was not fully orphaned and had a close relationship in childhood with her brother and sisters. Winifred Gérin speaks of the 'emotional powerhouse' of this period, however, attributing this in part to their reading of Romantic literature which was then at its height.[17] Charlotte Brontë herself refers to childhood as the 'Burning Clime' and the children's early writings are much preoccupied with love and passion.[18] Elizabeth Gaskell remarks also on the influence of the isolated surroundings in which the Brontës were brought up on Charlotte's imagination, for 'children leading a secluded life are often thoughtful and dreamy' and wont to transform their experiences of nature and people into 'things so deeply significant as to be almost supernatural'.[19] Jane's mental and physical sufferings at Lowood are certainly those of Charlotte Brontë at Cowan Bridge, however, a fact so evident that a controversy about the portrayal of the school was generated in the pages of the *Halifax Guardian* between June and August 1857. The school had apparently changed after the Brontës' time there and, indeed, a vindication of William Carus Wilson and his establishment appears in *Thorneycroft Hall* (1864), a novel by Emma Jane Warboise who later attended the school. It is true that Charlotte Brontë's portrayal of Lowood is based on her memory of experiences undergone as a young child, but this does not invalidate her indictment of the conditions and methods inflicted on the small pupils.[20] Indeed, her use of the adult narrator's voice corroborates the misery the child feels and makes the cruelty of such inhumanely applied Evangelicalism all the more striking. Jane's later experiences as a governess are also informed by Brontë's own experience, so that the novel can be seen as a cathartic working-through of all the author's experience of life up to the point of writing, allied, perhaps, to a degree of wish-fulfilment in the happy ending as Jane finds love and happiness as the wife of the maimed Mr Rochester.[21]

The same themes of rebellion, passion and rage, though very differently directed, are at the heart of Emily Brontë's *Wuthering Heights*, and are also mediated through child figures, though not through a child's eyes, since the 'story' is narrated at two removes from the actual events, via Nelly Dean and Mr Lockwood. Indeed, the central figures as children never appear in the present of the text, and only Heathcliff, in fact, is still living at the time that Lockwood, our narrator, learns of the events at the Heights and Thrushcross Grange. Although the reader is given a vivid picture of Catherine and Hindley Earnshaw and Heathcliff as children and young adults, we are never allowed direct access to their thoughts, for their actions and motives are presented and interpreted by Nelly, who has been both participant and witness in the complex web of relationships. Nevertheless, the portrayal of the childhood years not only present, on a naturalistic level, a vivid account of the effects of upbringing and environment on character, but also establish the fundamental characteristics and relationships which underlie and activate subsequent events. In many respects, these events duplicate childhood patterns, as the relationships and emotions of childhood remain fundamentally unchanged.

At the heart of the picture of the upbringing of the Earnshaw and Linton

children in the two radically different milieus of the Heights and the Grange
is a complex pattern of contrasts, between the primitive, emotional, violent
and neglectful and the refined, restrained and cherished.[22] Yet this is no
simple opposition of lifestyles, for the civilised restraint of the Grange is seen,
when it affects Catherine, who is essentially a child of the moors like Emily
Brontë herself, to result in repression and the perversion of natural vitality
leading to misery and, eventually, death, while, despite the chill gloom of the
Heights, the wildness of the moors for Catherine is at least synonymous with
freedom and passion.[23] The remoteness of the setting from the outside world
means that the themes and motifs noted in *Jane Eyre* are here transposed to
a milieu largely free from general and widely accepted social constraints.
Moreover, the orphaning of the children means that they remain largely
undirected and unrestrained in their language and behaviour by parental
authority and guidance.

Our first glimpse of the Earnshaw children comes through Catherine's
diary, perused by the exhausted and agitated Lockwood who has been forced
reluctantly to spend the night at Wuthering Heights. The first words he reads
clearly intimate future events, for they concern rebellion and link the child
Catherine with Heathcliff in alliance against her older brother, Hindley: '"An
awful Sunday!" commenced the paragraph beneath. "I wish my father were
back again. Hindley is a detestable substitute – his conduct to Heathcliff is
atrocious – Heathcliff and I are going to rebel – we took our initiatory step
this evening"'.[24] Their revolt against the harsh discipline imposed by Hindley
and religion personified in old Joseph, the frenetically Calvinist servant, as
they attempt first to retreat into a secret place to play after a lengthy sermon
and subsequently hurl their 'good books' across the room, results in a
separation of the two children which sends the diary writer into paroxysms of
weeping.[25] This episode, which was recorded some twenty-four years
previously, not only clearly foreshadows later events but demonstrates the
power of Catherine both over Lockwood's imagination, manifested in his vivid
'dream' of the waif at the window, and over Heathcliff who responds violently
to Lockwood's account of the dream.[26]

The tale recounted by Nelly, who grew up with the Earnshaw children at
the Heights as a servant, begins, since its purpose is to explain to Mr
Lockwood the history of his grim neighbour, with the discord caused by the
arrival of the child Heathcliff at Wuthering Heights. Old Mr Earnshaw, on
returning from a visit to Liverpool, produces from under his greatcoat a 'dirty,
ragged, black-haired child' found wandering, starving and homeless, in the
streets, introducing him to his dumbstruck family as '"a gift of God; though
it's as dark almost as if it came from the devil"' (p. 45). The motif of the
orphaned and rejected child, introduced here to emphasise the mystery
attached to Heathcliff's origins and to alert pity, is to become a seminal theme
throughout the novel.[27] The victim's start is hardly auspicious, as Nelly's

repeated references to him as 'it' suggest: he speaks only 'gibberish', Mrs Earnshaw is reluctant to take in the 'the gypsy brat', and the children are alienated by his intrusion and the consequent damage or loss of their promised presents. Catherine's spirit, temper and unfeminine ways are already apparent at the age of 6 in her choice of a riding-whip (her brother Hindley, aged 14, requests a fiddle) and her spontaneous response of spitting at the interloper. The consequences of Mr Earnshaw's altruistic action are far-reaching for, by giving the urchin the name (Heathcliff) of a son who died in childhood, increasingly favouring him above both Hindley and Catherine and protecting him from the persecution of the former, he gradually changes Heathcliff's anomalous position into one of power. Thus Nelly tells us '"from the very beginning, he bred bad feeling in the house"' (p. 46). The myth of the changeling of folklore who brings bad luck continues to be associated with Heathcliff – even at the end, Nelly wonders whether he is really a devil.

However, while Hindley regards him as 'a usurper of his parents' affections and his privileges' (p. 46), a view which embitters and warps his character, Catherine quickly becomes Heathcliff's ally and friend. Even Nelly's initial hatred is softened by the patient and uncomplaining nature of Heathcliff, although she is aware that this springs from sullenness and hardness, not gentleness. Mr Earnshaw's partiality remains inexplicable to Nelly, although she perceives anxiously the apparent insensibility to gratitude of Heathcliff and his growing awareness of his power: '"conscious he had only to speak and all the house would be obliged to bend to his wishes"' (p. 47) (a state of affairs which may explain his rage at his failure, later, to get his own way).[28] It is significant, however, that the ill-treatment and injustices Heathcliff undergoes are the result of a situation not of his own making, and the relatively passive child is quite unlike the vengeful figure of later. Nelly's explication of Heathcliff's pride and 'black tempers' is juxtaposed with examples of Hindley's viciousness as Mr Earnshaw's defence of his favourite becomes more violent with the degenerating temper of his last days until the conflict between the two results in Hindley being sent away to college and Heathcliff and Catherine are thrown more exclusively into each other's company.

The depiction of Catherine at this stage is interesting, for the characteristics attributed to her as a child – her liveliness, strong emotions, capacity for mischief and her capricious tormenting energy (Nelly describes her as a '"wild, wicked slip"' who '"liked exceedingly to act the little mistress"' but is quick to weep with those she upsets) – are to persist in adulthood. Catherine's friendship with Heathcliff is founded on the intense, asexual exclusivity of childhood ('"The greatest punishment we could invent for her was to keep her separate from him"' p. 49) and quickly becomes an instrument for baiting her father, '"showing how her pretended insolence, which he thought real, had more power over Heathcliff than his kindness: how the boy would do her bidding in anything, and *his* only when it suited his own inclination"' (p. 49). This loyalty and closeness to the point of identification with Heathcliff, in that an injury done to him makes her suffer too, even when that injury is inflicted by herself, and her easy assumption of power over Heathcliff's will, are fundamental to their relationship and continue to inform Catherine's behaviour throughout the novel.[29] His presence and her love for him make her increasingly rebellious against her father's authority, hardened to his irritated rejection of her and scornful of the notion of repentance, behaviour patterns which she endeavours to repeat in her adult life but which doom her to frustration and despair in the social context of her marriage to Edgar Linton.[30] Just as the removal of her brother from the scene allows her to achieve domination over the household, however, the death of old Mr Earnshaw, which brings Hindley and his young bride back to Wuthering Heights, thus restoring the patriarchal hold of the rightful heir, changes the balance of power once more.

Catherine and Heathcliff are alienated by Hindley's preoccupation with his wife, Frances, while his old hatred prompts him to tyrannise Heathcliff, striving to degrade and marginalise him by depriving him of his education and his status as a member of the family. The theme of dispossessed orphan is now extended to Catherine, for Hindley and Frances (not the wicked stepmother of fairy-tale but more like a child herself) are quite inadequate as surrogate parents, such that her isolation is mitigated only by her friendship with Heathcliff. Indeed, her plight now mirrors his, for both are subject to Hindley's fits of temper and Joseph's curses and left to their own devices, as '"unfriended creatures"' both of whom soon '"promised fair to grow up as rude savages"' (p. 52). Their close bonding thus directly results from the physical and psychological abuse and emotional deprivation they experience, their only joy to '"run away to the moors in the morning and remain there all day"' (p. 52), for they are frequently banished from the living-rooms and thus exiled from the family circle. Brontë thus establishes sympathy for her protagonists, for the seeds of their passion are sown in the innocence of oppressed childhood, just as their childish energy and vitality attract the reader, appealing perhaps to a nostalgia for childhood too soon overlaid by adult socialised restraints. It is important to note that, though developed through close proximity and mutual anguish and lived close to nature, their relationship remains an entirely innocent one sexually – although Catherine's disgust at the kissing and love-talk of Hindley and Frances suggests a dawning glimmer of sexual awareness – for her later miseries ensue from her failed attempt to continue this relationship, cemented in childhood, into an adult world where sexuality and gendered behaviour inevitably enter into male/female relationships.

It is through escaping from the uncongenial atmosphere at the Heights that Catherine and Heathcliff make their first ill-fated visit to Thrushcross Grange, fired by the curiosity to see whether the Linton children 'passed their

Sunday evenings standing shivering in corners, while their father and mother sat eating and drinking, and singing and laughing' (p. 53). What they see as they peep through the windows of the Grange is indeed a contrast to their own lives for, despite the splendid gold and crimson interior shimmering with warmth and light which prompts their envy, the Linton children, Edgar and Isabella, are squabbling over a dog, shrieking and weeping in separate corners of the room in a manner quite alien to Catherine and Heathcliff. Ironically, it is Heathcliff who reports this incident to Nelly, voicing his scorn ('"When would you catch me wishing to have what Catherine wanted? or find us by ourselves, seeking entertainment in yelling and sobbing, and rolling on the ground, divided by the whole room?"', p. 54), for the accident which befalls Catherine, who is chased and injured by a dog and kept at the Grange, is the beginning of the division between them. The different treatment meted out by the Lintons to the two children from the Heights begins the process of their social awareness, for Catherine, as a neighbour's daughter, is pampered as a 'young lady' while Heathcliff, initially viewed as a gypsy and potential thief, is dismissed as a 'wicked boy, at all events' because of his obscure origins, clothes and language.[31] His response is symptomatic of his growing tendency to live up to the expectations of those he despises, for their approbrium makes him curse all the more vociferously.

Catherine's first experience of life at the Grange acts as a painful initiation into a phase of her life which separates her from her past and from her childhood companion. It is significant that she is cosseted as an invalid for she is indeed crippled by the genteel and civilised young-ladyhood the Lintons inflict upon her.[32] Although she responds readily to the fine clothes and admiration which form part of Mrs Linton's plan of reform, it is clear that her vitality ebbs as she becomes more elegant and gracious. Her return after five weeks underlines the change in terms which, with their implications of artifice and restriction, suggest that despite the approval of the Earnshaws, her transformation into a stereotypical beauty is one of loss rather than gain:

> 'instead of a wild hatless savage jumping into the house, and rushing to squeeze us all breathless, there lighted from a handsome black pony a very dignified person, with brown ringlets falling from the cover of a feathered beaver, and a long cloth habit, which she was obliged to hold up with both hands that she might sail in.' (p. 57)

The emotional tension apparent in her spontaneous greeting of Heathcliff and her rueful laughter at the effect of his dirtiness on her dress illustrate the extent to which her acquired femininity is indeed a barrier between them. Yet her subsequent unease whenever her friendship with the Lintons is confronted with her loyalty to Heathcliff demonstrates that, although she enjoys her new life, she regrets the passionate freedom of self implicit in her childhood on the moors and embodied in the untamed and uncultivated presence of Heathcliff.

At 15 Catherine, '"the queen of the countryside"', haughty, headstrong and full of ambition, is said by Nelly to have adopted '"a double character without exactly intending to deceive anyone"' (p. 68). Though repressing her instincts in polite company, she is contemptuous of Edgar for his weakness when Heathcliff throws hot apple sauce in his face at the Heights and 'in purgatory' when Heathcliff is locked in a garret and starved. Her confused feelings erupt in outbursts of temper and regret: her protestation that '"I did nothing deliberately"' (p. 73) after the quarrel with Nelly during which she hits Edgar and, ironically, moves their relationship onto a more intimate footing, is symptomatic of Catherine's wilful behaviour throughout. Nelly calls Catherine '"a marred child"' here, and in some respects she never transcends the volatility and egotism of childhood, as her later repeated blaming of others, uncontrolled weeping, petulance and verbal violence, all characteristic of childish tantrums, demonstrate. Her initiation as a 'young lady' thus fragments her personality, as reflected in the different names Lockwood sees written on the window-sill.

Once Catherine has made the choice of marrying Edgar Linton and is separated from Heathcliff both physically and by social propriety, her torment results from her awareness that she cannot reach him and, by implication, her lost childhood state again. It is not just the loss of Heathcliff but the loss of selfhood embodied in their shared past which eventually drives her to her death. Such an outcome is, in fact, intimated in Catherine's well-known speech to Nelly, in which her youthful naivety and wilful blindness prevent her from comprehending that marriage to Edgar, a commitment to the adult world and standards of behaviour, is incompatible with a continuation of her childhood union with Heathcliff.[33] Although her new socialised self acknowledges that '"it would degrade me to marry Heathcliff now"' (p. 81), her instincts endorse a relationship which derives from a more profound and deeply entrenched affinity than her feelings for Edgar which are based on her emerging sexuality and the attraction of his social position and wealth. Her uncontrollable grief at Heathcliff's disappearance and the fever she contracts watching for him with childlike stubbornness in the storm foreshadow her later illness when a more irrevocable separation is brought about by her own actions.

Indeed, her realisation, after her marriage, that the two relationships cannot coexist, just as our childhood selves are inevitably eclipsed by the socialised codes of adulthood, quite literally drives her 'out of herself', such that she sees herself as an outcast and exile. Her dream of being in heaven and offending the angels by weeping, such that they fling her out onto the heath where she wakes sobbing for joy, confirms her sense of irretrievable loss. Her breakdown is signalled by a reversion to childhood scenes and a yearning to repair the damage inflicted by adulthood: '"I wish I were a girl again, half savage and hardy, and free; and laughing at injuries, not maddening under them! Why am I so changed?"' (p. 116). The language of both Catherine and Heathcliff in their last interview before her death is charged with the raw emotion of the frustrated and angry child. The waif at the window in Lockwood's 'dream' can thus be seen as the spirit of the child Catherine, wandering the scenes of her childhood in search of her lost home, although the name by which she calls herself is that of the married Catherine Linton, Heathcliff's reaction revealing, moreover, that it is the Catherine of childhood with whom he seeks to be reunited.[34]

The first visit to the Grange is a catalyst in Heathcliff's fortunes too, for, when his shame at the contrast between his appearance on her return to the Heights causes him to seek Nelly's help in making him presentable, it is clear that his desire to resemble Edgar is an acknowledgement of his essential and unalterable difference from the socially acceptable. 'Being good' is clearly associated with '"make me decent"' (p. 59). Like many young literary females, Heathcliff mourns his failure to match up to the conventional stereotype of fair good looks which traditionally promise romantic and social success. Indeed, Nelly invokes the clichés of romance to encourage the boy, turning the mystery of his origins in his favour ('"Who knows but your father was an Emperor of China, and your mother an Indian queen . . ."', p. 61). Despite his attempts to socialise himself, the violent rejection he receives from Hindley, whose behaviour also resembles that of a recalcitrant child, only ferments his bitterness such that as Catherine's emerging womanhood blossoms in adolescence, so Heathcliff declines:

> 'His treatment of the latter [Heathcliff] was enough to make a fiend of a saint. And, truly, it appeared as if the lad *were* possessed of something diabolical at that period. He delighted to witness Hindley degrading himself past redemption; and became daily more notable for savage sullenness and ferocity.' (p. 67)

At 16, Heathcliff allows himself to sink to a brutish level and appears to take pleasure in exciting aversion. His relationship with Catherine changes too, for, having sensed and internalised her ambivalence towards him, he now recoils suspiciously from her caresses, and it is shortly after this that he leaves Wuthering Heights. Thus his childhood experience of cruelty and injustice, with the little power and self-esteem he once had now stripped away by Hindley, is compounded by rejection by his sole support and love, leading to a naked and extravagant desire for revenge, in itself characteristic of a thwarted child but highly destructive in the empowering adult world. It is significant that, as a man, Heathcliff uses the next generation of children, Cathy Linton, Linton Heathcliff and Hareton Earnshaw, as an instrument of that revenge.

Through these children, Emily Brontë also explores the way in which the characteristics of parents are reproduced, blended and modified in their offspring. Catherine's death follows closely upon the premature birth of her child who, as a puny infant neglected by her distraught father, has an unpropitious start to life.[35] Though named after her mother and having her dark eyes, the fair skin and yellow curls which are her Linton inheritance suggest a more conventional femininity. Nevertheless, although the fierce emotions of her mother are tempered in her character, she too has a 'perverse will'. A child of civilisation, Cathy seems perfectly contented in her protected, reclusive life which is bounded by the walls of the park such that she has no knowledge of Wuthering Heights or the world outside. Yet the desire she expresses as an adolescent to visit the sunlit tops of Peniston Crag, a desire associated with the attainment of womanhood ('"Then I can go, too, when I am a woman"', p. 166), gradually becomes an obsession forging a link with her mother's past. Her father's refusal to allow the journey, which would take her past the Heights, can thus be seen as an attempt to arrest the process of maturation which might expose his child to the same dissatisfaction and longing for freedom as her mother, and inevitably bring about her loss to himself. Her obedience and dutifulness as a child also create a trusting complacency in Nelly Dean which is frustrated by Cathy's wilful escape, at 13, from the park during her father's absence. Nelly's horrified exclamation, '"What will become of her?"' (p. 167), evokes not only an immediate physical danger but the unknown female world beyond puberty. Significantly, it is Cathy's first act of disobedience which brings her to Wuthering Heights where she is discovered by the distraught Nelly 'perfectly at home' in her mother's old chair by the hearth. That at heart she remains a socialised child of strictly limited naughtiness is apparent in her sulky tears at Nelly's reproaches and her casual assumption of superiority to Hareton, whom she mistakes for a servant. The frank reproofs of Hareton and the servant at her arrogance, so different from the indulgent petting she is used to at the Grange, cause her energetic wilfulness to collapse, her distress compounded by the shock of the revelation that the uncouth Hareton is her cousin, a fact carefully concealed by her father.

Cathy's first meeting with Hareton on the moors is, in fact, a propitious one, until she alienates him by her manner, for he reveals to her 'the mysteries of the Fairy Grove, and twenty other queer places' (p. 172). It is tempting to see this as an intimation of sexual awakening, but it is also the introduction, significantly by an Earnshaw, of the child of culture to the world of nature which inspired her mother's soul. Their union at the end of the novel, when Cathy has taught Hareton to read, thus helping him to shake off 'the clouds of ignorance and degradation' (p. 267) and assume his birthright, is seen as a restoration of order, a fulfilment of the frustrated union between Catherine and Heathcliff.

The next child in this complex web of relationships is Linton, the child of Isabella and Heathcliff, a pale, weak, effeminate boy who appears to take almost entirely after his mother's family. Unlike the ethereal delicacy of the idealised child invalid, his sickly peevishness derives from the self-pity of the orphan cosseted by an unhappy and embittered mother, and soon turns to the vicious spite of the powerless when he falls into the clutches of his vengeful father, a suggestion perhaps that he has in fact inherited the worst characteristics of both parents. The reader is drawn initially to pity Linton, especially when, in response to his father's incontestable rights, he is reluctantly delivered to the Heights, an act which seems like a betrayal, albeit undeliberate, of his innocence. Linton's dread and bewilderment at Heathcliff's derision is touchingly portrayed and foreshadows the psychological abuse which he is to suffer as a tool in his father's task of destruction and revenge: '"That is the sole consideration which can make me endure the whelp: I despise him for himself, and hate him for the memories he revives"' (p. 180). When Linton and Cathy meet again, aged 16, the contrast between the languid, passive youth and the active, blooming young woman could not be more marked but their renewed relationship threatens, ironically, to fulfil Heathcliff's plan to marry the cousins and thus gain control of both properties. The manipulativeness of Heathcliff and the protectiveness of Edgar Linton are thus both, in their different ways, attempts to control their children's lives on the basis of their own old grudges, rendering deeply ironical Cathy's declaration that '"Linton and I have no share in your quarrel"' (p. 186).

When Cathy is lured to Wuthering Heights because Linton is allegedly dying of love for her, the latter's true inheritance is seen in the physical and moral decline which manifests itself in his childishly unrestrained behaviour, the 'mere peevishness of an indulged plague of a child, determined to be as grievous and harrassing as it can' (p. 205). Cathy's desire to nurture Linton and her awareness of her power over him is a perverse reflection of her mother's power over his father. It is, furthermore, the egotistical wilfulness inherited from Catherine and the same attraction to a male who is the opposite to herself in every way, which draw Cathy every night, in secret, to the Heights and lead to her eventual incarceration there by Heathcliff. His treatment of his son at this stage is indeed 'diabolical' as he manipulates him by violence to entice Cathy away from her home to their gloomy meetings on the moors. Nelly Dean voices the shock that contemporary readers, accustomed to the literary convention of romanticised sick-bed behaviour, must have experienced: '"I could not picture a father treating a dying child as tyrannically and wickedly as I afterwards learned Heathcliff had treated him, to compel this apparent eagerness . . ."' (p. 219). Though speaking of 'my children', Heathcliff brings about their marriage by force not to secure the family, but to destroy it. This is reflected in the two halves of the locket containing the portraits of her parents which Cathy breaks apart, for by this unhappy union Heathcliff succeeds in rending, symbolically, that of his beloved Catherine and his rival Edgar Linton.

It is through Hareton, the son of Hindley and Frances, that Heathcliff's plans are finally thwarted. As a child, Hareton is cowed by the drunken, erratic violence of his father and neglected and despised, with Nelly as his only champion. Having saved the child's life when Hindley drops him from the top of the stairs, Heathcliff's grudging regard for Hareton seems to stem from his awareness that, in some ways. the boy is a reflection of himself, unwanted and dispossessed. His determination to keep him a brute, depriving him of education and moral instruction, can thus be seen as complex in motivation – as a desire for revenge on the Earnshaws, and, perhaps, on his earlier self who failed to keep Catherine's love, or, a more positive aim, as an attempt to create the child of nature he feels his own son should have been. Heathcliff admits to Nelly, when he is struck by the similar eyes of Hareton and Cathy, that Hareton '"seemed a personification of my youth, not a human being"', a constant reminder of '"the ghost of my immortal love, of my wild endeavours to hold my right; my degradation, my pride, my happiness, and my anguish"' (p. 268). His growing agitation at Hareton's relationship with Cathy suggests his awareness that the youth's future will be different from his own adulthood. Paradoxically, Hareton remains fond of Heathcliff and defends him despite all he has done. As a youth, Hareton is characterised as 'good things lost amid a wilderness of weeds . . . yet notwithstanding, evidence of a wealthy soul, that might yield luxuriant crops under other and favourable circumstances' (p. 171), a clear indication of his potential for warmth and intelligence which the love and pity of Cathy cause to emerge. The prospect of their union, humanised and civilised but lived in harmony with nature, is enhanced by Nelly's description of them, bent over a book together, '"animated with the eager intent of children; for though he was twenty-eight and she eighteen, each had so much novelty to feel and learn, that neither experienced or evinced the sentiments of sober disenchanted maturity"' (p. 267). Their childish qualities are seen, this time, to portend a vital, positive good.

Thus it can be argued that the portrayal of childhood reaches its most far-reaching and significant level in *Wuthering Heights*, for it functions on both a naturalistic *and* a symbolic level. The vitality of Catherine and Heathcliff creates an empathy in the reader which makes it difficult for their later behaviour to be judged impartially. Moreover, the development of the children is seen to be determined by environmental and social factors, thus repudiating the idea of innate characteristics. The implications of this portrayal of childhood can be seen to have not only literal, human significance but also a cosmic, divine one, reflecting Emily Brontë's visionary response to the dilemmas of human existence and the individual's relationship to the universe and to God. Her Gondal poems confirm her Romantic view of childhood as a time associated with beauty, freedom and energy when the soul is still not totally divorced from its first home in heaven, but also one of vulnerability and impending pain, for the process of growing to adulthood carries with it the dissipation of joy and liberty, the loss of innocence and goodness and an imprisoning of the soul:[36]

> Sleep not, dream not; this bright day
> Will not, cannot last for aye;
> Bliss like thine is bought by years
> Dark with torment and with tears
>
> I love thee, boy; for all divine,
> All full of God thy features shine
> Darling enthusiast, holy child,
> Too good for this world's warring wild,
> Too heavenly now but doomed to be
> Hell-like in heart and misery
>
> And what shall change that angel brow
> And quench that spirit's glorious glow?
> Relentless laws that disallow
> True virtue and true joy below.[37]

Adulthood is, indeed, seen in terms of an evil overshadowing the innocent child, more forcefully and threateningly than Wordsworth's 'shades of the prison house'.[38] The following extract from a poem written in July 1837, which expresses this horror, also intriguingly foreshadows *Wuthering Heights* in many of its images.

> I saw thee, child, one summer's day
> Suddenly leave thy cheerful play,
> And in the green grass, lowly lying,
> I listened to thy mournful sighing.
> . . .
> The anxious prayer was heard, and power
> Was given me, in that silent hour,
> To open to an infant's eye
> The portals of futurity.
> . . .
> He hears me: what a sudden start
> Sent the blood icy to that heart;
> He wakens, and how ghastly white
> That face looks in the dim lamplight.
>
> Those tiny hands in vain essay
> To thrust the shadowy fiend away;
> There is a horror on his brow,
> An anguish in his bosom now;
> . . .
> Poor child, if spirits such as I
> Could weep o'er human misery,
> A tear might flow, aye, many a tear,

To see the road that lies before,
To see the sunshine disappear,
And hear the stormy waters roar,
Breaking upon a desolate shore,
Cut off from hope in early day,
From power and glory cut away.

But it is doomed, and morning's light
Must image forth the scowl of night,
And childhood's flower must waste its bloom
Beneath the shadow of the tomb.[39]

The Gondal poems illustrate the effects of this calamitous process, as the 'melancholy boy' becomes the 'iron man' whose 'stormy breast' contains no remorse which might 'half unchain his soul from hell'.[40] As in *Wuthering Heights*, the affinity with nature is seen as an essential part of the 'paradise' of childhood, its glory echoing that of heaven:

The soft unclouded blue of air,
The earth as golden green and fair
And bright as Eden's used to be:
That air and earth have rested me

Laid on the grass I lapsed away,
Sank back again to childhood's day;
All harsh thoughts perished, memory mild
Subdued both grief and passion wild.[41]

The 'iron man's' degree of alienation from innocence and goodness is measured by the fact that, once responsive to nature, he is now cold, distant and unmoved:

Though storms untold his mind have tossed,
He cannot utterly have lost
Rememberance of his early home –
So lost that not a gleam may come; . . .
. . .
Unmarked, I gazed; my idle thought
Passed with the ray whose shine it caught;
One glance revealed how little care
He felt for all the beauty there . . .[42]

Love would seem to be the only means of redemption for the imprisoned soul – significantly, *human* love, not divine love of the traditional sort, and a love which, as the poem above suggests and *Wuthering Heights* confirms, is inseparable from a communion with nature.[43]

Thus it is possible to see the dispossessed orphan children of *Wuthering Heights* as human souls cast out into the world by God and the anguish caused by the separation of Heathcliff and Catherine as a paradigm of the increasing despair of the soul at separation from heaven.[44] The desire to return to childhood implicit in Catherine's dreams can be seen to re-enact the desire of the soul to get back to its primal state. However, the characters of *Wuthering Heights* rage against their Creator, like disobedient children against a stern father, and yearn for union with each other and with nature rather than for union with God, a preference which encapsulates Emily Brontë's own rejection of conventional religious views and her visionary religion of nature, inextricably bound up with childhood and passion. Thus, the report of the child at the end of *Wuthering Heights* that he has seen the ghosts of 'Heathcliff and a woman' up on the moors suggests a reunion of their souls in eternity just as their bodies are, in accordance with Heathcliff's order, to be reunited and merged in the grave.[45]

While the novels of the Brontës are concerned with the plight of the orphan, conflicts experienced by the protagonist of *The Mill on the Floss* (1860) derive largely from the emotional pressures of a close-knit family. George Eliot's novel explores in painful detail the problems of 'growing up female' and finding fulfilment in a society which has very firm and traditional views on the role of a woman. As in *Middlemarch* (1872), she depicts a young female who is 'different' from the social norm in her longing for a fulfilling and independent existence but who is trapped in an environment which offers 'no coherent social faith and order' to encourage and guide the 'ardently willing soul'.[46] The depiction of Maggie Tulliver's childhood and adolescence was criticised as over-long and self-indulgent (indeed George Eliot confessed that she was 'beguiled' by the childhood sequences) but it is in fact fundamental to the central theme of repressed intelligence and potential, for in her upbringing and family relationships lie the formative elements of Maggie's personality and the origins of the inner conflict which exacerbates her struggle against the narrow-mindedness and incomprehension of her environment.[47]

Most commentators on George Eliot's work accept that there is a significant autobiographical element in *The Mill on the Floss*, as in *Middlemarch*, although the fate of the protagonists of both novels in no way parallels that of their author.[48] This points to an important element in female-authored novelistic lives, namely that such narratives tend to depict failure rather than success, and thus reveal not so much the authors' own experience as their awareness of themselves as exceptions and their desire to portray the greater generality of women's experience.[49] In discussions of *The Mill on the Floss*, however, special emphasis is usually laid on George Eliot's relationship with her brother Isaac with whom she shared a loving childhood, but from whom she became estranged when he could not accept, first, her rejection of the family religion and then her position as common-law wife of George Henry Lewes.[50] It is indeed possible, though not, in terms of appreciating the text, essential, to conclude that the trauma of separation and the longing for reconciliation had a significant influence on her portrayal of the childhood of the Tulliver children and Maggie's conflict and fate which are closely bound up with her feelings for her brother Tom.[51] Moreover, Eliot's original title for the novel was to be 'Sister Maggie', thus focusing attention on the sibling relationship, and the joy and pain of their shared childhood experiences are so exquisitely evoked as to suggest an intimate personal involvement with her subject.[52] Precisely the same sentiments are evoked in a poem of 1869, (published 1874) entitled 'Brother and sister' (a relationship she describes as 'always one of my best loved subjects') which portrays, in an overtly sentimental manner, the memory of a young female child's loving dependence on and respectful adoration of an older brother, and mirrors in many respects the essence of Maggie Tulliver's feelings for Tom:[53]

> I cannot choose but think upon the time
> When our two lives grew like two buds that kiss
> At lightest thrill from the bee's swinging chime
> Because the one so near the other is.
>
> He was the elder and a little man
> Of forty inches, bound to show no dread,
> And I the girl that puppy-like now ran,
> Now lagged behind my brother's larger tread.
>
> I held him wise, and when he talked to me
> Of snakes and birds, and which God loved the best,
> I thought his knowledge marked the boundary
> Where men grew blind, though angels knew the rest.
>
> If he said 'Hush!' I tried to hold my breath
> Whenever he said 'Come!' I stepped in faith . . .[54]

The speaker acknowledges the significant impact of that closeness on her later life ('Those hours were seed to all my good . . .', verse 5), of the lessons learned in shared activities in which she is both taught and protected by her brother, and of their mutual delight in nature and each other's company. Her idealisation of this childhood relationship, recreated in memory, is contrasted fleetingly in the closing lines with the awareness of its transitory nature and her present regret, although all the pain of loss cannot obliterate the enduring value of the past:

> Till the dire years whose awful name is Change
> Had grasped our souls still yearning in divorce,
> And pitiless shaped them in two forms that range
> Two elements which sever their life's course.
>
> But were another childhood-world my share,
> I would be born a little sister there.[55]

Maggie Tulliver's role as 'little sister' is underlined at the start of the novel in a scene which not only establishes her 'difference', but is full of omens of future conflict. As her parents discuss plans for Tom's future schooling, Mr Tulliver's opinion that it is 'a pity' that his daughter should be the brighter child ('"Too cute for a woman, I'm afraid"') encapsulates the view of his society that intelligence is not only a waste but may be a positive disadvantage in terms of a female's future prospects: '"It's no mischief much while she's a little un, but an over-'cute woman's no better nor a long tailed sheep: she'll fetch none the bigger price for that"' (pp. 59–60). While Mr Tulliver's attitude towards Maggie is a mixture of pride at her cleverness and anxiety ('"a woman's no business wi' being so clever, it'll turn to trouble, I doubt"', p. 66), his wife's view is revealing for its clear association of 'goodness' with conformity: '"Yes, it *is* a mischief while she's a little un, Mr. Tulliver, for it all runs into naughtiness. How to keep her in a clean pinafore two hours together passes my cunning"' (p. 60).[56] Mrs Tulliver's description of Maggie reveals that the source of her discontent with her daughter is that physically she does not conform to the ideal of a neat, demure young female, a failing which Mrs Tulliver feels most acutely as a reflection upon herself. The pejorative vocabulary she applies so abundantly to Maggie emphasises the extent of this 'crime' in the eyes of Mrs Tulliver, for whom social decorum, domestic trivia and conventional, respectable appearances are obsessions:

> 'I'm sure the child's half an idiot i' some things, for if I send her upstairs to fetch anything, she forgets what she's gone for, an' perhaps 'ull sit down on the floor i' the sunshine and plait her hair an' sing to herself like a Bedlam creatur' . . .' (p. 60)

Mr Tulliver's defence of his child ('"she's a straight, black-eyed wench as anybody need wish to see"') is met by the objection that 'her hair won't curl' (p. 60). The irony that Maggie's 'wrongness' is inherent even in her physical make-up (her thick, heavy hair and dark, gypsyish skin suggesting a changeling), and hence something over which she has no control, is under-lined by Eliot's description of her as 'this small mistake of nature' when she enters the room, and the injustice of this view is apparent in the explicit contrast of the attractive naturalness of Maggie, whose incessant tossing of her head to keep her unruly mane of hair out of her eyes is reminiscent of a small Shetland pony, with the artifice of her admired cousin Lucy with her '"row o' curls round her head, an' not a hair out o'place"' (pp. 60–1). Moreover, the very fault for which Mrs Tulliver blames her daughter here is revealed to be the result of an inappropriate attempt to impose the same artifice on Maggie, for Mrs Tulliver, 'desiring her daughter to have a curled crop, "like other folks' children"', had had it cut too short in front to be pushed behind the ears' (p. 61). Indeed, Mrs Tulliver's shallow values and deficiencies as a role model and source of support for her daughter are made clear by Eliot in the devastating description of her as 'from the cradle upwards . . . healthy, fair, plump and dull-witted – in short, the flower of her family for beauty and amiability' (p. 62).

Maggie's eagerness to show off her quick intelligence is apparent in the scene where she explains to her father's visitor a picture of a witch-ducking, a powerful image of female 'difference' and its fate which foreshadows Maggie's own. This episode also echoes an amusing anecdote allegedly told by George Eliot about herself. The young Mary Ann Evans, who was 'very early possessed with the idea that she was going to be a personage in the world', insisted at the age of 4 on playing the piano, without knowing a single note, to impress the servants 'with a proper notion of her acquirements, and generally distinguished position'.[57] Maggie's energy and enquiring nature, which make her the noisy, clumsy antithesis of pretty, quiet, obedient Lucy, further illustrate her difference from the desired stereotype of budding femininity. Her first words in the novel, a vehement rejection of her mother's admonition that she should tidy herself and get on with her patchwork, reveal moreover an intuitive awareness of the inadequacy of such traditional sedentary female activities. '"It's foolish work", said Maggie, with a toss of her mane – "tearing things to pieces to sew 'em together again. And I don't want to do anything for my aunt Glegg, I don't like her"' (p. 61). That such wilful deviation from the 'right' path of socially sanctioned role behaviour patterns is indeed, in this environment, likely to 'turn to trouble' is prefigured in Mrs Tulliver's further complaint which not only reflects the moralists' method of frightening children into submission (see the poem at the head of Chapter 1) but, in fact, accurately predicts what Maggie's end is to be: '"where's the use o' my telling you to keep away from the water? You'll tumble in and be drownded some day, an' then you'll be sorry you didn't do as mother told you"' (p. 61).

The reader's sympathy for Maggie is intensified as she is shown to be isolated as an object of constant derision and reproach in her extended family of uncles and aunts, whose narrow, materialistic and oppressive views are regarded as law in the Tulliver household. That such criticism has moreover been internalised by Maggie is evidenced by her own sense of wrongness implicit in her despair at the triumph of blonde, pretty heroines in books and in her envy of Lucy:

> she was fond of fancying a world where the people never got any larger than children of their own age, and she made the queen of it just like Lucy, with a little crown on her head and a little sceptre in her hand – only the queen was Maggie herself in Lucy's form. (p. 117)[58]

Her rage and frustration manifest themselves in outbreaks of rebellion: the violent treatment of an old wooden doll on which Maggie inflicts vicarious punishment, her running away to join the gypsies, and the furious chopping off of her hair, with Tom's assistance, which seems, briefly, a deliverance till

Tom's laughing remark that she looks 'like the idiot we throw our nutshells to at school' (p. 120), opens her eyes to the enormity of what she has done. This last episode illustrates a duality in Maggie's character which is to inform every dilemma she encounters in later life: her sense of injustice at the criticism she receives coexists with a longing for approval from the very people whose values she rejects. Thus, 'she didn't want her hair to look pretty – that was out of the question, she only wanted people to think her a clever little girl, and not to find fault with her' (p. 121). Tom's reaction provokes immediate regret for her impulsive action and grief at the prospect of further derisive rejection from her family. Through the devastation of her misery Eliot evokes the impact of apparently trivial sorrows in childhood, the depth of which can be easily underestimated by adults whose memory of their own early years has dimmed:

> Every one of those keen moments has left its trace, and lives in us still, but such traces have blent themselves irrecoverably with the firmer textures of our youth and manhood; and so it comes that we can look on at the troubles of our own children with a smiling disbelief in the reality of their pain ... Surely if we could recall that early bitterness, and the dim guesses, the strangely perspectiveless conception of life that gave the bitterness its intensity, we should not pooh-pooh the griefs of our children. (p. 122–3)

Eliot's text is a plea, like Charlotte Brontë's, for compassion for the emotional torments children are capable of undergoing, rather than an indictment of the physical abuse and neglect at the hands of society more commonly depicted by her contemporaries. In a letter to her friend, Sara Hennel, she wrote in 1844 that 'Childhood is only the beautiful and happy time in contemplation and retrospect – to the child it is full of deep sorrows, the meaning of which is unknown', a perception which reveals a far more realistic view of childhood than that of the Romantics.[59]

The only real solace in Maggie's life is her relationship with Tom, whom she worships and whose love and approval she craves. Their different responses are delightfully portrayed in moments such as Tom's return from school in chapter 5: 'he submitted to be kissed willingly enough, though Maggie hung on his neck in rather a strangling fashion, while his blue-gray eyes wandered towards the croft and the lambs and the river . . .' (p. 84).[60] Like the little girl in Eliot's poem, Maggie feels unqualified admiration at Tom's 'superiority', instinctively privileging his male knowledge of worms, fish, birds and how padlocks work, her delight in his company tempered always, however, by the fear of displeasing him. Though also capable of affection and protectiveness towards his little sister, Tom, while he too can be wilful, rarely gives way to impulse, 'having a wonderful, instinctive discernment of what would turn to his advantage or disadvantage' (p. 121) which, in addition to his inherent advantage of being male, ensures him the approval of his family. The following passage brilliantly exposes their different natures and foreshadows the eventual outcome of their development into adulthood:

> He was one of those lads that grow everywhere in England, and, at twelve or thirteen years of age, look as much alike as goslings – a lad with light-brown hair, cheeks of cream and roses, full lips, indeterminate nose and eyebrows – a physiognomy in which it seems impossible to discern anything but the generic character of boyhood – as different as possible from poor Maggie's phiz, which nature seemed to have moulded and coloured with the most decided intention. But that same Nature has the deep cunning which hides itself under the appearance of openness, so that simple people think they can see through her quite well, and all the while she is secretly preparing a refutation of their confident prophecies. Under these average boyish physiognomies that she seems to turn off by the gross she conceals some of her most rigid, inflexible purposes, some of her most unmodifiable characters, and the dark-eyed, demonstrative, rebellious girl may after all turn out to be a passive being compared with this pink and white bit of masculinity with the indeterminate features. (pp. 84–5)

Even in childhood there is, then, evidence that the open, independent, vital qualities of Maggie may be subdued by the intransigence of Tom, whose lack of imagination, intelligence and compassion and 'desire of mastery' make him absolutely inflexible in his view of right and wrong. Her vulnerability to his opinion is manifested in her crushing grief when, for misdemeanours like forgetting to feed his rabbits so that they die, he punishes her by the means he knows will afflict her most: the withholding of his love. Although his anger speedily dissolves, Maggie's willingness to submit to his will and sacrifice her own desires confirms George Eliot's statement that 'it is a wonderful subduer, this need of love, this hunger of the heart' (p. 91). It is Tom's apparent preference for the company of Lucy during a visit of the aunts and uncles that drives Maggie to distraction, her raging figure following them across the fields at a distance, 'looking like a small Medusa with her snakes cropped' (p. 161), until the torment of being repeatedly excluded by Tom explodes in the vengeful pushing of 'poor little pink and white Lucy' in the mud.[61] George Eliot's gently humorous description underlines the relativity of experience allowing the reader to share what for the child is an intense sense of betrayal and misery.

Although such deliberate manipulation of Maggie through her feelings crystallises in adulthood into an attempt to control and subdue her by constant carping and disapproval of her friendships and, ultimately, rejection of her as 'dishonoured' because of her supposed elopement with Lucy's suitor, Stephen Guest, it is an over-simplification to condemn Tom as completely heartless. Indeed, George Eliot protested at criticism that she painted Tom only in a bad light, for it is clear that he too is a victim of his upbringing, having learnt patriarchal attitudes at an early age ('he was very fond of his sister, and meant always to take care of her, make her his housekeeper and punish her when she did wrong', p. 92) but he lacks the imaginative flexibility to see the injustices inherent in his society's over-rigidified moral code.[62] Moreover, the effect of the extended portrayal of their childhood days when Tom can also defend and comfort Maggie modifies our later view of Tom and above all renders credible Maggie's continuing love for her brother and her desire for his approbation, which tug against her own impulses in her subsequent dilemmas.

The spontaneous quality of their happy days when they fish and explore the natural world together is touchingly described and is seen, in Wordsworthian terms, to be an enduring joy of the kind which feeds the language of the imagination,

> the language that is laden with all the subtle inextricable associations the fleeting hours of our childhood left behind them. Our delight in the sunshine on the deep-bladed grass to-day might be no more than the faint perception of wearied souls, if it were not for the sunshine and the grass in the far-off years, which still live in us, and transform our perception into love. (p. 94)

In her evocation of Maggie's attachment to her home, Eliot captures the child's imaginative interpretation of reality: thus, the spiders' webs in her father's mill, which is 'a little world apart from her outside everyday life' look like 'faery lace-work' with their dusting of meal and the scuttling creatures themselves like 'lady spiders shocked at each other's appearance' (p. 80). This picture also justifies the importance Maggie, and Eliot, attach to roots, which becomes a significant factor in Maggie's later conflicts. Even a trivial object can acquire importance in adulthood because it evokes a memory of a similar feature of childhood, 'the long companion of my existence, that wove itself into my joys when joys were vivid' (p. 222).

Both children are, in fact, utterly believable and complex creations. Eliot's publisher, John Blackwood, thought that Tom was a 'very lifelike' boy, which comparison with another Tom, the idealised protagonist in a near contemporary novel, Thomas Hughes' *Tom Brown's Schooldays* (1857) confirms.[63] Eliot moreover avoids the temptation to make her protagonist idealised or unrealistically superior, frequently subjecting her to a gentle irony as in the delightful scene where Maggie behaves in an arrogant and high-handed way to a group of bemused gypsies whom she has naively and patronisingly presumed will welcome her on the grounds of her superior knowledge as their new queen. Even Lucy, who is presented through the adults' eyes as the epitome of goodness, neatness and acquiescence, evades her stereotype by contradicting her mother's assertion that she would not want to stay alone at the Tullivers' and, at Tom's urging, enjoys the rare treat of disobedience in straying away across the fields to the pond.

As in the poem 'Brother and sister', home life is disrupted by schooldays, which are seen as an important influence on the growing child. It is significant that the narrative focuses on Tom's education and that we learn virtually nothing of Maggie's schooling for it apparently contributes little to her development, while she covets the more academic learning to which Tom is unwillingly exposed. Even as a child, Maggie intuits that knowledge is the gateway to freedom, although the kind of 'thumbscrew' cramming Tom receives at Mr Stelling's school, where classics and geometry are seen as a *sine qua non* of a gentleman's upbringing, proves, in fact, to be of little use to him when he needs to find work to rescue the family's fortunes. Ironically, it is Maggie who could intellectually benefit most from such an education: her lively imagination responds to the Latin grammar and Euclid which reduce Tom, whose talents are of a more practical nature, to a 'girl's susceptibility' with a sense of helpless inadequacy which shakes his normal self-satisfaction. For the first time, Tom undergoes what has become a way of life for his sister, the oppressive sense of being 'all wrong somehow' (p. 204). Tom is, in fact, seen in a most sympathetic light here, his spirits further depressed as he has to undergo not only Maggie's patronising pity but also her manifest ability to surpass him in mastering the work. His cross response to her cocky assertion that she means to be a clever woman ('"Oh, I dare say, and a nasty conceited thing. Everybody'll hate you"', p. 216) is less of a dampener to her aspirations, however, than his tutor Mr Stelling's view of girls' academic potential: '"They can pick up a little of everything, I dare say . . . They've a great deal of superficial cleverness; but they couldn't go far into anything. They're quick and shallow"' (pp. 220–1). Although George Eliot deflates Mr Stelling's arrogance in her subsequent description of Maggie as 'this small apparatus of shallow quickness', Maggie's mortification at this swift branding of her 'quickness' as just a further sign of inferiority is vividly communicated to the reader.

Eliot's depiction of Tom's relationship with his fellow pupil, Philip Wakem, nearly two years his senior, throws considerable light on his character as well as offering a realistic portrait of a young invalid. Their initial meeting, as the two boys metaphorically circle each other, is deftly drawn. Tom's prejudice against Philip, motivated by family loyalty because of his father's enmity with lawyer Wakem and aggravated by a childish fear and suspicion of his deformity, is rapidly modified by his fascination with Philip's drawings. For his part, Philip, who with his pallor and girlish appearance seems superficially to have the stereotypical attributes of the literary invalid, feels a 'bitter complacency' at 'the promising stupidity of this well-made, active looking boy' (p. 235) and is not without a desire to impress with his mental superiority. The spurts of 'peevish susceptibility' due to his sense of his own deformity are accurately and perceptively detailed by Eliot, as is the mutual uneasiness in each other's company this causes:

every glance seemed to him to be charged either with offensive pity or with ill-repressed disgust – at the very least it was an indifferent glance; and Philip felt indifference as a child of the south feels the chill of a northern spring. Poor Tom's blundering patronage, when they were out of doors together, would sometimes make him turn upon the well-meaning lad quite savagely, and his eyes, usually sad and quiet, would flash with anything but playful lightening. No wonder Tom retained his suspicion of the hunchback. (p. 240)

It is this sensitivity, need for love and frustration at the externally imposed and irredeemable limitations to his potential which draw Philip to Maggie, in whose dark eyes he instinctively recognises the gleam of 'unsatisfied intelligence and unsatisfied, beseeching affection' (p. 253). Maggie, too, initially drawn to Philip because of her tenderness for vulnerable creatures, a trait which emanates from her own sense of helplessness, is attracted by his cleverness and sensitivity. In later years, the sisterly affection inextricably mingled with pity which she feels for him, and his tendency to play on this in their meetings, complicate a potentially more intimate relationship already threatened by Tom's disapproval which is to create a major dilemma for Maggie's conscience.

The breach in the precarious friendship between the boys when Tom accuses Philip of being the son of a rogue is only partially and temporarily healed by Philip's kindness to Tom after his accident. Fuelled with the desire to emulate the warriors of old, Tom, having persuaded his drill-master to let him borrow his sword, attempts to impress Maggie with his masculine posturing, and when the sword falls and injures his foot, it is only Philip who intuits the unspoken dread of permanent lameness uppermost in Tom's mind. Like Harriet Martineau in *The Crofton Boys*, Eliot does not treat the subject of infirmity with an affected sentimentality. Tom's fear and, upon reassurance, his vaunting of his own bravery, are natural and spontaneous, as is Philip's appreciation of Tom's state of mind.

It is, in fact, their father's failure in his law-suit and consequent loss of the mill and their home which herald the end of childhood for Maggie and Tom. The reduction of the patriarchal figure in their lives to a helpless and bewildered man, broken physically and mentally, significantly alters the course of their lives, annihilating the family's expectations of Tom's academic career and initiating a long, sad period of depression and self-deprivation for Maggie, her longings to achieve something constantly thwarted by family needs.[64] This transition is marked by Eliot in words which emphasise the difference between childhood and adulthood:

They had gone forth together into their new life of sorrow and they would never more see the sunshine undimmed by remembered cares. They had entered the thorny wilderness, and the golden gates of their childhood had for ever closed behind them. (p. 270)

These words are paralleled by the description of their death by drowning in the flood at the end of the novel when, after years which for Maggie, in her search for selfhood, are full of conflict between her own desires and duty, exemplified by the ties of the past and embodied in Tom, they die clasped in each other's arms. The complexity of inferences in the narration of the ending deny the view that this is simply a 'nostalgia for lost childhood' novel, although some of the vocabulary may suggest this, for there are strong implications that Maggie has been finally overwhelmed by the forces in her society which oppress her and that death is the only way out of her impasse. Maggie's plight may also be complicated by Eliot's own longing for reconciliation with her brother and her doubts about achieving it. Certainly her final choice of images suggests the joy and peace of reconciliation, a concept associated for Maggie, as for the author herself, with childhood:

> The boat reappeared, but brother and sister had gone down in an embrace never to be parted, living through again in one supreme moment the days when they had clasped their little hands in love, and roamed the daisied fields together. (p. 655)

It is an intriguing fact that few women writers tackled the problems of the woman as creative artist in their fiction. Even Maggie Tulliver's aspirations are vague and her creative intelligence never focuses on any clear objective. Sarah Grand's *The Beth Book* (1897), subtitled *Being a study of the life of Elizabeth Caldwell Maclure, a woman of genius*, departs radically from this apparent reluctance to get too close to personal experience or to explore areas with which the majority of their readers might not be able to identify or which might even alienate their sympathy, and charts the intellectual, emotional and artistic growth of the protagonist in the face of the social and internal pressures of a Victorian upbringing from the moment of her birth.[65] Sarah Grand (the pen-name of Frances McFall, 1854–1943) is one of the most important and readable of the 'New Woman' novelists who, at the end of the nineteenth century, overturned many literary and moral conventions to illustrate the inequities, prejudices and pernicious treatment to which young females were subjected and to demand new intellectual, social and, most disturbing of all to contemporary critics, sexual freedom for women through their outspoken and controversial novels.[66]

The extensive portrayal of Beth's early years is justified by the author on the grounds that, in her view, every incident or impression experienced in childhood, no matter how trivial, is vital in the development of the individual and hence is related in detail, not only because

> in several instances it seems to me that the impression left by some observation or incident on her baby mind, made it possible for her to do many things in after life which she certainly never would have done but for those early influences

but also to illustrate that 'had there been any there with intelligence to interpret, they probably would have found foreshadowings of all she might be, and do, and suffer: and that would have been the time to teach her' (p. 11). Grand constantly stresses the importance of upbringing in moral development and of studying the individual's early years in order to understand character. The novel, with its episodic structure within the linear framework of Beth's growing-up, is thus, as the subtitle indicates, less a fiction than a case history of a temperament.

Since it is sympathetic and constructive guidance that the warm, loving, energetic and inquisitive Beth lacks throughout her formative years, it is largely through impressions that her character matures in her solitary exploration of the world around her. Her spontaneous and instinctive response to nature, to other people's idiosyncrasies and to situations in which she finds herself are conveyed directly to the reader in a constant shifting between the child's and the adult narrator's viewpoint. The earliest incidents illustrate the awakening of her awareness of self and are common to many descriptions of childhood in their evocation of the different perspective of the child's world: walking unsteadily between gigantic flowers, the instantaneous distraction from the misery of a hot, dusty walk by a clump of tiny yellow flowers growing by the roadside, and the sudden panic of finding herself left behind by her nurse. Her adamant assertion that the spots of colour on a clutch of bird's eggs had appeared overnight, contrary to her nurse's assertions that they had always been there, evoke the child's intense but limited powers of observation, like Harriet Martineau's experience with the sea.

There is a problem inherent in Grand's presentation, however, for she can rarely resist the temptation to interpret, as intrusive omniscient narrator, the significance of what she has portrayed. Thus, for example, Beth's chagrin at being scoffed at by her mother and older sister Mildred for her own ignorance when she is fired by enthusiasm to teach the children of a poor local family is followed by the redundant remark: 'and so her mother checked her mental growth again and again instead of helping her to develop it' (p. 27). A further and more fundamental problem in the text is created by Grand's insistence on Beth's 'genius', an aspect which might with justification be viewed uncomfortably, given that the novel is blatantly autobiographical, but which also raises complications in her assertion of Beth's ability to triumph over her circumstances and thus provide a new role model for the reader who might in every other respect have been able to identify with her problems in life.[67] Beth's 'genius', described variously as her 'further faculty' or 'the vision and the dream' which comes upon her at moments of intense engagement with the natural environment, is emphasised from the moment of her birth. The seventh child of a weary and anxious mother who is resigned to her 'lot' as the long-suffering wife of a heedless, nagging husband, Beth arrives in the world 'unassisted and without welcome' and for the first three months cries incessantly, 'as if bewailing her advent' (p. 9). Yet, Grand tells us, despite this inauspicious beginning, Beth 'was born to be a child of light' and 'all the time that light which illumines the spirit was being bestowed upon her in limitless measure' (p. 10).

A sensitive and perceptive child, Beth's imagination is easily stimulated, her senses are acute, and 'from the first her memory helped itself by the involuntary association of incongruous ideas' (p. 17): thus, a particular Chopin waltz conjures up the smell of black beetles because she first heard it being played overhead while she chased and killed beetles on the kitchen hearth of her first school, and she is nauseated by bread and butter after consuming some while watching a cat eat a mouse. As before, the child's reactions are both evoked *and* explained by the narrator. She also appears to see things others cannot with her 'inner eye': when the family leave Ireland, after Mr Caldwell's death, Beth 'sees' a hanged man on Gallows Hill, a claim derisively dismissed by her family but which awes her nurse as a demonstration of a kind of sixth sense. Indeed, it is this apparent ability which, allied to her outspoken manner and easy adoption of the more vivid aspects of the local brogue, causes her Irish neighbours to fear her as a 'devil', giving rise to one of the more improbable episodes in the book in which Beth almost becomes the victim of superstitious violence when an aggrieved local man attempts to shoot her with a silver bullet. Certainly Beth seems endowed at times with what amounts to an extra sense, a psychic power which she cannot articulate fully but which allows her to sense impending deaths or the arrival of bad news. The linking of the child with the world of the supernatural and secret powers has become a popular and disturbing theme, as in, for example, Henry James' *The Turn of the Screw* and many twentieth-century novels and films which explore the potential for horror of the juxtaposition of evil and innocence, but for Grand, this association is not destructive or harmful, acting rather as a strategy for signifying female difference, energy and power.

This 'further faculty' is seen at its most extreme in early childhood: Grand attributes to Beth both a strange dream of her ancestors which is interpreted as a 'hereditary memory', and a vision of being expelled violently from an 'indescribable, hollow space' which seems to be a memory of the trauma of birth (p. 27–8). As Beth grows older, and her intellectual faculties develop, her visionary power becomes weaker. 'The vision and the dream' become more commonly a rather vague way of describing the subjective moments when Beth feels at one with the universe through her awareness of the beauty and harmony of nature. Indeed, the first awakening of her 'further faculty' at the age of 5 is one such moment, and is remembered by Beth as confirmation of her opinion that 'Genius to her was yet only another word for soul' (p. 16). Grand enlists Wordsworth's view of the child to underline Beth's specialness when she writes that Beth retained all her life a vague consciousness 'of a condition anterior to this, a condition of which no tongue can tell, which is not to be put into words, or made evident to those who have no recollection' (p. 28). Every kind of experience is seen to feed her 'genius': thus her grief at her father's death is seen as a 'fertilising essence', and all her pains are transmuted into something 'subtle, mysterious, invisible' (p. 81).

Despite these undeniably intrusive and portentous claims, the portrayal of Beth as a child is a thoroughly delightful and credible one. The reader relishes her verbal sallies against the pompous and patronising Uncle James who gives a home to the fatherless Caldwell family, his meal-time lectures reduced to chaos by Beth's enthusiastic responses, artless questions and deliberately malicious remarks which discomfort and deflate the adults struggling to preserve their social masks.[68] Her moments of suffering, even for trivial things which, as George Eliot noted, seem catastrophic to a child, are most vividly represented when her perspective is adopted: the humiliation she experiences at having to wear a cast-off jacket of her brother's, her terror of beetles after one presumed dead twines itself round her finger, and her extreme self-consciousness on entering Uncle James' house for the first time ('Family portraits . . . seemed to have been watching [Great Aunt Victoria] complacently until the travellers entered, when they all turned instantly and looked hard at Beth', p. 89). There is also mental anguish from causes which can be seen from women's autobiographical writings to be common female experience: the sense of isolation and estrangement, despair at being the object of constant nagging and recriminations, shame at her ignorance, and the dread engendered by Great Aunt Victoria's strong Calvinism, such that Beth is racked with terror at the thought of her friends and loved ones burning in hell.

As with Maggie Tulliver, Beth's greatest antagonist in her early days is her mother, although here the conflict is more intense and painful. Mrs Caldwell, a product of the time when women unquestioningly accepted everything inflicted on them as 'God's will', nevertheless manifests her frustration and her sense of impotence, especially in her impoverished widowhood, in neurotic attacks on Beth, the most rebellious of her children, while at the same time seeking to perpetuate the same concept of womanhood for her daughters. Beth's honesty, outspokenness, stubbornness and energy are construed unrelentingly as rudeness and naughtiness, and she is psychologically and physically abused by her mother in a manner which almost succeeds in killing her spirit. Although the beatings drive her to such despair that on one occasion she leaps off the end of the pier into the sea to escape her mother's anger, she endures them with a stoicism beyond her years. Objectively, there is perhaps much to drive a nervous and overstretched mother to distraction: Beth invites a crowd of strangers into the house for an animated conducted tour of their possessions, wanders around alone at dawn and lures her younger sister Bernadine onto the roof, leaving her stranded and terrified. Yet because Beth's activities are also viewed from her perspective, they are seen to be the consequences of lively curiosity, the desire to experiment and a total lack of direction for her restless intelligence. Moreover, with an even-handedness which transcends the conventional alternatives of the parent as infallible or irredeemably flawed, Grand does not condemn Mrs Caldwell, evoking rather our pity for her lack of capabilities and self-respect, as a victim of a lifetime of repressed womanhood. The absence of supportive love and approval, so frequently lamented by women writers in their own childhood, explains Beth's lack of sense of self-worth and her enduring tendency to internalise her emotions. Like Maggie, Beth yearns to please the mother who oppresses her, although her rebellions are more overt because she does not suffer from the inner dilemma which afflicts Eliot's protagonist, following her own concept of truth despite perpetual conflict.

Beth's isolation is scarcely mitigated by the fact that she is not an only child: her older brothers, at school in England, are as absent from the text as they are from her life, apart from Jim, whose privileges, as a boy, impinge inexorably on Beth's life: thus a small bequest from Great Aunt Victoria, intended for Beth's education, is hijacked to subsidise his gentlemanly activities in bar and billiard-room. In one recollection involving Jim, Grand captures the common trick played by memory of collapsing several occasions into one, for there is snow on the ground as Beth sets bird-snares with Jim, yet after she has cut his head open with a hurled block of wood, she recalls him visiting her in her solitary confinement and (with apparent disregard for seasonality), shooting ripe gooseberries across the floor like marbles. Though longing to share his pursuits, Beth encounters the same patronising male attitude towards girls as Maggie meets with Tom: her fury at his assertion that girls cannot be taught because they have no brains elicits the retort that 'when you grow up . . . you'll be just the sort of long-tongued shrew, always arguing, that men hate' (p. 154). (Beth trumps this, however, by querying the correctness of his grammar.) Although the younger Bernadine, a passive, gullible and treacherous creature, is Beth's only accomplice and occasional victim, the almost ritualistic mutual battering of the two young girls is a sad reflection of the role played by violence in their lives as a means of self-expression and control.

The scant attention that Beth receives paradoxically prompts development, for being forced to learn from practical experience saves her 'further faculty' from destruction, but her solitary apprenticeship also leads to a fragmented identity like that reported by many women in their memoirs, although Beth leads not just a double but a triple life of desultory lessons and coercion, her own carefree activities and an incessant indulging in dreams and imagination. The fantasy roles she invents for herself and acts out for others are attempts at forging an attractive persona as well as a means of escaping her present self and, though productive of trouble in the short term, also externalise her emotions and foreshadow her talents and later roles in life. The scene in which she frightens Bernadine by acting a sorceress in a darkened attic can be seen, like the episode of the silver bullet, and her reputation as a public disturber of the peace, to symbolise her 'difference', while her role as founder of the 'Secret Service of Humanity' which entrances a group of local girls, testifies to her natural leadership and gift for persuasive rhetoric. When her adventures finally lead her into serious debt, her impassioned gesture of atonement of having her hair cropped short like a boy repudiates both the artificial, external glamour of her fantasies and the image of femininity endorsed by her mother. As with Maggie, her failure to live up to this image is a constant source of friction, making her feel all wrong.

Her behaviour is certainly unfeminine by contemporary standards and testifies to her love of unfettered physical movement and resourceful independence – she hunts rabbits, fights like a boy, speaks her mind, and visits a menagerie dressed as a boy with two male companions. Despite the materially and spiritually impoverished and humiliating conditions of her everyday life which threaten to 'distort, if not actually destroy, all that was best, most beautiful and most wonderful in her character' (pp. 175–6) by forcing her into lies and deceit, the most admirable qualities developing in Beth throughout childhood are precisely those which would customarily have been seen as 'masculine' virtues: love of thoroughness, fearless honesty, courage, active loyalty, decisiveness and the tendency to listen and weigh carefully all the facts of a situation without prejudice or emotion before forming an opinion. These were, in fact, all the attributes of a 'New Woman', in direct opposition to the traditional feminine attributes embodied in Mrs Caldwell.

Grand's very open indictment of the Victorian age's attitudes to rearing its daughters, particularly the systematic repression of individuality and activity, is, however, rather curiously juxtaposed with an endorsement of orderly domesticity and feminine refinement, which are equated with a 'higher life'. These are the real legacy of Great Aunt Victoria, whose instruction is clearly valorised by the author who describes the quiet and loving attentiveness to the needs of others that she inculcates in Beth as the 'most charming traits' in her character. This bears fruit later in Beth's life, when, despite her independence in London and involvement with the Women's Movement, she is still able to describe a period spent caring for a sick male friend as 'the homiest time' of her life (p. 504). Thus, Grand's demand for opportunity and individual fulfilment for women is never divorced from her sanctioning of the 'sacred' role of service implicit in marriage and motherhood, just as Beth's career as a speaker for the Women's Movement is ultimately crowned by the appearance of a mate.

Beth's creative talent survives the daily rigours and emotional deprivation of her life through its link with her 'further faculty' and the instinctive response to music and nature. Her ability to compose spontaneous poems and weave magical tales fascinates other young people and makes them willing slaves to her will while ensuring her the reputation, especially among adults, of being 'odd'. Interestingly, Beth's path diverges to some extent from that of her creator later in life, for when Beth, trapped in a desperately unhappy marriage, attempts to write, she discovers that this is not the right path for her talents and ultimately achieves her success through the spoken rather than the written word. This is further foreshadowed by Beth's childhood urge to proselytise which emerges strongly again during a religious phase at school at the age of 14, her eloquence and ardour ('like one inspired') giving rise to the teachers' hopes that she might do great work. Ironically, this is indeed to be the case, but the word Beth will preach is not the word of God, for she is soon repelled by what she sees as the injustices and inconsistencies of religion, but the discourse of feminism.

Grand's indictment of the contemporary education system is among the most comprehensive and rigorous to be found anywhere in nineteenth-century fiction. Although during her first experience of institutionalised education, at the age of 6 in a day school in a little Irish seaport where much of her time is spent in solitary confinement for 'breaches of the peace' (p. 16), her lively spirit unable even then to endure restriction and rigid discipline, she makes little progress with her book learning, it is made clear that, in Rousseau-istic tradition, her senses are sharpened to acuteness by every experience she absorbs: 'The books of nature and of life were spread out before her, and she was conning their contents to more purpose than anyone else could have interpreted them to her in those days' (p. 19).

Her abilities are seen to transcend conventional academic attainments and the need for an adult mentor, although she has the potential to succeed in this respect too, as when, at 13, she becomes intrigued by the air of superiority of Jim's male friends because of their knowledge of Latin grammar and classical texts, and sets out to study them too. Unlike Maggie Tulliver, Beth does not privilege such male preserves as the gateway to intellectual freedom, finding such knowledge useful only in that it 'imposed upon the boys' and makes them think her clever. Her Latin lessons in fact end abruptly when her tutor uses sophistical moral arguments to persuade her to embrace him. What Beth *really* learns at this period is 'how inferior in force and charm mere intellect is to spiritual power' (p. 275), so that, rejecting the stultification of a classical education, she cultivates rather the originality of her mind.

The process of the development of 'genius' is severely put to the test at the first school she attends in her teens, St Catherine's Mansion, the Royal Service School for Officers' Daughters, which threatens to stunt her talents with its repressive and superficial regime, by which potential is quashed, effort mocked and physical health endangered by inactivity and poor diet. There is no physical cruelty here, as at Lowood, but Beth's bodily and mental health declines under the pedagogical ethos which seeks to make life like a punishment. Subsequently, at a finishing school in London ('a regular forcing house for the marriage market', p. 316), she is exposed to the worldly talk of the other girls and begins to learn what being a woman means, but also is treated as an individual and given access to a more refined and cultivated world by the high-minded and exemplary mistresses. Beth, paradoxically, responds well to the teaching of 'showy accomplishments' deemed essential for young ladies, and the work begun by Great Aunt Victoria is continued by one particular teacher, who knows how to curb Beth's exuberance and direct her energy into profitable channels, such that the most valuable part of her education is 'the strengthening of every womanly attribute' (p. 319). This is cut short, however, when she is recalled home because of the death from meningitis of her sister Mildred, and shortly afterwards, though still little more than a child, marries a man she scarcely knows, partly to escape and partly to please her enthusiastic mother.[69]

The careful detail with which Grand records Beth's experience over so many pages of this extraordinary novel allows the reader to share the unfolding of her life, despite the intrusive and occasionally pompous authorial intrusions, and the account of her childhood years, where the foundations of her character and of everything that happens later are laid, is in many respects the most fascinating part of the text. Arguably, Beth becomes a more remote figure as she approaches young womanhood, and the emphasis on her genius and physical and spiritual superiority removes her further and further from the average reader's realm of experience. Any idealisation is effectively countered, however, by the appalling sufferings to which Beth is exposed in her marriage to the unappetising, gross, insensitive and faithless Dan Maclure.

Beth is, ultimately, a memorable character, and an unusual one too, for from childhood she engages dynamically with life and succeeds, becoming on the last page a woman who 'has it all', personal fulfilment in her chosen career, public admiration, loyal friends and a loving partner, while retaining the childlike qualities of freshness of perception, frankness and sensitivity. This novel is perhaps the best example of a female version of the male *Bildungsroman* where all the aspects of the protagonist's public and private life combine, after errors and trials, in harmony at the end.[70]

Sarah Grand uses the development of a child to similar effect in *The Heavenly Twins* (1893), although in this more diffuse narrative, the twins of the title are only a part of her onslaught on contemporary attitudes towards women.[71] The role of the twins, Angelica and Diavolo, is nowhere better stated than in the short passage cited at the head of the novel: '"They call us the Heavenly Twins". "What, signs of the Zodiac?" said the Tenor. "No, signs of the times", said the Boy.' (The Boy is in fact the very young, newly married Angelica, who establishes a close relationship with a romantic young man, while escaping from her household in male attire.)

The personalities of the twins are established in lively childhood scenes in order to underline Grand's plea for a radical reassessment of attitudes towards the upbringing and education of young people, especially females. When small, the twins seem temperamentally alike and are inseparable, but it becomes apparent that, in many respects, gender roles are reversed, for Angelica, the taller, stronger, more intelligent and dynamic of the two, is 'the organiser and commander of every expedition'.[72]. She is also, like other literary antitheses of the conventional 'ideal' of femininity, dark-haired, boisterous, untidy and outspoken, while the fair-haired Diavolo, though always ready to follow her lead, is chivalrous, courteous and passive when on his own.

Their aristocratic home is continual mayhem: the moat has to be filled in to avoid accidents and windows barred to prevent expeditions in search of adventure. They are deemed uncontrollable, the opposite of the fictional 'good child' in every respect, for they are disruptive, noisy and disobedient, but also, unlike the 'scamps' so popular in the late nineteenth century, greedy and violent, appropriating things that do not belong to them, and telling lies. Their first appearance is in a scene that begins conventionally, as they intrude on an adult dinner party, two small figures in their nightgowns, 'their forefingers in their mouths, their inquisitive noses tilted in the air and their bright eyes round with astonishment' (p. 9), but quickly becomes subversive for, far from being patronised by the adults, they dominate and destroy the social situation, scrambling across the dinner table to examine the glass centre-piece, smashing plates, glasses and decanters, till Diavolo accidentally stabs himself in the leg with a pocket-knife, severing the femoral artery, and the occasion degenerates into disarray. They are subsequently seen pelting local schoolchildren with boiled sweets, insulting visiting clergymen, attacking their tutor, galloping like furies around the countryside, swapping clothes and getting drunk at a wedding, and, like Beth, constantly embarrassing adult company by their questions and candid observations. Although they generally think and act as one, they also fight each other continually, and it is Angelica who most often initiates the aggression, scratching, kicking and banging the head of her long-suffering brother in their 'quarrels' over the rights of primogeniture.

Despite this objectively alienating behaviour, they are also presented as endearing, not in any 'cute' or sentimental way, but in their openness and honesty, their willingness to discuss and analyse what they and others have done and admit their faults, their loyalty and fundamental sense of honour. Reader response is manipulated by the approval of the twins' courage, imagination and vivacity by the more enlightened characters in the text.

Grand's central point becomes clear as the twins grow into their early teens and the differences of gender begin to intrude and cause uneasiness in their relationship. This is not seen as just a question of social conditioning, however, for Angelica, who initially resists the inevitability of growing up, clinging to childhood as she clings to her short dresses, begins to feel the stirrings of emotions and longings which distance her from her brother and cause bewilderment to both. At 15, although she has 'no coquettish or womanly ways' (p. 245), the changes in her temperament become more marked, as her delight in teasing and tormenting gives way to greater sensitivity and sympathy. Yet despite the tentative desires to appear more adult, the old ways of childhood are still seen by Angelica as synonymous with freedom of self-expression: thus when her unexpected appearance in a long dress, her hair coiled neatly upon her head, shocks and distresses Diavolo, her reaction is characteristically spontaneous, for she rejects her finery at once, promising that such womanly garb can only be a disguise and that '"I'll be just as bad as ever in it"' (p. 275). This scene reveals her awareness of the fundamental incompatibility of her real self with conventional feminine images and behaviour, just as her adventuring in male clothing, continued into young adulthood, symbolises her rejection of gender stereotyping and the restrictions imposed on females.

Angelica's growing understanding of how her society regards and treats its women, her initiation into 'the world of anguish', is at the heart of the novel. Her horror at the plight of Edith, a victim of insanity due, like the sickly deformity of her child, to a sexually transmitted disease contracted from her husband, awakens her to the shocking consequences of the expectation that girls should be kept in ignorance and encouraged to acquiesce unquestioningly in their family's wishes. In this respect too, Angelica is the leader and educator of Diavolo, recruiting him in adolescence as a supporter of the cause of women. A lingering remnant of their childhood relationship, as well as an ironic reversal of social power structures, is nicely signalled in the remark that 'she was teaching him to respect women . . . when he didn't respect them, she beat him; and this made him thoughtful' (p. 255). The insistence on his gentle and caring nature explains his ready sympathy with the plight of women, for he has the makings of a 'New Man', like Beth's eventual partner and the small number of male characters who stand in contrast to the selfish, brutish and opinionated (and socially sanctioned) behaviour of the other men who populate this novel.

Like Beth, Angelica is an embryonic 'New Woman' even in childhood, while her social position and personal dynamism empower her in the pursuit of individual freedom. The last glimpse we have of the twins is, however, intriguing, for the reversal of roles suggested in childhood is, in fact, only partially fulfilled. Diavolo, who seems more 'feminine' physically and temperamentally throughout, resigns his commission in the army and devotes himself to caring for his grandfather, the old Duke. Angelica is 'a splendid specimen of hardy, healthy, vigorous young womanhood' (p. 602) but has also been brought to realise, after the tragic death of her friend, the Tenor, for which she feels partially responsible, the 'blessing of a good man's love' (p. 551) and to appreciate her husband's good influence in curbing her faults. Thus, as in the *The Beth Book*, Grand endorses, in the last analysis, her respect for marriage as 'the ideal state'.[73]

The foregrounding of the female child in such texts not only allows for an exploration of the implications of the gender stereotyping which social forces imposed on young females, but the figure of the child can be seen as a paradigm of the condition of womanhood itself, with its energy, aspirations and potential but relative powerlessness and vulnerability to exploitation and oppression. The novels considered here in fact privilege the notion of 'difference' to some extent. The strong-willed, assertive, lively, boisterous or outspoken child, the opposite of the ideal of demure femininity, appears as a positive representation, subverting conventional expectations and positing new, more vital role models. Their vitality and resistance to criticism, and the overwhelming moments of unhappiness and isolation they all experience, underpin the critique of adult attitudes and behaviour. If the fates of some of these characters seem to reflect a compromise, the qualities of the 'different' child being modified to effect a 'happy ending' in line with traditional values, this may reflect the author's own desires and realisation that, in being 'different' themselves, something was missing from their lives, as much as their awareness of the lack of alternative opportunities for self-fulfilment. The tragic fate of others is a powerful indictment of society's attitudes towards 'difference' and, moreover, can be seen to reflect the metaphorical death of the self in which the alternative course, unquestioning submission to the debilitating forces that society brought to bear on its children, especially the females, could result.

Conclusion

Speaking of books for the young, Isabelle Jan asserts that many of the child-heroes of the eighteenth and nineteenth centuries refused to come to life, having no freedom of action or sensitivity, responding only to exterior motivations, and were, in short, 'mere pretexts', at the mercy of the author's whim or obsessions.[1] It is true that the child figure was very widely used by female and male writers in books for both a juvenile and an adult readership as a symbol or a vehicle for a didactic secular or religious message, yet it would be unfair to assume that in such cases the child character never transcends a stereotype. As the preceding discussion reveals, the most powerful and affecting of such texts are precisely those in which the individuality of the child is not totally subsumed in its symbolic value. Even when making use of literary stereotypes, many women writers also frequently succeeded in investing a considerable degree of plausibility in their literary children, an awareness of childish capabilities, games, desires and reactions which may be explained by their greater day-to-day experience and observation of children, for even when they did not have children themselves, they often had experience of helping to educate and bring up younger siblings or taught in local day or Sunday schools. They also often demonstrate a sensitivity to the psychological stresses of family relationships and appear more aware than their male counterparts of the effects of gender stereotyping from an early age.

It is clear that the image of the innocent child which came to dominate in the nineteenth century was often a very subjective one, corresponding less to the reality of childhood than to the adult's need of a comforting or inspiring mythology.[2] The tender vulnerability of the child had enormous appeal for male and female writers and readers alike as a symbol of a sense of insecurity and defencelessness in the face of the uncertainties of a rapidly changing world, and especially of the obscurely threatening implications of a dehumanising materialistic and mechanised society.[3] The popularity, in particular, of the figure of the orphan, homeless, hungry and abandoned by family and society, also poignantly reflects the nineteenth-century concern with identity and origins (an especially intense preoccupation after the

181

publication of Charles Darwin's *On the Origin of Species by Natural Selection or the Preservation of Favoured Races in the Struggle for Life* in 1859).

Such a concern with identity and the relationship between the individual and society seems to have had even greater significance for women writers, many of whom display anxieties or resentment about being cast by society into narrow and limited roles. As has been seen, a large number of women chose to endorse social expectations in their imaging of young girls in their works, especially in the domestic novels, even when they may have had personal reservations or suffered themselves from dissatisfaction and a sense of repression. It is frequently less an unqualified endorsement, however, than an attempt to create revised versions of the image, or to show their young readers how to come to terms with their situation and find personal fulfilment and a degree of autonomy within traditional roles. For some, as consideration of their autobiographical writings reveals, this may also have represented an attempt to confirm in their own eyes the correctness of overcoming early rebellious instincts. A few, especially later in the century, challenged these expectations openly and demanded the right to develop the individual identity and to have more freedom of choice over their path in life.

The figure of the child not only mirrored women's subordinate social position (indeed, for legal purposes women were classed with minors), but their portrayal of the child at different stages in the century can be seen to reflect women writers' changing attitudes towards their own status. Thus, the shift from the docile, obedient, rational child of the early moral tales to the rebellious, outspoken and 'different' is a paradigm for women's rejection of the early desire to achieve recognition according to male criteria and assumption of a position of open questioning and revolt. It is possible to argue, moreover, that female rebellion was first mediated through the child figure because a degree of 'naughtiness', representing an assertion of the individual will and defiance of restraints, was more familiar and acceptable and hence less directly subversive.

Interest in the child figure also often corresponded to a very personal need to explore and recapture the innocence, happiness and freedom from adult restraints and responsibilities of the writer's own childhood, becoming a nostalgic or escapist journey into the past that both articulated a sense of loss and made the present tolerable. A considerable number of female- and male-authored portrayals of childhood have a strong autobiographical basis. Ironically, however, such a journey often found emotional problems and conflicts in childhood too, which opened up new areas of exploration of individual psychology and human relationships. The portrayal of childhood also, therefore, became a means of exorcising personal miseries or resentments of the past. Once again, with women writers, this answered a special need to explore their own difficulties in coping with specific problems of 'growing up female', many of which were, as their writing reveals, extremely common experiences. The impulse to write of their own childhood also became for some women writers, as has been seen, an important part of the wish to construct and promote a desirable image of the self. The evocation of admiration and sympathy for the child was an effective means of eliciting favourable reader response to the adult writer and her work in the face of anticipated criticism.

The positive aspects of the mythology of the innocent child were of obvious appeal to the creative artist: the sensibility, imaginativeness, originality, heightened perception, freshness of vision and closeness to nature vaunted by the Romantic poets were pressed into service as a potent image of the plight of the artist in an alienating and potentially hostile environment.[4] But there were negative implications too, which were increasingly apparent as this image of childhood became overworked during the course of the century. The cloying sentimentality of many portrayals of children has been noted, often reducing the child figure to a loosely constructed confection of stereotypical and predictable physical characteristics and behaviour patterns. As Coveney demonstrates, the symbol was susceptible to continuous deterioration through 'over-assertion and special pleading'.[5] There were other, more insidious, implications, however, in the case of the portrayal of young female children, where the insistence on the ideals of purity and innocence reflect rather an unhealthy repression of natural instincts and vitality, at best associated with passivity and self-abnegation, at worst with madness or even death. The Victorian age's awareness of the dangers of sexuality and the importance of protecting children, especially girls, from the outside world turned the notion of purity into an obsession. The sentimentality about these ideals thus masked anxieties about emotional and physical drives in children which instead became channelled into an intensification of domestic emotions.[6] It is significant that little girls in fiction were frequently portrayed as the embodiment of untainted innocence and spirituality and were favoured as the angelic instruments of redemption and regeneration by female and male authors alike. It is equally significant that such little girls often die young, thus being denied the possibility of development, which might expose them to worldly influences, in order to preserve their purity intact.

The prizing and encouraging of the childlike qualities of sweetness, ingenuousness and innocent virtue in adult women and the censure of sexual expression led, moreover, to an uneasy ambiguity in attitudes towards little girls who were seen to combine the purity of the child *and*, by association, that of the ideal female, an 'angel in the house' in the making.[7] Thus, the child as 'little mother' or 'little housewife' was a very popular type in female- and male-authored fiction. This blurred line between child and woman sometimes led, however, to a fascination with the visual appeal of miniature females which has distinctly erotic undertones, as the frequently provocative presentation of little girls and adolescents in Victorian art testifies.[8] The obsession of some male writers with little girls (John Ruskin's love for a 10-year-old at the age of 40, and Lewis Carroll's photographs of naked little girls in provocative poses, for example) is a disturbing aspect of the period and adds a further dimension to the exploitation of children by adults.[9] The depiction of 'womanly' attractions in the person of a child paradoxically represented a fascination with female sexuality, while ostensibly rendering safe its potential threat, just as the thriving trade in child prostitution in the nineteenth century was a response to the fear of sexually transmitted diseases. The actual result, however, was to sexualise the child further.[10]

There was a significant split, therefore, between the presentation of the female child as secular saint or 'angel' (see the literal representation of a child as angel in Sir Joshua Reynolds' 'Angel heads' of 1787 and the transformation of Annie into angel in her cousin's painting in Stretton's *The Children of Cloverley*) and the erotic implications of the beautiful, 'womanly' child, especially apparent in the visual arts, which modern readers find distasteful. Just as women writers, on the whole, did not uncritically endorse the attractiveness of childishness in women, so they did not exploit this aspect of the portrayal of little girls and are not preoccupied, in their works, with alluring physical attributes and seductively winsome manners. (The criticism of Blanche's coquettish behaviour in *The Daisy Chain*, discussed in Chapter 4, is an attack on precisely this idea.) Marie Corelli's treatment of Jessamine in *The Mighty Atom* comes closest to this kind of exploitation, demonstrating, perhaps, her highly developed commercial sense and willingnesss to pander to the demands of the market. As the texts discussed in Chapter 6 reveal, some women writers were not afraid to tackle the taboo subject of sex, exploring the implications of the nascent sexuality of their protagonists and the effects of repression of natural instincts, but here, significantly, the child is the subject of the enquiry rather than merely an object of voyeuristic urges.

It is arguable that women writers sometimes tended, conversely, to 'feminise' their male child characters, creating pretty, gentle, captivating little boys, thus neutralising the implications of masculinity and hence sexuality. Moreover, such boys are not infrequently seen to succeed in life by means of the 'feminine' attributes of patience, tolerance, compassion and faith. Significantly, in books for young readers by women writers, boys often feature as younger brothers, thereby underplaying their inherently more privileged male position and allowing an older sister to take the lead or play the 'little mother' role. In the texts discussed in Chapter 6 which were written largely for adults, however, boys are seen to oppress their sisters or cousins, like Tom Tulliver, Jim Caldwell or John Reed, revealing the authors' awareness of the pernicious effects of the inculcation of gender roles and expectations on young males and females alike. This is a subject which begs for further and more intensive study of both female- and male-authored texts.

The ideal of childlike innocence was also perceived to play an undesirable role in the imaging of young females as they grew towards adulthood. What Simone de Beauvoir calls a 'state of prolonged infancy', endorsed by society as a means of personal and social control over women, came increasingly under fire as the century progressed and women writers felt able to free themselves from social and literary expectations and to assert the need for young females to learn to develop their mental and physical capabilities, rather than to conform to preconceived models which were patronising and reductive.[11] A distinct shift in gendered behaviour developed in fiction, with young females becoming more energetic, dynamic and independent. In their autobiographies and semi-autobiographical novels, women often exploded the myth of innocence by revealing its origins in ignorance, inexperience and fear of natural instincts, and demonstrating through the patterns in their own lives the real-life consequences for the child and the adult of an upbringing subjected to such attitudes.

A further disconcerting aspect of the nineteenth-century portrayal of the child is the preoccupation with death which became common to religious and secular writers alike. There is no doubt that, to some extent, this reflected a grim fact of life and, particularly in religious families, was a common topic of interest. A copy of a juvenile periodical, *The Children's Friend* for 1862 (a volume chosen at random), contains a number of poems in which death is represented soothingly to a questioning child: thus a dead baby brother is seen as a butterfly bursting out of its chrysalis, a dying child worries about forgetting her prayers or wishes not to be adorned with flowers after her death because her Saviour's head was crowned with thorns, and several children yearn to be reunited in death with lost loved ones. A substantial number of the short articles and anecdotes also seek to instruct the child readers about heaven and urge them to aspire to deserve an eternal home there. Tales of exemplary death-beds of children and of the flight to heaven of a child's soul were also designed to ease the grief of real parents in an age when the infant mortality rate was high, and to comfort them with the thought that the spiritual purity of their child would ensure eternal bliss. As has been seen, the dying child as a literary device shifted from serving as a dramatic warning about the probable results of misbehaviour to a vehicle for a religious message, whether cautionary or exemplary, and became, eventually, merely a recognised means of engendering pathos and eliciting a sentimental response from the reader. The two most prevalent attitudes towards the child, the Romantic and the Evangelical, converged, as did female and male writers, in their recognition of the effectiveness of this theme.[12]

It is easy to understand the attractiveness of the dying child as a medium for social criticism. The love of pathos for its own sake has profound implications for the concept of innocence, however, for the Romantic image of the child as an embodiment of the potential of the best qualities of human beings became, in the second half of the century, an image associated, in some works by women and men, with the failure to grow up and withdrawal from life, an innocence which, paradoxically, is seen as better dead than exposed to real-life experience, indeed which can only survive through death. It has been said of Dickens that he gave 'vicarious possession' of innocence to his adult readers through their enjoyment of death-bed scenes, 'to compensate for their own lost childhoods'.[13] Coveney interprets this phenomenon as a negation of the Romantic idea, 'as if many placed on the image the weight of their own disgust and dissatisfaction, their impulse to withdrawal, and, in extremity, their own wish for death'.[14] Whether or not it is a symptom of personal or social malaise, the dying child was clearly successful bait in the commercial literary world and the exploitation of the theme in books for both adults and children remains one of the most disconcerting aspects of nineteenth-century literary history.

The portrayal of the child clearly changed in many significant ways throughout the century. In the early moral tales which depicted the child as the passive recipient of instruction, seen almost exclusively from the viewpoint of the adult narrator, when a voice was given to the child character, it was generally a voice with which few child readers would have been able fully to identify. There are, of course, exceptions to this, notably the work of Maria Edgeworth and Harriet Martineau, as discussed in Chapter 1. Although the emphasis on rational thought and discourse, at the expense of the imagination and experimentation with language of a real-life child, was a reflection of the age, it undoubtedly had further significance for many women writers for whom demonstrably well-founded anxieties about criticism and the desire to present a mature self-image contributed to a reticence about adopting a childlike voice in their narratives.[15] Later in the century, when the focus shifted more closely onto the child as individual, interest was generated in the child's own perception of, and response to, experience and writers were forced to confront the difficulties inherent in capturing this different world. In fact, throughout the century, we do find attempts by a number of women writers to capture the child's perspective in books for both adults and young people, if only intermittently or in a dual technique employing the viewpoints of both the experiencing child and the observing and reflecting adult.[16] The most successful in capturing the child's world in a wholly believable and unself-conscious manner are, arguably, those in which the adult narrator and the child protagonist are one and the same, as in *Jane Eyre*, and some of Juliana Ewing's works, like *Six to Sixteen*, *We and the World* and *Mrs Overtheway's Remembrances* (1869), in which an elderly adult relives childhood impressions and perceptions.

Many women certainly excelled in their portrayal of the child's viewpoint and language in their books for young readers, perhaps because they were more confident and less self-conscious when addressing a young audience than male writers were.[17] Writers like Juliana Ewing, Mary Louisa

Molesworth, Frances Hodgson Burnett and Edith Nesbit presented in their best works the child's view of life in language which a child might plausibly have used, displaying an admirable understanding of the child's thought processes and avoiding, for the most part, the pitfalls of idealisation and sentimentality. They overcame, in particular, the difficulties of depicting childish pleasure and happiness without seeming condescending. In this way, they succeeded in capturing the absolute present of childhood experience and created a new child-reader/author-relationship. Paradoxically, these same qualities earned them an appreciative audience among adults too. Frequently, the world they depict is bounded by the child's experience, a restricted world of the child where adults are shadowy figures or intruders. In *The Boys and I* (1883), for example, Mrs Molesworth, whose novels focus generally on the middle-class nursery world, depicts the heartache of three young children separated from their parents and the ways in which they learn to cope with the disruption to their routines, the sense of abandonment and isolation in their uncle's house in London and the incomprehension of adults. It is revealing that the first of these factors is, in fact, the one which exercises the children most. The story is narrated in retrospect by the oldest child, a girl, and Molesworth captures the earnest, self-conscious and scrupulous eagerness of the 14-year-old Audrey to tell it as a 'proper story' from the start:

> I was nine then – I mean I was nine at the beginning of the time I am going to tell you about, and now I am fourteen. Afterwards, I will tell you what put it into my head to write it down. If I told you now you wouldn't understand – at least not without my telling you things all out of their places – ends at the beginning, and middles at the end; and mother says it's an awfully bad habit to do things that way. It makes her quite vexed to see any one read the end of a book before they have really got to it. There aren't many things that make her really vexed, but that's one, and another is saying 'awfully', and I've just said it, or at least written it. And I can't score it through – I've promised not to score through anything, and just to leave it as it came into my head to write it all down.[18]

The different viewpoints of the children and the adults are fully acknowledged through Audrey's attempts to compare and contrast them. Her ready assumption of responsibility for her brothers, her protectiveness and willingness to stand up to adults despite her awareness of the relative impotence of the children are conveyed without condescension. The child's view is vindicated eventually when the adults acknowledge their mistakes and a happier family context is established. In many such children's books the child's viewpoint is adopted to voice a criticism of adult society's attitudes and assumptions, in direct opposition to the prevailing tone at the beginning of the century. Writers like Charlotte Brontë and Sarah Grand also exploited the effectiveness of this technique in their novels for adult readers, in which, while the adult narrator's voice is preserved, the child's perception of the treatment received at the hands of adults creates a more immediate and potent critique than mere authorial comment.

Attempts to portray the child's viewpoint led to greater awareness of the complexity of childhood experience and range of childish emotions and urges, including the capacity for spite, envy, hatred and violence and other undesirable concomitants of the child's absorption with self. Although these aspects were acknowledged by the didactic and Evangelical writers, they were seldom explored from the child's perspective. (It is intriguing to compare the Evangelical view of innate depravity with the recognition in twentieth-century texts like William Golding's *Lord of the Flies* or Susan Hill's *I'm the King of the Castle*, for example, of the child's capacity for evil.)

A highly popular form of narrative which the constraints of this study have obliged me to omit is the fantasy or allegorical tale. Although frowned on by the moralists, such imaginative fiction was reinstated in mid-century, largely by the phenomenal success with young and older readers alike of the surreal world of Lewis Carroll's *Alice in Wonderland* (1865). It is perhaps through the use of fantasy that a writer is best able to enter fully the imaginative world of the child and capture, for example, the child's irrational fears of the unknown and unexplained or the joys of a sense of all-powerfulness. Although the best-known writers of fantasies which enjoyed a dual readership were men, like Lewis Carroll, George Macdonald and J. M. Barrie, women were active in this sub-genre too. The stories of Frances Browne, Jean Ingelow and Dinah Craik were widely read and loved. Christina Rossetti's *Speaking Likenesses* (1874) is significant for its enactment in 'A Party in the Land of Nowhere' of the child protagonist's confrontation with her own faults and those of her siblings and friends through a fantasy which we are left to assume is a dream and hence emanating from her subconscious. During her birthday party where the children become fractious, selfish and quarrelsome, the disgruntled Flora, dissatisfied with everything that is done for her, falls asleep and is lured into a hollow tree to a terrifying parody of the party with a group of grotesque and fantastic creatures, where the hostile and arbitrary behaviour and games of the boys with their prickly quills and hooks and the sticky and slippery girls display a surprisingly aggressive eroticism.[19] The immense and continuing success of Edith Nesbit's novels like *Five Children and It* (1902), *The Phoenix and the Carpet* (1904) and *The Story of an Amulet* (1906) testifies to the allure of a recipe in which the everyday lives of very real children are merged with an escape into fantasy, by means of which the children learn to confront their true desires and needs.

Nesbit is also noteworthy for the fun she pokes at gendered behaviour and assumptions and her repeated allusions to, and parodies of, earlier literary assumptions and styles which would seem to be directed more at amusing an adult reader. Thus, in *The Wouldbegoods* (1901), in which the Bastable children are sent to a moated manor-house in the country 'to learn to be good' and decide to set up a secret society to encourage themselves, the spontaneous saintliness of many Evangelical literary children is nicely satirised in their discussions about the running of the Society of Wouldbegoods:

'I'm not sure we oughtn't to have put our foot down at the beginning', Dicky said. 'I don't see much in it, anyhow'.

'It pleases the girls', Oswald said, for he is a kind brother.

'But we're not going to stand jaw, and "words in season" and "loving sisterly warnings". I tell you what it is, Oswald, we'll have to run this thing our way, or it'll be jolly beastly for everybody'.

Oswald saw this plainly.

'We must do something', Dicky said; 'it's very, very hard though. Still, there must be *some* interesting things that are not wrong'.

'I suppose so', Oswald said, 'but being good is so much like being a muff, generally. Anyhow, I'm not going to smooth the pillows of the sick, or read to the aged poor, or any rot out of *Ministering Children*.'[20]

The inability of a visiting child, Daisy, to 'play' is attributed by the young narrator to her

reading the wrong sort of books partly – she has read *Ministering Children*, and *Anna Ross or, the Orphan of Waterloo*, and *Ready Work for Willing Hands* and *Elsie, or Like a Little Candle*, and even a horrid little blue book about the something or other of Little Sins.[21]

In children's books, in fact, as in their portrayal of children in books for adults, women writers in the second half of the century can often be found to be at their most subversive. As Juliet Dusinberre remarks: 'the first real rebels against Victorian stiffness were children and the first rebels in print wrote books for them'.[22]

Thus, women writers were not only responsible, to a considerable extent, for creating and developing the stereotypical images of children and childhood which prevailed in different guises throughout the century in different forms of literature, but also for revising and modifying those stereotypes in important ways, highlighting their inadequacies and the absurdities and iniquities of associated attitudes. Although, like male writers, they were influenced in many and differing ways by the beliefs and needs of their age and also by the particular restraints on themselves as women and writers, their contribution to the development of the theme is unique in its scope and variation, and their consciousness of their society's attitudes towards females which, in some cases, clearly determined, how, when and what they wrote, in others gave impetus and lasting significance to their portraits of the childhood world and of children attempting to find new values with which to understand and engage with the adult world and grow.

Notes

Numbers in bold type refer to items in the Bibliography.

Introduction

1. See David Grylls [**62**, p. 35]. Isabelle Jan claims that 'real human children continued to be virtually excluded from both adult and children's literature' until the middle of the nineteenth century [**77**, p. 90].
2. Peter Coveney [**27**, p. 162].
3. Robert Pattison [**103**, chs 4, 6].
4. Grylls [**62**, chs 3,4].
5. Richard N. Coe [**24**].
6. R. Kuhn [**86**].
7. See for example Philippe Ariès [**3**]; Lloyd de Mause (ed.) [**38**]; Ivy Pinchbeck and Margaret Hewitt [**107**, vol. 2]; James Walvin [**139**]. Linda Pollock [**108**] assesses many theories.
8. Walvin [**139**, p. 18].
9. Ariès [**3**, pp. 357, 396].
10. Coe [**24**, p. 11].
11. Ariès [**3**, pp. 127–9, 397].
12. Grylls [**62**, pp. 19–20].
13. Grylls [**62**, p. 22].
14. John Locke [**91**]. Locke is essentially concerned with the education of 'young gentlemen' but his basic ideas were taken to be more widely applicable.
15. 'Les plus sages s'attachent à ce qu'il importe aux hommes de savoir, sans considérer ce que les enfants sont en état de comprendre. Ils cherchent toujours l'homme dans l'enfant sans penser à ce qu'il est avant que d'être homme.' (Jean-Jacques Rousseau [**114**, 'Préface', p. 242]. 'Aimez l'enfance, favorisez ses jeux, ses plaisirs, son aimable instinct. Qui de vous n'a pas regretté cet âge où le rire est toujours sur les lèvres et où l'âme est toujours en paix? Pourquoi voulez-vous ôter à ces petits innocents la jouissance d'un temps si court qui leur échappe?' [**114**, Livre 2, p. 302].
16. 'Tout est bien sortant des mains de l'Auteur des choses, tout dégénère entre les mains de l'homme.' [**114**, Livre 1, p. 245].
17. Coveney [**27**, p. 46].
18. Grylls [**62**, p. 34].
19. See Vineta Colby [**25**, p. 95].
20. See Grylls [**62**, p. 23].
21. William Wordsworth, *The Prelude*, Book 5, lines 531–3 [**147**, p. 81].

22. Whither is fled the visionary gleam?
    Where is it now, the glory and the dream?'
    Ode on *Intimations of Immortality* (pub. 1807) [**148**, p. 460]. See Coveney [**27**, ch. 3] for a full discussion of Wordsworth's view of children.
23. See, for example, Adrian Vincent (ed.) [**136**].
24. See Blake's two contrasting poems on 'The chimney sweeper' and discussion in Coveney [**27**, ch. 2].
25. See my Chapter 2 for further discussion of this.
26. See note 7 above. Also illuminating is Grylls' discussion of periodical articles [**62**, ch. 2].
27. See also Walvin [**139**, p. 15], and some of the sketches in Blanchard Jerrold and Gustave Doré [**80**].
28. Sir James Kay-Shuttleworth, *Four Periods of Public Education* (1862), p. 121, cited in [**107**, vol. 2, p. 349].
29. See Walvin [**139**] for further discussion.
30. Anna Jameson, 'A revelation of childhood' [**76**, p. 117].
31. George Eliot, *The Mill on the Floss*, Penguin: Harmondsworth, 1985, p. 123. See Coe's description of the 'alternative world' of childhood [**24**, p. 1].
32. Wordsworth, Ode on *Intimations of Immortality*, lines 5, 8–9, [**148**, p. 460].
33. Katherine Mansfield, letter to Ida Baker, 29 August 1921 [**101**, p. 219].
34. Walvin recounts that Henry Mayhew was appalled to find so few 'childlike' qualities among the poor children he interviewed on the London streets in the 1850s and 1860s [**139**, p. 12].
35. Roy Pascal [**102**, p. 52].

Chapter 1

1. See Gillian Avery with Angela Bull [**8**] for a list of names of women writers, and Geoffrey Summerfield [**125**].
2. For example, Anna Barbauld's *Evenings at Home* (1792–96), *Lessons for Children* (1780) and *Hymns in Prose for Children* (1781), and Sarah Trimmer's *Fabulous Histories* (1786).
3. Cited in Patricia Demers and Gordon Moyles (eds) [**40**, pp. 135–7].
4. Jean-Jacques Rousseau: 'les enfants se moquent du corbeau, mais ils s'affectionnent tous au renard'. [**114**, p. 356].
5. Mary Wollstonecraft, *Original Stories from Real Life* (1788), in *The Works of Mary Wollstonecraft*, ed. Janet Todd and Marilyn Butler, Pickering: London, 1989, vol. 4, p. 359.
6. *Ibid.*, p. 401.
7. *Ibid.*, p. 413.
8. *Ibid.*, p. 370.
9. *Ibid.*, p. 388.
10. *Ibid.*, p. 389. The two children are allegedly based on the Kingsborough girls, to whom Wollstonecraft was governess, one of whom later assumed the name of Mrs Mason. See Eleanor Flexner [**52**, p. 272].
11. Mary Jane Kilner, *The Memoirs of a Peg-top* (c. 1805), cited in Avery and Bull [**8**, p. 16]. See also Mary Wollstonecraft in *Thoughts on the Education of Daughters* (1787):
    > Whenever a child asks a question, it should always have a reasonable answer given it. Its little passions should be engaged. They are mostly fond

of stories, and proper ones would improve them even while they are amused. Instead of this, their heads are filled with improbable tales, and superstitious accounts of invisible beings, which breed strange prejudices and vain fears in their minds. (*Works of Mary Wollstonecraft*, vol. 4, p. 10)

12. See Julia Briggs [**12**, pp. 231–3].
13. For biographical information, see Elizabeth Harden [**64**] and Vineta Colby [**25**].
14. Maria Edgeworth, *The Parent's Assistant* (1796), 3rd edn, J. Johnson: London, 1800, p. viii.
15. Richard and Maria Edgeworth, *Practical Education*, 2 vols, J. Johnson: London, 1798, vol. 1, pp. 335–8.
16. See Elizabeth McWhorter Harden [**65**] for further discussion.
17. Maria Edgeworth, *Simple Susan* in *Lazy Lawrence and Other Tales*, Watergate Classics: London, 1948, p. 110.
18. *Ibid.*, p. 117.
19. See Edgeworth, *Practical Education*, p. 167.
20. Sir Walter Scott called *Simple Susan* 'quite inimitable' [**61**, vol. 1821–23, p. 312].
21. Edgeworth, *Lazy Lawrence*, p. 37.
22. *The Purple Jar* appeared first in *The Parent's Assistant*, and subsequently in *Early Lessons* which comprised *Harry and Lucy, Frank, Rosamond* (1801), *Continuation of Early Lessons* (1814), *Rosamond: A sequel* (1821), *Frank: A sequel* (1822) and *Harry and Lucy, Concluded* (1825). *Early Lessons*, Routledge: London, n.d., p. 5.
23. *Ibid.*, p. 9.
24. See Briggs' discussion of this [**12**, pp. 230–1].
25.   I was honest, Mamma, when I returned his nuts to him; and he was honest when he returned my cherries. I liked him for being honest; and he liked me for being honest. I will always be honest about everything as well as about the nuts.
    Frank at his most childlike in Edgeworth, *Early Lessons*, p. 16.
26. *The Good French Governess, Moral Tales*, vol. 2, *Tales and Novels*, 18 vols, Baldwin & Cradock: London, 1832, vol. 3, p. 97.
27. See Colby, [**25**, p. 136]. See also Edgeworth's *Vivian*, in which the protagonist is critical of his mother who
    took too much, a great deal too much care of me; she over-educated, over-instructed, over-dosed me with premature lessons of prudence: she was so afraid that I should ever do a foolish thing, or not say a wise one, that she prompted my every word and guided my every action. So I grew up, seeing with her eyes, hearing with her ears, and judging with her understanding, till at length, it was found out, that I had not eyes, ears, or understanding of my own. (*Tales of Fashionable Life*, vol. III in *Tales and Novels*, vol. 8, p. 5)
    See also *Ennui, or Memoirs of the Earl of Glenthorn* in which a young man narrates his own story to show his misspent youth (*Tales of Fashionable Life*, vol. I in *Tales and Novels*, vol. 6).
28. Edgeworth, *Harrington, Tales and Novels*, vol. 9, p. 1.
29. See also *The Birthday Present*, and Mary Wollstonecraft's *Thoughts on the Education of Daughters* on the influence of servants on children left in their care: 'the first notions they imbibe are mean and vulgar. They are taught cunning, the wisdom of that class of people, and a love of truth, the foundation of virtue, is soon obliterated from their mind.' *The Works of Mary Wollstonecraft*, vol. 4, p. 9.
30. Edgeworth, *Harrington*, p. 4. One of Edgeworth's step-brothers, Henry, apparently suffered from such night terrors. See Summerfield [**125**, p. 130].

31. Edgeworth, *Harrington*, p. 5.
32. *Ibid.*, p. 7.
33. *Ibid.*, p. 9.
34. Colby [25, pp. 97–8].
35. Jane Austen, *Pride and Prejudice*, in *The Novels of Jane Austen*, ed. R.W. Chapman, Oxford University Press: Oxford, 1987, vol. 2, pp. 122–3.
36. Letter to Anna Austen, 9 September 1814, cited in R.W. Chapman (ed.) [22, p. 402].
37. Austen, *Northanger Abbey*, in *The Novels of Jane Austen*, vol. 5, pp. 13–14.
38. *Ibid.*, p. 14. Park Honan claims that the green slope corresponds to one at the rectory at Steventon where Austen lived as a child, and that Austen was trained to love the outdoors [72, p. 22].
39. Austen, *Mansfield Park*, in *The Novels of Jane Austen*. vol. 3, p. 13.
40. *Ibid.*, p. 19. Eva Figes claims that Fanny remains a dutiful child and never grows up [51, p. 105].
41. Angus Wilson [143, p. 207].
42. Mary Wollstonecraft, *Mary: A fiction*. Janet Todd (ed.) [133, p. 8].
43. *Ibid.*, p. 9. See R.M. Wardle [140, pp. 6–7].
44. Wollstonecraft, *Mary*, p. 8.
45. See Wardle [140]; Claire Tomalin [134] and Flexner [52] for corroborating biographical details.
46. Mary Shelley, *Matilda* [133, p. 157].
47. Todd suggests that these relationships may reflect many aspects of the shifting relationships between the Godwins and the Shelleys [133, p. xvii].
48. Susan Ferrier, *Marriage*, with Introduction by H. Foltinek, Oxford University Press: Oxford, 1977, p. 163.
49. The same fate befalls Tommy Merton in *Sandford and Merton* and other literary miscreants of the period.
50. *Jane Eyre*, *Middlemarch* and *The Mill on the Floss*, respectively.
51. See Valerie Sanders [117] and R.K. Webb [141] for details of Harriet Martineau's career.
52. Harriet Martineau, *Principle and Practice, or, The Orphan Family*, Wellington: Salop, 1827, pp. 1–2.
53. See Sanders for details of Martineau's illness and her awareness of the 'reduction to essentials' of a restricted life in a letter to Richard Monckton Miles, 4 December 1841, cited in [117, p. 89].
54. Harriet Martineau, *The Settlers at Home* in *The Playfellow*, G. Routledge: London, n.d., pp. 87–8.
55. See discussion of Marryat in Barbara Wall [138, pp. 45–8]. Sanders claims that Martineau's work looks forward to the adventure stories of Marryat and Arthur Ransome [117, p. 91].
56. See Martineau's *Letters to the Deaf: An essay by Harriet Martineau*, Tait's *Edinburgh Magazine*, 1834 and *Life in the Sick Room: Essays by an invalid*, Edward Moxon: London, 1844.
57. Martineau, *The Crofton Boys*, in *The Playfellow*, p. 417.
58. *Ibid.*, p. 440.
59. Harriet Martineau, *Autobiography*, with Memorials by Maria Weston Chapman, 2nd edn, Smith, Elder: London, 1877, vol. 1, p. 44.
60. *Ibid.*, vol. 1, p. 48.
61. *Ibid.*, vol. 1, p. 76.
62. *Ibid.*, vol. 1, p. 78.

63. Letter to Samuel Taylor Coleridge [92, vol. 1, p. 326].
64. William Wordsworth, *The Prelude or Growth of a Poet's Mind*, Book 5, lines 228–41, 436–9 [147, pp. 67–84].
65. Cited in Juliet Dusinberre [46, p. 42].
66. Briggs describes the sexist nature of such attacks which sometimes mocked the writer herself, as in the joke between Southey and Coleridge about Mrs Bare-Bald (Mrs Barbauld), as 'the saucy mockery of the schoolboy thumbing his nose at female authority' [12, p. 234].

Chapter 2

1. Sarah Trimmer, *Guardian of Education*, vol. I, 1802, p. 287.
2. See Margaret Nancy Cutt [32]. Cutt claims that the fact that no revolution occurred in England can be credited to the 'sobering influence' of Evangelicalism to some extent.
3. Samuel Pickering [105, p. 20].
4. *Ibid.*, p. 10. See also Cutt [32], Grylls [62] and Elizabeth Jay [78]. Hannah More's tracts had a circulation of two million in the first year of publication (Pickering [105, p. 27]).
5. It is, in fact, often difficult to determine at which age group the tracts were directed. See Avery and Bull [8, 81].
6. See Jay [78] and R.L. Wolff [145].
7. 'From liberty, equality and the rights of man, good Lord deliver *us*.' Hannah More in a letter to Horace Walpole, cited in Pickering [105, p. 51].
8. Pickering cites the *Methodist Magazine*'s view that novels were like 'a poisoned shirt presented to Hercules, a pestilent treasure' [105, p. 48].
9. Avery and Bull [8, p. 83].
10. William Makepeace Thackeray, 'Mme Sand and the New Apocalypse' [128, pp. 263–4]. George Eliot was critical of the 'oracular species' of women novelists too: 'the ability of a lady novelist to describe actual life and her fellow-men, is in inverse proportion to her confident eloquence about God and the Other World' ('Silly Novels by Lady Novelists', *Westminster Review*, vol. lxvi, October 1856 [47, pp. 300–24, 311].
11. Matthew 18: 2–6.
12. Sarah Trimmer, *The Good Schoolmistress*, in *Instructive Tales* (1831 edn), pp. 113–27. Cited in Cutt [32, pp. 9–10].
13. See Grylls [62, p. 23].
14. Hannah More, *Strictures on the Modern System of Female Education* (1799), New York, 1835, vol. vi, p. 36. William Wilberforce, in his *A Practical View of the Prevailing Religious System* (1797), is critical of parents who fail to instil the principles of faith in their children and are not watchful enough for childish manifestations of sin.
15. Sequels to *The History of the Fairchild Family* appeared in 1842 and 1847.
16. Naomi Royde Smith suggests that Mrs Sherwood's experience of oriental worship and justice in India fostered her pseudo-romantic taste for the macabre [122, p. 64], but her preoccupation with death certainly relates to her own grief at the loss of several of her children in India and, of course, the macabre is present in many folk- and fairy-tales.
17. Grylls argues that patriarchy was revived by the success of Evangelicalism [62, p. 90].

18. Mary Martha Sherwood, *The History of the Fairchild Family* (1818), 4th edn, J. Hatchard: London, 1819, pp. 269, 69.
19. *The History of the Fairchild Family*, Wells, Gardner, Darton: London, 1902, pp. iii–iv. The introduction, by Mary E. Palgrave, speaks of 'this new edition of a dear old book', but in fact the removal of everything that made Mrs Sherwood's book what it is alters it beyond recognition.
20. *Ibid.*, pp. 156–9.
21. Mrs Sherwood was not alone by far in this respect. See Henry Sharpe Horsley's poem 'A visit to Newgate', in *The Affectionate Parent's Gift, and the Good Child's Reward* (1828), which begins:
    The Father of two little boys
    Resolved one day to take
    A walk through Newgate with his lads
    Just for example's sake
    Cited in Demers and Moyles [**40**, p. 158].
22. Mary Martha Sherwood, *The History of Henry Milner: A little boy, who was not brought up according to the fashions of this world*, 3rd edn, J. Hatchard: London, 1826, p. 7.
23. *Ibid.*, pp. 22–4.
24. *Ibid.*, pp. 25–6.
25. *Ibid.*, p. 28.
26. *Ibid.*, p. 139 and p. 40.
27. David C. Harrison suggests that in *Praeterita* John Ruskin patterned what he chose to remember of his own life on *The History of Henry Milner*, because he felt it was suitable training for his own temperament [**68**, pp. 45–66].
28. Cutt suggests that Maria Charlesworth unwittingly contributed to this general disillusionment with her writing! Charlesworth had experience of this kind of charity work in Suffolk and had also tried it in London around 1850 [**32**, p. 55].
29. Maria Charlesworth, *Ministering Children: A tale dedicated to childhood* (1854), Seeley, Jackson and Halliday: London, 1868, p. iii.
30. *Ibid.*, p. 22.
31. *Ibid.*, p. 24. Avery claims that this makes *Ministering Children* 'the most unacceptable of all the tract books' [**8**, p. 90].
32. Cutt suggests that the scene of Mary Clifford's funeral may well have been influenced by that of Little Nell in Dickens' *The Old Curiosity Shop* [**32**, p. 66].
33. Charlesworth, *Ministering Children*, p. 176. Compare *The Old Curiosity Shop*: 'When Death strikes down the innocent and young, for every fragile form from which he lets the panting spirit free, a hundred virtues rise, in shapes of mercy, charity and love, to walk the world and bless it' [**43**, p. 544].
34. Charlesworth, *Ministering Children*, p. 214.
35. As one of the results of the Poor Law of 1834, parish relief was only given inside the workhouse, which segregated inmates and caused loss of self-respect because of the associated 'pauper taint'. Fear of the workhouse appears in many novels of the time. See also Anne Thackeray's article on 'Little paupers' in the *Cornhill Magazine*, vol. xxii, September 1870, in which she describes the benefits and drawbacks of a scheme of placing workhouse children with widows, spinsters and childless couples for a small amount of money. Her portraits of deprived children are heart-rending and confirm the pictures painted in contemporary literature [**127**].
36. Charlesworth, *Ministering Children*, p. 426.
37. See Flora Thompson, *Lark Rise to Candleford* [**130**, p. 387]. Charlesworth's niece,

Maud Charlesworth, ascribed her life's work with the Salvation Army to reading *Ministering Children*. Another niece, Florence Barclay, wrote *The Rosary* (1909) in which the characters are also an object lesson in living. See Cutt [32, pp. 171–81].

38. Hesba Stretton, *The Children of Cloverley*, Religious Tract Society: London, 1865, p. 129.
39. *Ibid.*, p. 189.
40. Charlotte Mary Yonge [149, p. 309].
41. Cited in Juliet Dusinberre along with other such criticisms [46, p. 51].
42. George Eliot, *Silas Marner: The weaver of Raveloe* (1861), *The Novels of George Eliot*, Blackwood: Edinburgh and London, 1878, vol. 3, p. 2.
43. *Ibid.*, p. 139.
44. *Ibid.*, p. 147.
45. *Ibid.*, p. 165.
46. Letter to John Blackwood, 24 February 1861 in Gordon S. Haight (ed.) [63, p. 382].
47. Eliot, *Silas Marner*, p. 164.
48. *Ibid.*, p. 158.
49. *Ibid.*, p. 104.
50. George Eliot, *Amos Barton*, in *Scenes of Clerical Life*, ed. Thomas A. Noble, Clarendon Press: Oxford, 1985, p. 67.
51. *Ibid.*, pp. 68–9.
52. See Colby on George Eliot's 'secular saints' [25, p. 204].
53. Peter Coveney claims that the use of the children is merely 'barbaric emotionality' to increase the 'sadistic tension' of the second half of the novel [27, p. 181].
54. Mrs Henry Wood, *East Lynne* (1861), Macmillan: London, 1909, p. 434.
55. *Ibid.*, p. 435.

Chapter 3

1. Hannah More knew the mining areas of the Mendip Hills, where she opened successful Sunday and day schools with her sisters (I. Kovacevic [84, p. 148]). See also Maria Edgeworth's story, *Lame Jervas* in *Tales and Novels*, 18 vols, Baldwin & Cradock: London, 1832, vol. 4, *Popular Tales*, in which a young trapper, after many misadventures, becomes a gentleman.
2. Hannah More, *The Lancashire Collier Girl: A true story*, in Kovacevic [84, p. 172].
3. *Ibid.*, p. 174.
4. *Ibid.*, pp. 169–70.
5. *Ibid.*, p. 172.
6. *Ibid.*, pp. 172–3.
7. First-hand evidence that children, especially boys, were seen as a valuable economic commodity is cited in E. Royston Pike [106, p. 167].
8. Sarah Trimmer, *The Economy of Charity, or An Address to Ladies concerning Sunday Schools* (1787).
9. John Dyer, *The Fleece*, III, lines 281–5, cited in Kovacevic [84, p. 78].
10. Kovacevic [84, p. 82].
11. J. Fielden, cited in Pike [106, p. 78].
12. See Alan Ereira [49, pp. 101 ff].
13. B. Leigh Hutchins and Amy Harrison [74, Appendix A, p. 304].
14. Pinchbeck and Hewitt [107, vol. 2, p. 404]; Ereira [49, p. 119].
15. Report of sub-commissioner R.H. Franks, Parliamentary Papers 1842, vol. xv, pp. 91–2, cited in Pike [106, p. 170].

16. Kovacevic argues that abuse of children was tolerated with equanimity in the early stages of industrialisation and that reform only came about once a sound economic basis had been established [**84**, p. 106].

17. Cutt [**32**, p. 109]. Ruskin accused Dickens of killing Little Nell 'like a butcher for the market' in 'Fiction Fair and Foul', *Macmillan's Magazine*, 1880 [**116**, vol. xxxiv, p. 275].

18. See Valerie Sanders who contrasts Dickens in this respect [**118**, p. 39]. Vineta Colby claims that only Dickens was as skilful in integrating fact and fiction [**25**, p. 222].

19. See Kovacevic [**84**, p. 219]. Louis Cazamian sees Martineau as cold towards the problems of the workers and too obsessed with economic factors, although she softened later in her career [**21**, pp. 57–8]. Charlotte Brontë described her as 'both hard and warm-hearted, abrupt and affectionate, liberal and despotic' in a letter to Ellen Nussey, 1850, cited in Elizabeth Gaskell [**53**, p. 437].

20. Kovacevic [**84**, p. 218].

21. Frances Eleanor Trollope [**135**, vol. 1, pp. 300–2].

22. Frances Trollope, *The Life and Adventures of Michael Armstrong: The factory boy* (1840), F. Cass: London, 1968, p. iv.

23. A review in the *Atheneum*, 10 August 1839, suggested that such books were dangerous and written 'for the purpose of scattering firebrands among the people'. Cited in Kovacevic [**84**, p. 101].

24. Trollope, *Michael Armstrong*, p. 21.

25. *Ibid.*, p. 237.

26. See Pike [**106**, pp. 137–54]; Walvin [**139**, ch. 4]; and the museum in the Apprentice House at Quarry Bank Mill, Styal, Cheshire.

27. Trollope, *Michael Armstrong*, p. 237.

28. *Ibid.*, p. 182. By the time the novel was written, such isolated mills were less common because factories were increasingly established in cities where children were able to live at home (Kovacevic [**84**, p. 101]).

29. *Ibid.*, p. 187.

30. *Ibid.*, p. 202.

31. *Ibid.*, p. 282. See Wordsworth's poem 'The Excursion', Book 8, lines 333–4: 'Can hope look forward to a manhood raised/On such foundations? "Hope is not for him!"' [**148**, p. 685].

32. See Cazamian [**21**, pp. 211–12] on this. Trollope, a middle-of-the-road Anglican, also wrote an anti-Evangelical novel, *The Vicar of Wrexhill* (1837) about a 'ranting, canting fanatic'.

33. Trollope, *Michael Armstrong*, p. 186.

34. Cazamian criticises the novel on stylistic grounds [**21**, pp. 236–7]. Frances Trollope in *Trollope* [**135**, p. 301].

35. Charlotte Elizabeth Tonna was editor of the *Christian Lady's Magazine*, among others, from 1843 to 1846. *The Wrongs of Women* contained *Milliners and Dress-Makers, The Forsaken Home, The Little Pin-Headers* and *The Lace-Runners*.

36. See I. Kovacevic and S.B. Kanner [**85**, pp. 152–73].

37. Tonna, *Helen Fleetwood* (1841), in *The Works of Charlotte Elizabeth*, 3 vols, M.W. Dodd, New York, 1844–5, vol. 2, p. 71.

38. *Ibid.*, p. 159.

39. *Ibid.*, p. 69.

40. Tonna, *The Little Pin-Headers*, reproduced in Kovacevic [**84**, p. 340].

41. *Ibid.*, p. 345.

42. *Ibid.*, p. 344.

43. *Ibid.*, p. 331. Royston Pike cites many examples of sadistic behaviour by overseers [106].

44. Tonna, *The Little Pin-Headers*, p. 326.

45. *Ibid.*, p. 320.

46. *Ibid.*, p. 329.

47. See *The Perils of the Nation: An appeal to the legislative, the clergy and the higher middle classes* (1843). Tonna shared the same fear as her contemporaries of working-class action, seeing socialism as a 'moral Gorgon' and the 'last effort of Satanic venom' in *Helen Fleetwood*, p. 168.

48. See Cutt [32, p. 35].

49. The novel was accused of calumny by Manchester manufacturers in the *Manchester Guardian* of 28 February and 7 March 1849.

50. Elizabeth Gaskell, *Mary Barton: A tale of Manchester life* (1848), Penguin: Harmondsworth, 1975, p. 61.

51. *Ibid.*, p. 96.

52. *Ibid.*, p. 116.

53. *Ibid.*, p. 98. Gaskell's depiction is corroborated by evidence in the works of Friedrich Engels and Sir James Kay-Shuttleworth. See Gary S. Messinger [96].

54. Elizabeth Gaskell, *Mary Barton*, p. 460.

55. Elizabeth Gaskell, *The Three Eras of Libbie Marsh*, in *Four Short Stories*, ed. Anna Walters, Pandora: London, 1983, pp. 25–6.

56. *Ibid.*, p. 45.

57. *Ibid.*, p. 46.

58. *Ibid.*, p. 47.

59. See Cutt [32, pp. 37–42].

60. The term 'street arab' was allegedly coined by Charlotte Yonge. See R.L. Wolff [145, p. 242]. See Walvin [139, pp. 67–70] on street children in London.

61. See Cutt [32, chs 8 and 9]. Thomas Barnardo homes were set up for the rescue of children, Octavia Hill worked to found decent housing, the Booths offered spiritual help through the Salvation Army and Maria Rye devised schemes to send destitute children to adoptive homes in Canada.

62. Grylls remarks that, ironically, 'power-over-parents first crept into literature through the chapel door' [62, p. 93].

63. There is a stained-glass window featuring Jessica in memory of Hesba Stretton in the parish church of St Laurence, Church Stretton, Shropshire.

64. Hesba Stretton, *Jessica's First Prayer* (1867), in *Novels of Faith and Doubt: A Garland series of Victorian fiction*, no. 45, ed. R.L. Wolff, Garland: New York and London, 1976, p. 12.

65. Wolff claims that Jessica is by nature an Evangelical, since she calls confidently on a personal God whom she summons as a father and who answers her prayer [145, p. 242].

66. Stretton, *Jessica's First Prayer*, pp. 61–2.

67. *Ibid.*, p. 80.

68. Hesba Stretton, *Little Meg's Children* (1868), in *Novels of Faith and Doubt*, no. 45, pp. 10–11.

69. *Ibid.*, p. 24.

70. *Ibid.*, p. 63.

71. *Ibid.*, p. 33.

72. *Ibid.*, p. 16.

73. Hesba Stretton, *Alone in London* (1869), in *Novels of Faith and Doubt*, no. 45, p. 127.

74. Hesba Stretton, *A Thorny Path* (1879), Religious Tract Society: London, n.d., p. 173.
75. Silas Hocking [**70**, pp. 15–16].
76. Cutt [**32**, p. 156].
77. Cutt [**32**, p. 168]. *A Peep behind the Scenes* was made into a film in 1918. Cutt calls it a 'most unlikely hybrid: an Evangelical fairy-tale' [**32**, p. 167].
78. Mrs O.F. Walton, *A Peep behind the Scenes* (1877), Religious Tract Society: London, n.d., pp. 14–15.
79. *Ibid.*, p. 113.
80. *Ibid.*, p. 191. 'The Good Shepherd' is first on the list of the Religious Tract Society's Coloured Scripture Cartoons as advertised at the back of Hesba Stretton's *The Children of Cloverley*.

Chapter 4

1. Leonore Davidoff and Catherine Hall [**35**, p. 74].
2. Davidoff and Hall suggest that incipient panic about the conditions of women working in the mines was the motivation for many such works [**35**, pp. 182–4].
3. *Ibid.*, p. 180.
4. See Mark Spilka [**123**, p. 167].
5. Ann Taylor, *Reciprocal Duties of Parents and Children*, Taylor & Hessey: London, 1818, p. 176.
6. *Ibid.*, p. 167.
7. Martineau, *Autobiography*, vol. 3, p. 3; *Blackwood's Magazine*, April 1846, p. 413, cited in Kathleen Tillotson [**132**, p. 131]. In this respect, the portrayal of the child mirrored the development of the novel in the shift from concern with external behaviour to inner emotions and dilemmas.
8. Colby [**25**, pp. 31–2].
9. Hannah More, *Essays on Various Subjects Principally Designed for Young Ladies* (1777), C. Whittingham: Chiswick, 1824, p. xv.
10. Avery and Bull [**8**, p. 66].
11. Cited in Gillian Avery [**5**, p. 68].
12. Catherine Sinclair, *Holiday House: A book for the young* (1839), Ward, Lock: London, 1901.
13. *Ibid.*, p. 73.
14. *Ibid.*, p. 145.
15. *Ibid.*, p. 320.
16. Smith [**122**, p. 187].
17. Cited by Margaret Kennedy [**81**, p. 41]. The novels are thought to be a lampoon on the Clapham Sect, a group of strict Evangelicals, but Kennedy argues that Mozley ignores the side of Evangelicalism which promoted service to humanity, like the work of William Wilberforce. Mozley was the sister of Cardinal Newman and strongly disapproved of his secession to Roman Catholicism.
18. Harriet Mozley, *The Fairy Bower or, the History of a Month* (1841), cited in Avery and Bull [**8**, p. 74].
19. Kimberley Reynolds [**112**, p. 98].
20. See Avery and Bull [**8**, ch. 3] for discussion of the Victorian child, and Nina Auerbach [**4**, p. 147].

21. Yonge [**149**, pp. 309–10]. She also remarked that children reading such tales of
    pious deaths might well conclude that it was 'dangerous to be good', in the *Monthly
    Packet*, 1852.
22. Charlotte Mary Yonge, *The Daisy Chain or, Aspirations: A family chronicle* (1856),
    reprinted with an Introduction by Barbara Dennis and Afterword by Georgina
    Battiscombe, Virago: London, 1988, pp. xi–xii.
23. Ruth Harris [**67**, p. 78]. See Barbara Wall's discussion of Yonge's 'governess'
    voice in her books for younger children [**138**, pp. 79–81].
24. Yonge, *The Daisy Chain*, p. 7. Ethel's continued habit of 'grumbling' at the end
    provokes a suspicion that there may have been an unconscious ambivalence on
    Yonge's part despite her overt endorsement of traditional gender roles. Cristabel
    Coleridge claims that Yonge lived in an atmosphere of mingled ardour and
    submission all her life in *Charlotte Mary Yonge. Her Life and Letters*, Macmillan:
    London, New York, 1903.
25. Charlotte Mary Yonge, *Scenes and Characters* (1847), Macmillan: London, 1886,
    p. 60.
26. Elizabeth Missing Sewell, *The Experience of Life* (1853), in *Novels of Faith and
    Doubt: A Garland series of Victorian fiction*, no. 26, ed. R.L. Wolff, Garland: New
    York and London, 1972, p. 2.
27. *Ibid.*, p. 8.
28. Elizabeth Missing Sewell, *The Autobiography of Elizabeth Missing Sewell*, ed.
    Eleanor Sewell, Longman: London, 1907, p. 15. 'Sarah's troubled mind was a
    record of my own personal feelings, but I had no Aunt Sarah to comfort me' (p.
    115).
29. Sewell, *The Experience of Life*, p. 24.
30. *Ibid.*, p. 10. Although the events of the novel are invented, money troubles also
    affected Sewell's family.
31. *Ibid.*, p. 9, p. 7.
32. *Ibid.*, p. 9. Sewell uses the same expression of her own home in her autobiography
    (p. 4).
33. *Ibid.*, p. 19.
34. Juliana Ewing, *Six to Sixteen*, Society for Promoting Christian Knowledge:
    London, 1875, p. 12.
35. *Ibid.*, p. 22.
36. *Ibid.*, p. 172.
37. *Ibid.*, p. 296.
38. Juliana Ewing, *We and the World*, in *Aunt Judy's Yearly Volume*, ed. H.K.F. Gatty,
    George Bell: London, 1878, p. 11.
39. *Ibid.*, p. 470.
40. J.S. Bratton [**11**, p. 200].
41. Florence Montgomery, *Misunderstood* (1869), Macmillan: London, 1909, p. 50.
42. *Ibid.*, pp. 75–6.
43. *Ibid.*, p. 65.
44. *Ibid.*, p. 37.
45. *Ibid.*, p. 187.
46. *Ibid.*, p. 205.
47. Coveney includes discussion of Marie Corelli in a chapter entitled 'Reduction to
    Absurdity' and waxes almost vicious in his accusations of 'intellectual mauling',
    'mental mediocrity' and 'consummate vulgarity' [**27**, pp. 184–93].
48. Marie Corelli, *Boy: A Sketch*, Hutchinson: London, 1900, p. 8.
49. *Ibid.*, p. 17.

50. *Ibid.*, p. 65.
51. *Ibid.*, p. 17.
52. *Ibid.*, p. 304.
53. Marie Corelli, *The Mighty Atom*, Hutchinson: London, 1896.
54. *Ibid.*, pp. 8–9.
55. *Ibid.*, p. 70.
56. *Ibid.*, p. 298.
57. *Ibid.*, p. 310.

Chapter 5

1. See Valerie Sanders' discussion of these problems [117].
2. For evidence of this see Sanders [117] and Estelle C. Jelinek [79].
3. Sanders [117, p. 67].
4. See Sanders [117, p. 53].
5 Mary Martha Sherwood, *The Life and Times of Mrs Sherwood*, ed. F.J. Harvey Darton, Wells, Gardner, Darton: London, 1910, p. 34. Further page references to this work will be given in parenthesis in the text. That back-braces were common is suggested by the paintings of the Drummond children in Susan Lasdun [87]. Naomi Royde Smith includes the following intriguing sentence in her citation of this extract, which, although she claims to be quoting from the 1910 edition of *The Life and Times of Mrs Sherwood*, does not appear in the copy I have consulted:
> it only wanted one to tell me that I was hardly used to turn this healthy discipline into poison, but there was no such person to give this hint, and hence the suspicion never, as I remember, arose in my mind that other children were not subjected to the same usage as myself.

[122, p. 28].
6. Smith cites the following passage which, as above, does not appear in the 1910 edition consulted: 'that which was laid up in the future for the little wild girl who was educated in the woods of Stanford, was not an everyday life, and for such therefore, she was not fitted, by an all-wise Providence' [122, p. 29]. This might refer to her life in India, but certainly hints at a sense of herself as special and the expression 'little wild girl' suggests a romanticising of the facts presented in the autobiography.
7. A shockingly undisciplined boy, reminiscent of the Noble children, the lesson of courtesy she is taught by her father when she hesitates to help an old man pick up his bundle of sticks, and the extraordinarily dressed Mme de Pelévé all appear in *The History of the Fairchild Family*.
8. Charlotte Elizabeth Tonna, *Personal Recollections*, 2nd edn, Seeley, Burnside & Seeley: London, 1843, pp. 1–3. Further page references to this work will be given in parenthesis in the text.
9. Sanders cites some interesting examples which suggest that daydreaming was seen as more healthy and constructive in males than in females [117, pp. 58–9].
10. See Sanders [117, p. 67] for further discussion of this.
11. Sewell, *The Autobiography*, p. 16. Further page references to this work will appear in parenthesis in the text.
12. Sewell specifically states this (*ibid.*, p. 116).
13. 'Autobiography' in Christabel Coleridge [26, pp. 1–119; 62–3]. Further references to this work will be given in parenthesis in the text.

14. Coleridge asserts that 'she lived so much in the life of her family that her history cannot be picked out and separated from theirs' [26, p. 120].
15. Frances Hodgson Burnett, *The One I Knew the Best of All: A memory of the mind of a child*, illustrated by Reginald B. Birch, Charles Scribner: New York, 1893, Preface, p. vii. Further page references to this work will be given in parenthesis in the text.
16. Coleridge, *Charlotte Mary Yonge*, p. 107.
17. Mrs Sherwood's account in her autobiography of the deaths of her children in India is an extremely moving one.
18. Martineau was criticised by George Eliot, among others, for what was regarded as egotistical self-exposure. See Sanders [117, p. 8, p. 17].
19. Martineau, *Autobiography*, vol. 1, p. 9. Further page references to this work will be given in parenthesis in the text.
20. Sanders claims that more women than men admit to this in their autobiographies, with the exception of male members of the Romantic movement, like Lamb, De Quincey and Leigh Hunt [117, p. 60].
21. The deep impression made by this memory is evident in the fact that she recreates the episode in her novel *Deerbrook* (1839).
22. Martineau, *Autobiography*, vol. 2, p. 324.

> The lamplighter's torch on a winter's afternoon, as he ran along the street, used to cast a gleam, and the shadows of the window frames on the ceiling; and my blood ran cold at the sight, every day, even though I was on my father's knee, or on the rug in the middle of the circle round the fire.

(Harriet Martineau, *Household Education*, Edward Moxon: London, 1849, p. 98).
23. See Sanders [118, pp. 139–41] for comparison with *The Mill on the Floss* and *Jane Eyre* and my Chapter 5.
24. Sewell, *The Autobiography*, p. 10.
25. *Ibid.*, p. 34; Sherwood, *The Life and Times of Mrs Sherwood*, p. 147.
26. Martineau advocates domestic manual labour as beneficial in *Household Education*, although she claims that she disliked sewing for a long time because it was irritating and exhausting (p. 310). Obituary of Charlotte Brontë reproduced in [94, p. 365]: 'She was as able at the needle as at the pen. The household knew the excellence of her cookery before they heard of that of her books.'
27. Martineau's failure to see the sea is described in *Letters on the Laws of Man's Nature and Development*, p. 161. This childish frustration was experienced by the present writer when she could not 'see' the giant panda in the cage at London Zoo!
28. Hannah Lynch, *Autobiography of a Child*, W. Blackwood: Edinburgh and London, 1899. Further page references to this work will be given in parenthesis in the text.
29. Burnett also sees 7 as an important age for the awareness of new experiences (*The One I Knew*, p. 93).

Chapter 6

1. Charlotte Brontë, *Jane Eyre*, Penguin: Harmondsworth, 1985, p. 115. Further page references will be given in parenthesis in the text.
2. This is typical of autobiographical reminiscences where an important event or period looms large in the memory and hence in the narrative, leading, perhaps, to a telescoping of time and the eclipsing of other memories.
3. See Anne Brontë's poem, 'An Orphan's Lament' of 1841, which concludes:

Where shall I find a heart like thine
While life remains to me,
And where shall I bestow the love
I ever bore for thee?
(*The Poems of Anne Brontë*, ed. Edward Chitham, Macmillan: London, 1979, p. 78–9).

4. Sandra M. Gilbert and Susan Gubar [**56**, p. 34].
5. Elizabeth Rigby in the *Quarterly Review*, vol. 84 (December 1848), pp. 173–4, cited in Gilbert and Gubar [**56**, p. 338].
6. Rigby [**56**, p. 337].
7. Gilbert and Gubar see this description as embodying the 'Victorian superego', with overtones of Little Red Riding-Hood [**56**, p. 344].
8. Charlotte Brontë arrived at the Clergy Daughters' School at Cowan Bridge in August 1824 at the age of 8, and was placed at the bottom of the school because she was the youngest. Her older sisters, Maria and Elizabeth, were already there. See Winifred Gérin [**54**, pp. 1–5].
9. William Carus Wilson's stories in *The Child's First Tales* (1836) and his periodical *The Children's Friend* expound precisely these views, especially the idea that early death is a great protector from sin. See Gérin [**54**, p. 13].
10. The Clergy Daughters' School at Cowan Bridge had been conceived 'with vision and daring', with many of the progressive educationalists of the day, including Hannah More and William Wilberforce, among the subscribers. There were clearly serious problems, however. Charlotte Brontë blamed the school for the deaths of Maria and Elizabeth; indeed, Elizabeth Gaskell sees her portrait of the school as that of 'an unconsciously avenging sister' [**53**, p. 104]. The carelessness of the cook and the poor quality of the food were confirmed by Arthur Bell Nicholls in a contribution to the controversy about the portrayal which appeared in the *Halifax Guardian*, June–August 1857. The letters of the participants in the controversy are reproduced in Clement Shorter (ed.) [**120**, vol. 2, Appendix VIII].
11. Helen Burns is generally accepted to be a portrait of Maria Brontë, who was also untidy, abstracted and mystical. She had poor health and was ill-treated at Cowan Bridge by one teacher in particular. See Gérin [**54**, p. 14]. Gaskell claims that Charlotte Brontë was indignant about this to her dying day [**53**, p. 104].
12. Brontë was, in general, reserved about religion. The anxieties generated by the Calvinist beliefs of her Aunt Branwell had resulted in adolescent crises of religious melancholia for Charlotte, Branwell and Anne. In 1836, she wrote to Ellen Nussey 'if the Doctrine of Calvin [the predestination of the elect and the damned] be true, I am already an outcast' (Gérin [**54**, pp. 33–4]).
13. In a letter to William S. Williams of 28 October 1847, Brontë wrote:
    You are right in having faith in the reality of Helen Burns; she was real enough. I have exaggerated nothing there. I abstained from recording much that I remember respecting her, lest the narrative should sound incredible. Knowing this, I could not but smile at the quiet self-complacent dogmatism with which one of the journals lays it down that 'such creations as Helen Burns are very beautiful but very untrue'. (Thomas James Wise and John Alexander Symington [**144**, vol. 2, p. 150]).
    Jane's inablity to share Helen's feelings are interesting therefore and relate to Brontë's own anger and grief.
14. There was an epidemic of typhus at Cowan Bridge in April 1825. Maria was already weakened by tuberculosis before she went to school and her death in May 1825 was not due to the epidemic. Elizabeth went into decline in May, although

she escaped the fever, and died in June 1825. See Gérin [**54**, p. 16].

15. Mr Brontë's letter to the school after Maria's death states that 'she exhibited during her illness many symptoms of a heart under divine influence' (Gérin [**54**, p. 15]). The fortitude of Elizabeth was also commended by the prototype of 'Miss Temple' (a Miss Ann Evans) who nursed her in her room (Gaskell [**53**, p. 108]).

16. William Carus Wilson's school also changed for the better after the Brontës' time there. Gaskell writes that she feels 'sorry' about the picture Brontë paints [**53**, p. 99], yet her account of Wilson's attitude towards the quality of the food and the epidemic confirm it [**53**, p. 106].

17. Gérin [**54**, p. 40].

18. Fragment of an Angrian manuscript *c.* 1839 in the Parsonage Museum (Bonnell Collection, no. 125).

19. Gaskell [**53**, p. 120].

20. See discussion of this in Jay [**78**, pp. 252 *passim*]. Arthur Bell Nicholls claimed that 'To the day of her death "Currer Bell" maintained that the picture drawn in *Jane Eyre* was on the whole a true picture of Cowan Bridge School, as she knew it by experience' (letter to the *Halifax Guardian* cited in Shorter [**120**, p. 448]).

21. Gérin [**54**, p. 332].

22. See David Cecil's discussion of the 'children of calm' and the 'children of storm' in 'Emily Brontë and Wuthering Heights', in Thomas A. Vogler (ed.) [**137**, pp. 102–5].

23. In her biographical note to *Wuthering Heights*, Charlotte Brontë writes of Emily's love of the moors around Haworth: 'her native hills were far more to her than a spectacle; they were what she lived in and by, as much as the wild birds, their tenants, or as the heather, their produce'. (Emily Brontë, *Wuthering Heights* (1847), Penguin: Harmondsworth, 1953, p. xiv).

24. *Wuthering Heights*, p. 32. Further page references will be given in parenthesis in the text.

25. Emily Brontë completely rejected her Aunt Branwell's Calvinist faith (see Stevie Davies [**37**, pp. 11–12]).

26. See poem dated 14 October 1837 in Emily Brontë, *The Complete Poems of Emily Jane Brontë*, ed. C.W. Hatfield, Columbia University Press: New York, 1941, p. 51, in which a similar dream is described:

> My couch lay in a ruined Hall,
> Whose windows looked on the minster-yard
> Where chill, chill whiteness covered all –
> Both stone and iron and withered sward.
>
> The shattered glass let in the air,
> And with it came a wandering moan,
> A sound unutterably drear
> That made me shrink to be alone.
>
> One black yew-tree grew just below –
> I thought its boughs so sad might wail;
> Their ghostly fingers flecked with snow
> Rattled against an old vault's rail.
>
> I listened – no; 'twas life that still
> Lingered in some deserted heart:
> O God! What caused the shuddering shrill,
> That anguished, agonising start?

27. Gérin suggests that Branwell's account of his visit to Liverpool in August 1845, when he saw shiploads of Irish immigrants unloading in the docks, may have inspired this description. Pictures in the *Illustrated London News* showed dirty, dark, ragged children who only spoke Erse [55, p. 226].

28. One reason frequently put forward for Mr Earnshaw's partiality is that Heathcliff might be an illegitimate son, but this is not a particularly helpful interpretation and lacks substantiation. A dark, swarthy orphan figure appears in both Charlotte and Branwell's early stories in the Angria and Gondal sagas.

29. Gilbert and Gubar suggest that he is the 'body' who does her will [56, p. 265].

30. Stevie Davies interprets this as not only adolescent revolt, but rebellion against God the Father [36, p. 25].

31. Davies sees Heathcliff's position as a paradigm of Calvinist reprobation, thus predestined as 'lost', while Mr Earnshaw's favouritism could be seen as a parody of 'election', thus 'chosen' for salvation [36, p. 142].

32. Frances, too, is a model young lady who is diseased. See Gilbert and Gubar [56, p. 268].

33.   If all else perished and *he* remained, *I* should still continue to be; and if all else remained, and he were annihilated, the universe would turn to a mighty stranger: I should not seem a part of it. My love for Linton is like the foliage in the woods: time will change it, I'm well aware, as winter changes the trees. My love for Heathcliff resembles the eternal rocks beneath: a source of little visible delight, but necessary. Nelly, I *am* Heathcliff! (Emily Brontë, *Wuthering Heights*, p. 81)

34. Gérin reports that Branwell told of their sister Maria crying outside the windows twenty years before the writing of *Wuthering Heights* [55, p. 10].

35. Davies sees this as the 'huge cost' paid by Catherine in her innocent desire to attain the forbidden world of lost childhood, which is mitigated by the doubling of the plot in her child [36, p. 44].

36. See Irving H. Buchen [14, pp. 63–70] for discussion of this.

37. Poem headed A.A.A. (Emily Brontë, *The Complete Poems*, pp. 121–2).

38. Wordsworth, Ode on *Intimations of Immortality*, lines 67–8 [148, p. 460].

39. Emily Brontë, *The Complete Poems*, pp. 39–40.

40. From poem headed 'Lines', 28 April 1839, *ibid.*, pp. 104–6.

41. *Ibid.*, pp. 104–5.

42. *Ibid.*, pp. 105–6.

43. See Gérin [55, p. 223] and Buchen [14] for full discussion of this.

44. Thus Catherine's words like 'exile' and 'hell'. See Buchen [14, p. 68].

45. Davies sees the ultimate preference for Mother Earth over Father God as symptomatic of the 'sublime act of filial, literary and religious disobedience' which is *Wuthering Heights* [36, p. 18].

46. George Eliot, Prelude to *Middlemarch* (1872), Penguin: Harmondsworth, 1976, p. 25; *The Mill on the Floss*, Penguin: Harmondsworth, 1985. Page references will be given in parenthesis in the text.

47. In reply to criticism by Bulwer-Lytton, George Eliot remarked that 'the *epische Breite* into which I was beguiled by love of my subject in the first two volumes caused a want of proportionate fullness in the treatment of the third, which I shall always regret', cited in Ruby V. Redinger [111, p. 423].

48. See Redinger [111] for example. John Walter Cross, Eliot's husband, uses quotations from and echoes of *The Mill on the Floss* to describe Mary Ann Evans' own childhood in his 'Introductory Sketch of Childhood', stating that 'the early part of Maggie's portraiture is the best autobiographical representation we can

have of George Eliot's own feelings in her childhood' although he also states that there are so many fictitious elements that it would be 'absolutely misleading to trust to it as a true history' [**30**, p. 16].

49. When asked to write an autobiography, Eliot said:

> The only thing I should care much to dwell on would be the absolute despair I suffered from of ever being able to achieve anything. No-one could ever have felt greater despair, and a knowledge of this might be a help to some other struggler. (cited in Cross [**30**, p. 18])

50. See Redinger [**111**, p. 345]. Cross plays this down, writing that all that happened in real life between brother and sister was that 'as they grew up, their characters, pursuits and tastes diverged more and more widely' [**30**, p. 16]. In a letter to Isaac of 26 May 1880, Eliot wrote 'our long silence has never broken the affection for you which began when we were little ones', cited in *ibid.*, p. 17. Ironically, Cross was indebted to Isaac for much of the information concerning their childhood (*ibid.*, Preface, p. vi).

51. Redinger asserts that the novel was written 'to confess and defend herself' [**111**, p. 346].

52. Lewes told Blackwood of George Eliot weeping while writing the book (Redinger [**111**, p. 419]). Coveney dislikes what he calls such 'uncritical mingling' of her own experience with that of her child characters [**27**, p. 163].

53. Haight (ed.) [**63**, vol. 5, p. 403].

54. 'Brother and Sister', in *The Legend of Jubal and Other Poems Old and New*, in *The Works of George Eliot*, W. Blackwood: Edinburgh, 1874, pp. 197–207. Redinger claims that the poem was written 'in expiation' of *The Mill on the Floss* [**111**, p. 61].

55. The role of sister taxed the energies and emotions of many women writers, as the experiences of the Brontës, Elizabeth Sewell and Harriet Martineau testify.

56. The structure of the Evans' family was different from the Tullivers. There was an older sister, Christiana, and the parents were unlike the Tullivers. Cross asserts nevertheless that the young Mary Ann was her father's favourite, while Isaac was that of his mother [**30**, p. 9].

57. Cross [**30**, p. 7].

58. Lucy may have been based on Chrissie. Described by George Eliot as 'meek and passive' (Haight, [**63**, vol. 1, p. 117]), she was a favourite with her maternal aunts and uncles because she was always clean and neat (Cross [**30**, p. 9]).

59. Letter to Sara Hennel, 3 March 1844 (Haight [**63**, vol. 1, p. 173]).

60. Cross says of Mary Ann that 'she used always to be at his heel, insisting on doing everything he did' [**30**, p. 8]. He was told by Isaac of her delight at his homecoming from school and her eagerness to hear of all he had been doing and learning [**30**, p. 9].

61. Cross claims that the most salient trait in Mary Ann's character was

> the absolute need of some one person who should be all in all to her, and to whom she should be all in all. Very jealous in her affections, and easily moved to smiles or tears, she was of a nature capable of the keenest enjoyment and the keenest suffering, knowing 'all the wealth and all the woe' of a pre-eminently exclusive disposition. [**30**, p. 8].

62. Eliot claimed in a letter to William Blackwood that Tom was 'painted with as much love and pity too' (Haight [**63**, vol. 3, p. 299]).

63. John Blackwood wrote to William Blackwood on 12 December 1859 that 'The heroine a child as yet is very good and quaint and the hero is a wonderful picture of a boy and lifelike contrast to the sort of Tom Brown ideals of what boys are', cited in R.P. Draper (ed.) [**45**, p. 31].

64. Eliot herself nursed both parents at 16 and is described by Cross at this period as a 'full and passionate nature and hungry intellect shut up in a farmhouse in the remote country' [30, p. 17]. His description of her acquisition of ultra-Evangelical attitudes at her school in Coventry echoes Maggie's self-dramatising response to Thomas à Kempis:

> Miss Evans, as she now was, could not rest satisfied with a mere profession of faith without trying to shape her own life – and it may be added, the lives around her, in accordance with her conviction. The pursuit of pleasure was a snare; dress was vanity; society was a danger. [30, p. 16]

65. Sarah Grand, *The Beth Book: Being a study of the life of Elizabeth Caldwell Maclure, a woman of genius*, Virago: London, 1980. Further references will be given in parenthesis in the text.
66. See Gail Cunningham [31] and Lloyd Fernando [50].
67. Grand was, in fact, seen as a 'misunderstood genius' by George Bernard Shaw, George Meredith and Mark Twain. See Gillian Kersley [82] for details of her life.
68. After her father's death in 1861, Grand's family moved from Ireland to live near relatives in Yorkshire. See Elaine Showalter's Introduction to Grand, *The Beth Book*, p. xiii.
69. Grand also married at 16, 'to escape from school' (*ibid.*, p. xiii).
70. See Dickens' *David Copperfield* and *Great Expectations*, for example. Grand was a member of the Women Writers' Suffrage League and Mayoress of Bath at the end of her life.
71. The first edition of *The Heavenly Twins* sold out in a month (Cunningham [31, p. 57]).
72. Sarah Grand, *The Heavenly Twins* (1893), Heinemann: London, 1906, p. 7.
73. 'A chat with Sarah Grand', *Woman: Literary supplement*, 2 May 1894, pp. 1–2.

Conclusion

1. Jan [77, p. 90].
2. Peter Green describes this as a 'glutinous yearning for purity' which stemmed from the desire for the relief of guilt or gratification of the ego in his study of Kenneth Grahame [59, p. 161].
3. Jan argues that only when the child was perceived as a victim at the hands of adults did the child appear as hero in children's fiction [77, p. 92].
4. See Robert Louis Stevenson's description of the child in his essay 'Child's Play' (1878) which reflects a poetic sensibility: 'They walk in a vain show, and among mists and rainbows; they are passionate after dreams and unconcerned about realities' [124, pp. 222–44].
5. Coveney, [27, p. 33].
6. See Dusinberre [46, p. 28] and Spilka [123, p. 168].
7. See Auerbach [4, p. 131].
8. See Susan P. Casteras [20, p. 40].
9. Spilka reports that young men at Oxford used to invite little girls to tea-parties [123, p. 175].
10. Joan Crossley, 'The end of innocence' [71, p. 74].
11. Simone de Beauvoir [10, p. 142].
12. Grylls remarks that 'youngsters in fiction, exploited by both of these literary conventions, were unlikely to survive long' [62, p. 41].
13. Spilka [123, p. 175].

14. Coveney [27, p. 193].
15. Briggs [12, p. 248].
16. Rosemary Lloyd in her book on childhood in nineteenth-century French literature, published as I completed this study, comes to similar conclusions about the nature of the techniques employed in male- and female-authored texts in France [90].
17. See Barbara Wall [138, p. 79].
18. Mary Louisa Molesworth, *The Boys and I*, G. Routledge: London, 1883, pp. 1–2.
19. Briggs calls this 'the uninhibited violence [and] inverted logic of a Freudian nightmare' [12, p. 243].
20. Edith Nesbit, *The Wouldbegoods* (1901), Puffin: London, 1950, p. 34.
21. *Ibid.*, p. 64.
22. Dusinberre, [46, p. 94]. Dusinberre traces the considerable influence of children's books on early twentieth-century experimental writing.

Bibliography

Abel, Elizabeth, Marilyn Hirsch and Elizabeth Langland, *The Voyage In: Fictions of female development*, New England University Press: Hanover, 1983. [1]

Agress, Lynn, *The Feminine Irony: Women on women in early nineteenth century English literature*, University Press of America: Lanhom, 1978. [2]

Ariès, Philippe, *Centuries of Childhood*, trans. R. Baldick, Penguin: Harmondsworth, 1986. [3]

Auerbach, Nina, *Romantic Imprisonment: Women and other glorified outcasts*, Columbia University Press: New York, 1985. [4]

Avery, Gillian, *Childhood's Pattern: A study of the heroes and heroines of children's fiction 1770–1950*, Hodder & Stoughton: London, 1975. [5]

Avery, Gillian, *Mrs Ewing*, Bodley Head: London, 1961. [6]

Avery, Gillian and Julia Briggs (eds), *Children and their Books: A celebration of the work of Iona and Peter Opie*, Clarendon Press: Oxford, 1989. [7]

Avery, Gillian with Angela Bull, *Nineteenth Century Children*, Hodder & Stoughton: London, 1965. [8]

Battiscombe, Georgina and Marghanita Laski (eds), *A Chaplet for Charlotte Yonge*, Cresset Press: London, 1965. [9]

Beauvoir, Simone de, *The Second Sex*, trans. H.M. Parshley, Penguin: Harmondsworth, 1974. [10]

Bratton, J.S., *The Impact of Victorian Children's Fiction*, Croom Helm: London, 1981. [11]

Briggs, Julia, 'Women writers and writing for children: From Sarah Fielding to E. Nesbit' in Gillian Avery and Julia Briggs (eds), *Children and their Books: A celebration of the work of Iona and Peter Opie*, Clarendon Press: Oxford, 1989, pp. 221–50. [12]

Brownell, David, 'The two worlds of Charlotte Yonge', in J.H. Buckley (ed.), *The Worlds of Victorian Fiction*, Harvard University Press: Cambridge, MA and London, 1975. [13]

Buchen, Irving H., 'Emily Brontë and the metaphysics of childhood and love', *Nineteenth Century Fiction*, vol. 22 (June 1967), pp. 63–70. [14]

Buckley, J.H. (ed.), *The Worlds of Victorian Fiction*, Harvard University Press: Cambridge, MA and London, 1975. [15]

Butler, Marilyn, *Maria Edgeworth: A literary biography*, Clarendon Press: Oxford, 1972. [16]

Calder, Jenni, *Women and Marriage in Victorian Fiction*, Thames & Hudson: London, 1976. [17]

Cameron, Eleanor, *The Green and Burning Tree*, Little, Brown: Boston and Toronto, 1962. [18]

Carpenter, Humphrey, *Secret Gardens: A study of the golden age of children's literature*, Allen & Unwin: London, 1985. [19]

Casteras, Susan P., *Images of Victorian Womanhood in English Art*, Farleigh Dickinson University Press: Rutherford, 1987. [20]

Cazamian, Louis, *The Social Novel in England 1830–1850*, Routledge & Kegan Paul: London, 1973. [21]

Chapman, R.W. (ed.), *Jane Austen's Letters*, Oxford University Press: London, 1969. [22]

Coe, Richard N., 'Reminiscences of childhood: Approach to a comparative mythology', *Proceedings of the Leeds Literary and Philological Society*, vol. xix, part vi, 1984. [23]

Coe, Richard N., *When the Grass was Taller: Autobiography and the experience of childhood*, Yale University Press: New Haven and London, 1984. [24]

Colby, Vineta, *Yesterday's Woman: Domestic realism in the English novel*, Princeton University Press: Princeton, NJ, 1974. [25]

Coleridge, Christabel, *Charlotte Mary Yonge: Her life and letters*, Macmillan: London, 1903. [26]

Coveney, Peter, *The Image of Childhood: The Individual and Society: A study of the theme in English literature*, Penguin: Harmondsworth, 1967. [27]

Cox, D.R. (ed.), *Sexuality and Victorian Literature*, Tennessee Studies in Literature, no. 27, University of Tennessee Press: Knoxville, 1984. [28]

Crosland, Margaret, *Beyond the Lighthouse: English women novelists in the twentieth century*, Constable: London, 1981. [29]

Cross, John Walter, *George Eliot's Life as Related in her Letters and Journals*, W. Blackwood: Edinburgh and London, n.d. [30]

Cunningham, Gail, *The New Woman and the Victorian Novel*, Macmillan: London, 1978. [31]

Cutt, Margaret Nancy, *Ministering Angels: A study of nineteenth century Evangelical writing for children*, Five Owls Press: Wormley, 1979. [32]

Cutt, Margaret Nancy, *Mrs Sherwood and her Books for Children*, Oxford University Press: London, 1974. [33]

Darton, F.J. Harvey, *Children's Books in England: Five centuries of social life*, Cambridge University Press: Cambridge, 1966. [34]

Davidoff, Leonore and Catherine Hall, *Family Fortunes: Men and women of the English middle class 1780–1850*, Hutchinson: London, 1987. [35]

Davies, Stevie, *Emily Brontë*, Key Women Writers Series, ed. Sue Roe, Harvester Wheatsheaf: Hemel Hempstead, 1988. [36]

Davies, Stevie, *Emily Brontë: The artist as free woman*, Carcanet: Manchester, 1983. [37]

De Mause, Lloyd, (ed.), *The History of Childhood: The evolution of parent–child relationships as a factor in history*, Psychohistory Press: New York, 1974. [38]

Demers, Patricia (ed.), *A Garland from the Golden Age: An anthology of children's literature from 1850–1900*, Oxford University Press: Toronto, 1983. [39]

Demers, Patricia and Gordon Moyles (eds), *From Instruction to Delight: An anthology of children's literature to 1850*, Oxford University Press: Toronto, 1982. [40]

Dickens, Charles, *David Copperfield*, ed. Nina Burgis, Oxford University Press: Oxford, 1981. [41]

Dickens, Charles, *Great Expectations*, Pan: London and Sydney, 1974. [42]

Dickens, Charles, *The Old Curiosity Shop*, Oxford University Press: Oxford, 1987. [43]

Dickens, Charles, *Oliver Twist*, ed. K. Tillotson, Oxford University Press: Oxford, 1966. [44]

Draper, R.P. (ed.), *George Eliot: The Mill on the Floss and Silas Marner: A casebook*, Macmillan: London, 1977. [45]

Bibliography 211

Dusinberre, Juliet, *Alice to the Lighthouse: Childrens' books and radical experiments in art*, Macmillan: Basingstoke, 1987. [46]
Eliot, George, 'Silly Novels by Lady Novelists', *Essays of George Eliot*, ed. Thomas Pinney, Routledge & Kegan Paul: London, 1963. [47]
Empson, William, *Some Versions of Pastoral*, Chatto & Windus: London, 1935. [48]
Ereira, Alan, *The People's England*, Routledge & Kegan Paul: London, 1981. [49]
Fernando, Lloyd, *New Women in the Late Victorian Novel*, Pennsylvania University Press: Pennsylvania, 1977. [50]
Figes, Eva, *Sex and Subterfuge: Women writers to 1850*, Macmillan: London, 1982. [51]
Flexner, Eleanor, *Mary Wollstonecraft: A biography*, Penguin: Baltimore, MD, 1972. [52]
Gaskell, Elizabeth, *The Life of Charlotte Brontë*, ed. Alan Shelston, Penguin: Harmondsworth, 1975. [53]
Gérin, Winifred, *Charlotte Brontë: The evolution of genius*, Oxford University Press: Oxford, 1969. [54]
Gérin, Winifred, *Emily Brontë: A biography*, Clarendon Press: Oxford, 1971. [55]
Gilbert, Sandra M. and Susan Gubar, *The Mad Woman in the Attic: The woman writer and the nineteenth century literary imagination*, Yale University Press: New Haven and London, 1979. [56]
Gordon, Felicia, *A Preface to the Brontës*, Longman: London and New York, 1989. [57]
Gordon, J.B., 'The Alice books and metaphors of Victorian childhood', in R. Phillips (ed.), *Aspects of Alice: Lewis Carroll's dream child as seen through the critics' looking-glasses*, Penguin: Harmondsworth, 1974. [58]
Green, Peter, *Kenneth Grahame, 1859–1932*, John Murray: London, 1959. [59]
Green, Roger Launcelyn, *Tellers of Tales: Children's books and their authors from 1800–1964*, Kaye & Ward: London, 1969. [60]
Grierson, H.J.C. (ed.), *Letters of Sir Walter Scott*, 12 vols, Constable: London, 1932–7. [61]
Grylls, David, *Guardians and Angels: Parents and children in nineteenth century literature*, Faber & Faber: London and Boston, 1978. [62]
Haight, Gordon S. (ed.), *The George Eliot Letters*, 9 vols., Oxford University Press: London, 1954. [63]
Harden, Elizabeth, *Maria Edgeworth*, Twayne English Author Series no. 375, Twayne: Boston, 1984. [64]
Harden, Elizabeth McWhorter, *Maria Edgeworth's Art of Prose Fiction*, Studies in English Literature, no. lxii, Mouton: The Hague, 1971. [65]
Hardyment, Christine, 'Looking at children', in Sara Holdsworth and Joan Crossley (eds), *Innocence and Experience: Images of children in British art from 1600 to the present*, catalogue of exhibition at Manchester City Art Gallery, September–November 1992, Pale Green Press: Manchester, 1992. [66]
Harris, Ruth, 'Children and Charlotte Yonge', in Georgina Battiscombe and Marghanita Laski (eds), *A Chaplet for Charlotte Yonge*, Cresset Press: London, 1965. [67]
Harrison, David C., 'Ruskin's *Praeterita* and landscape in Evangelical children's fiction', *Nineteenth Century Fiction*, vol. 44, no. 1 (June 1989), pp. 45–66. [68]
Hazard, Paul, *Books, Children and Men*, trans. Margaret Mitchell, The Horn Book Inc.: Boston, 1967. [69]
Hocking, Silas, *Her Benny: A tale of Victorian Liverpool* (1879), Gallery Press: Liverpool, 1968. [70]
Holdsworth, Sara and Joan Crossley (eds), *Innocence and Experience: Images of children in British art from 1600 to the present*, catalogue of exhibition at Manchester City

Art Gallery, September–November 1992, Pale Green Press: Manchester, 1992. [71]

Honan, Park, *Jane Austen: Her life*, Weidenfeld & Nicolson: London, 1987. [72]

Houghton, Walter, *The Victorian Frame of Mind 1830–1870*, Yale University Press: New Haven, CT, 1957. [73]

Hutchins, B. Leigh and Amy Harrison, *History of Factory Legislation*, King: Westminster, 1903. [74]

Inglis, F., *The Promise of Happiness: Value and meaning in children's fiction*, Cambridge University Press: Cambridge, 1981. [75]

Jameson, Anna, 'A revelation of childhood', in *A Commonplace Book of Thoughts, Memories and Fancies, Original and Selected*, Longman, Brown, Green and Longman: London, 1854. [76]

Jan, Isabelle, *On Children's Literature*, trans. C. Storr, Allen Lane: London, 1973. [77]

Jay, Elizabeth, *The Religion of the Heart: Anglican Evangelicism and the nineteenth century novel*, Clarendon Press: Oxford, 1979. [78]

Jelinek, Estelle C., *Women's Autobiography: Essays in criticism*, Indiana University Press: Bloomington, 1980. [79]

Jerrold, Blanchard and Gustave Doré, *The London of Gustave Doré*, Wordsworth: Ware, 1987. [80]

Kennedy, Margaret, 'Harriet Mozley: A forerunner of Charlotte Yonge', in Georgina Battiscombe and Marghanita Laski (eds), *A Chaplet for Charlotte Yonge*, Cresset Press: London, 1965. [81]

Kersley, Gillian, *Darling Madame*, Virago: London, 1983. [82]

Kipling, Rudyard, *Something of Myself for My Friends Known and Unknown*, Macmillan: London, 1951. [83]

Kovacevic, I., *Fact into Fiction*, Leicester University Press/University of Belgrade: Leicester, 1975. [84]

Kovacevic, I. and S.B. Kanner, 'Blue Book into novel: The forgotten industrial fiction of Charlotte Elizabeth Tonna', *Nineteenth Century Fiction*, vol. 25 (September 1970), pp. 152–73. [85]

Kuhn, Reinhard, *Corruption in Paradise: The child in Western literature*, for Brown University Press by University Press of New England: Hanover, New Hampshire and London, 1982. [86]

Lasdun, Susan, *Making Victorians: The Drummond children's world 1827–1832*, Victor Gollancz: London, 1983. [87]

Laski, Marghanita, *Mrs Ewing, Mrs Molesworth and Mrs Hodgson Burnett*, A. Barker: London, 1950. [88]

Lejeune, Philippe, 'Autobiography in the third person', *New Literary History*, vol. 9 (1977). [89]

Lloyd, Rosemary, *The Land of Lost Content: Children and childhood in nineteenth century French literature*, Clarendon Press: Oxford, 1992. [90]

Locke, John, 'Some Thoughts concerning Education', *The Educational Writings of John Locke*, ed. J.W. Adamson, Edward Arnold: London, 1912. [91]

Lucas, G.V. (ed.), *The Letters of Charles Lamb*, 3 vols, Dent: London, 1935. [92]

Maison, Margaret, *Search your Soul, Eustace: A survey of the religious novel in the Victorian age*, Sheed & Ward: London, 1961. [93]

Martineau, Harriet, *Biographical Sketches*, Macmillan: London, 1869. [94]

Mayhew, Henry, *London Labour and the London Poor*, (1861–62), 4 vols, Cass: London, 1967. [95]

Messinger, Gary S., *Manchester in the Victorian Age: The half-known city*, Manchester University Press: Manchester, 1985. [96]

Moers, Ellen, *Literary Women*, The Women's Press: London, 1978. [97]

More, Hannah, *Essays on Various Subjects Principally Designed for Young Ladies*, C. Whittingham: Chiswick, 1824. [98]

More, Hannah, *Strictures on the Modern System of Female Education* (1799), New York, 1835. [99]

Muir, Percy, *English Children's Books 1600–1900*, B.T. Batsford: London, 1954. [100]

O'Sullivan, Vincent (ed.), *Katherine Mansfield: Selected letters*, Oxford University Press: Oxford and London, 1990. [101]

Pascal, Roy, *Design and Truth in Autobiography*, Harvard University Press: Cambridge, MA, 1960. [102]

Pattison, Robert, *The Child Figure in English Literature*, University of Georgia Press: Athens, USA, 1978. [103]

Phillips, R. (ed.), *Aspects of Alice: Lewis Carroll's dream child as seen through the critics' looking-glasses*, Penguin: Harmondsworth, 1974. [104]

Pickering, Samuel, *The Moral Tradition in English Fiction 1785–1850*, University Press of New England: Hanover, NH, 1976. [105]

Pike, E. Royston, *Human Documents of the Industrial Revolution in Britain*, Allen & Unwin: London, 1966. [106]

Pinchbeck, Ivy and Margaret Hewitt, *Children in English Society*, 2 vols, Routledge & Kegan Paul: London, 1969. [107]

Pollock, Linda, *Forgotten Children*, Cambridge University Press: Cambridge, 1985. [108]

Pollock, Linda, *A Lasting Relationship: Parents and children over three centuries*, Fourth Estate: London, 1987. [109]

Ratchford, Fanny, *A Web of Childhood*, Oxford University Press: Oxford, 1941. [110]

Redinger, Ruby V., *George Eliot: The emergent self*, Alfred A. Knopf: New York, 1975. [111]

Reynolds, Kimberley, *Girls Only? Gender and popular children's fiction in Britain 1880–1910*, Harvester Wheatsheaf: Hemel Hempstead, 1990. [112]

Robertson, Priscilla, 'Home as a nest: Middle class childhood in nineteenth century Europe', in Lloyd de Mause (ed.), *The History of Childhood: The evolution of parent–child relationships as a factor in history*, Psychohistory Press: New York, 1974. [113]

Rousseau, Jean-Jacques, *Émile ou de l'éducation*, *Oeuvres complètes*, vol. 4, Gallimard: Paris, 1969. [114]

Rowbotham, Judith, *Good Girls Make Good Wives: Guidance for girls in Victorian fiction*, Blackwell: Oxford, 1989. [115]

Ruskin, John, 'Fiction Fair and Foul', *The Works of John Ruskin*, ed. E.T. Cook and Alexander Wedderburn, George Allen: London, 1908. [116]

Sanders, Valerie, *The Private Lives of Victorian Women: Autobiography in nineteenth-century England*, Harvester Wheatsheaf: Hemel Hempstead, 1989. [117]

Sanders, Valerie, *Reason over Passion: Harriet Martineau and the Victorian novel*, Harvester: Brighton, 1986. [118]

Shine, Muriel, *The Fictional Children of Henry James*, University of North California Press: Chapel Hill, 1968. [119]

Shorter, Clement (ed.), *The Brontës: Life and letters*, 2 vols, Hodder & Stoughton: London, 1908. [120]

Showalter, Elaine, *A Literature of their Own: British women novelists from Brontë to Lessing*, Princeton University Press: Princeton, 1977. [121]

Smith, Naomi Royde, *The State of Mind of Mrs Sherwood*, Macmillan: London, 1946. [122]

Spilka, Mark, 'On the enrichment of poor monkeys by myth and dream; or, how

Dickens Rousseauisticised and pre-Freudianised Victorian views of childhood', in D.R. Cox (ed.), *Sexuality and Victorian Literature*, Tennessee Studies in Literature, no. 27, University of Tennessee Press: Knoxville, 1984. [123]

Stevenson, Robert Louis, 'Child's Play' (1878), *Virginibus Puerisque and Other Papers*, Chatto & Windus: London, 1891. [124]

Summerfield, Geoffrey, *Fantasy and Reason: Children's literature in the eighteenth century*, Methuen: London, 1984. [125]

Taylor, Ann, *Reciprocal Duties of Parents and Children*, Taylor & Hessey: London, 1818. [126]

Thackeray, Anne, *Toilers and Spinners and Other Essays*, in *The Works of Miss Thackeray*, vol. vii, Smith, Elder: London, 1890. [127]

Thackeray, William Makepeace, *The Paris Sketch-Book*, Collins: London and Glasgow, n.d. [128]

Thomas, Keith, 'Children in early modern England' in Gillian Avery and Julia Briggs (eds), *Children and their Books: A celebration of the work of Iona and Peter Opie*, Clarendon Press: Oxford, 1989. [129]

Thompson, Flora, *Lark Rise to Candleford*, Oxford University Press: London, New York and Toronto, 1979. [130]

Tillotson, Geoffrey and Kathleen Tillotson, *Mid-Victorian Studies*, Athlone Press: London, 1965. [131]

Tillotson, Kathleen, *Novels of the 1840s*, Clarendon Press: Oxford, 1955. [132]

Todd, Janet (ed.), *Mary, Martha and Matilda*, Pickering & Chatto: London, 1991. [133]

Tomalin, Claire, *The Life and Death of Mary Wollstonecraft*, Weidenfeld & Nicolson: London, 1975. [134]

Trollope, Frances Eleanor, *A Memoir of Frances Trollope: Her life and literary work*, 2 vols, Richard Bentley: London, 1895. [135]

Vincent, Adrian (ed.), *Victorian Watercolours: Children*, Bloomsbury Books: London, 1987. [136]

Vogler, Thomas A. (ed.), *Twentieth-Century Interpretations of Wuthering Heights*, Prentice Hall: Englewood Cliffs, NJ, 1968. [137]

Wall, Barbara, *The Narrator's Voice: The dilemma of children's fiction*, Macmillan: London, 1991. [138]

Walvin, James, *A Child's World: A social history of English childhood 1800–1914*, Penguin: Harmondsworth, 1982. [139]

Wardle, R.M., *Mary Wollstonecraft: A critical biography*, Richards Press, University of Kansas: London, 1951. [140]

Webb, R.K., *Harriet Martineau: A radical Victorian*, Heinemann: London, 1960. [141]

Wheeler, Michael, *English Fiction of the Victorian Period 1830–90*, Longman Literature in English Series, Longman: London and New York, 1985. [142]

Wilson, Angus, 'Dickens on children and childhood', in M. Slater (ed.), *Dickens 1970*, Chapman & Hall: London, 1970. [143]

Wise, Thomas James and John Alexander Symington, *The Brontës: Their lives, friendships and correspondance in four volumes*, Basil Blackwell: Oxford, 1932. [144]

Wolff, R.L., *Gains and Losses: Novels of faith and doubt in Victorian England*, John Murray and Garland: New York, 1977. [145]

Wolff, R.L., 'Some erring children in children's literature: The world of Victorian religious strife in miniature', in J.H. Buckley (ed.), *The Worlds of Victorian Fiction*, Harvard University Press: Cambridge, MA and London, 1975. [146]

Wordsworth, William, *The Prelude or Growth of a Poet's Mind*, ed. Ernest de Selincourt, Oxford University Press: London, New York and Toronto, 1933. [147]

Wordsworth, William, *Wordsworth: Poetical Works*, ed. T. Hutchinson, revised by E. de Selincourt, Oxford University Press: London, New York and Toronto, 1971. [148]
Yonge, Charlotte Mary, 'Children's literature of the last century', *Macmillan's Magazine*, vol. xx, May–October, 1869. [149]

Index